BIG DATA
AND HEALTH
ANALYTICS

BIG DATA
AND HEALTH
ANALYTICS

EDITED BY
KATHERINE MARCONI

The Graduate School
University of Maryland University College

HAROLD LEHMANN

School of Medicine
The Johns Hopkins University

CRC Press
Taylor & Francis Group
Boca Raton   London   New York

CRC Press is an imprint of the
Taylor & Francis Group, an **informa** business
AN AUERBACH BOOK

CRC Press
Taylor & Francis Group
6000 Broken Sound Parkway NW, Suite 300
Boca Raton, FL 33487-2742

Printed on acid-free paper
Version Date: 20141023

International Standard Book Number-13: 978-1-4822-2923-3 (Hardback)

Visit the Taylor & Francis Web site at
http://www.taylorandfrancis.com

and the CRC Press Web site at
http://www.crcpress.com

Contents

SECTION II

SECTION III

Foreword

Karen Bandeen-Roche

Over much of history, the generation of data was the cost-limiting step for the advancement of science. Tycho Brahe labored for decades in collecting the celestial observations that Johannes Kepler ultimately would use to deduce his laws of planetary motion. The last hundred years have witnessed huge data-related investments in field after field, whether in the vast accelerators that have been crucial to modern advancements in particle physics, satellites that have surveyed both our planet and the cosmos, technologies through which we can now sequence the genome, hundreds of thousands of persons who have been assessed through public health cohort studies and social science surveys, or efforts to implement exhaustive electronic medical records. With infrastructure increasingly in place, the costs of biomedical data collection plummeting, and crowd-sourcing exploding, the cost-limiting paradigm has inverted. Data availability is outstripping existing paradigms for governing, managing, analyzing, and interpreting those data.

Forces to meet this new demand are strengthening throughout our society. Academically, we have seen the genesis of the field of "data science." Industry demand for data scientists is skyrocketing. Government agencies such as the National Science Foundation and National Institutes of Health (NIH) are investing hundreds of millions of dollars toward producing the workforce, norms, methods, and tools needed to reap the benefits of "big data"—collections increasingly of terabyte scope or even larger. The NIH, for example, has established a new associate directorship of data science who, among other responsibilities, will oversee the "Big Data to Knowledge" (BD2K) program. BD2K will make investments, largely through grants, to "enable biomedical scientists to capitalize more fully on the Big Data being generated by those research communities".

In 2013 requests for information were issued, and workshops bringing together big data experts and leaders were convened to prioritize areas for investment, including ones to consider workforce training and development. One loud-and-clear message from the training workshop was that the science needed is **interdisciplinary**, including no less than computer science, statistics, applied mathematics, engineering, information science, medicine, physics, public health, and "domain" sciences such as biology, neuroscience, and social science. A second was that training must go beyond creating experts in these fields—even ones with specialty skills in big data. Rather, what is desperately needed is training to create effective **teams** spanning these fields, as well as **transdisciplinary** or "pi-shaped" people who cross boundaries with depth in two or more fields. Finally, we seem to be moving toward a reality in which data-intensive activity will touch all areas of science, so that training will increasingly need to span all possibilities of depth—from needing merely to be "conversant" to those who can adeptly apply existing tools for dealing with big data to experts who will create the new methods and tools that are urgently needed if our expertise in utilizing the data is to catch up with the volume and complexity of the data itself.

This volume targets crucial members of the teams who will be needed to unlock the potential of big data: health care and medical professionals, scientists and their students. It engages and grounds its readers in the issues to be faced by showing how health care practitioners and organizations are linking data within and across their medical practice on scales that only now have become possible. It also elucidates the realities of moving from medical and administrative records to useful information and the innovative ways that this can be accomplished.

An initial seven chapters sketch the landscape of biomedical big data, and in so doing, communicate the enormous diversity of data sources and types that are contributing to modern health care practice and research environments, and the massive challenges and needs that are posed by their effective integration and dissemination. They also expose us to the many uses to which these data are being applied, ranging from clinical decision-making and risk assessment, to mentorship and training to promote transformation of health care through effective data usage, to the assessment of social risks for poor health and the use of resulting measures to target interventions and investments.

A subsequent eight chapters then examine critical aspects relating to the data side of the equation, including governance, architecture, public policy issues that affect the use and usefulness of big health care, and the use of emerging information-capture technologies to leverage not only newly accruing data but also existing data. A concluding section samples the space of analytics tools—for interactive visualization; in the open source domain, and specifically the statistical software package "R"; and for leveraging so-called "unstructured" data such as images and text-based reports.

I expect that readers will enjoy the nontechnical language and case-study presentation by which challenges of big health care data are presented by the authors of the chapters to follow. Embedded links to websites, videos, articles, and other online content that expand and support the primary learning objectives for each major section of the book, which are provided, excitingly further expand readers' horizons of learning. In assembling this volume, its contributors have provided an accessible, excellent foundation for further specialized study in health analytics and data management.

List of Contributors

Ritu Agarwal
Robert H. Smith School
    of Business
University of Maryland
College Park, Maryland

Ruth Atukunda
Institute of Human Virology
University of Maryland School
    of Medicine
Kampala, Uganda

Sean Barnes
Department of Decision,
    Operations, and Information
    Technologies
Robert H. School of Business
University of Maryland
College Park, Maryland

Barbara Bastien
Institute of Human Virology
 University of Maryland School
    of Medicine
 Port-au-Prince, Haiti

Margrét V. Bjarnadóttir
Decision, Operations, and
    Information Technologies
Robert H. Smith School
    of Business
University of Maryland
College Park, Maryland

Christopher Broyles
Methodist University
Fayetteville, North Carolina

Lanette Burrows
Project Director
Futures Group International
Washington, DC

Kenyon Crowley
Center for Health Information
    and Decision Systems (CHIDS)
Department of Decision,
    Operations, and Information
    Technologies
Robert H. Smith School
    of Business
University of Maryland
College Park, Maryland

Dilhari R. DeAlmeida
Department of Health
    Information Management
School of Health and
    Rehabilitation Sciences
University of Pittsburgh
Pittsburgh, Pennsylvania

Linda Dimitropoulos
Center for the Advancement of
    Health IT (CAHIT)
RTI International
Chicago, Illinois

Matthew Dobra
Department of Financial
 Economics
Methodist University
Fayetteville, North Carolina

Donald A. Donahue, Jr.
Diogenec Group
Washington, DC
University of Maryland University
 College
Adelphi, Maryland

**Martine Etienne-Mesubi
MPH, DrPH**
Institute of Human Virology
University of Maryland School
 of Medicine
Baltimore, Maryland

Roland Grad
Department of Family Medicine
McGill University
Montreal, Quebec, Canada

Lynda R. Hardy
University of Maryland University
 College
Adelphi, Maryland

Kim S. Jayhan
LexisNexis Risk Solutions
Bolingbrook, Illinois

QianRan Jin
Robert H. Smith School
 of Business
University of Maryland
College Park, Maryland

Bruce Johnson
Consultant
Red Wing, Minnesota

Eva Karororo
Institute of Virology
University of Maryland
Kigali, Rwanda

John A. Kellum
Center for Assistance in Research
 using eRecord (CARe)
Critical Care Medicine
School of Medicine
University of Pittsburgh
Pittsburgh, Pennsylvania

Patience Komba
Institute of Virology
University of Maryland
Dar es Salaam, Tanzania

David T. Marc
Department of Health Informatics
 and Information Management
The College of St. Scholastica
Duluth, Minnesota

Peter Memiah
Institute of Human Virology
University of Maryland School
 of Medicine
Baltimore, Maryland

Jamie Meuser
Department of Family and
 Community Medicine
Centre for Effective Practice
Toronto, Ontario, Canada

Tamra Meyer
Office of the Surgeon General
US Army
Washington, DC

Megan Monroe
Institute for Advanced Computer
    Studies
University of Maryland
College Park, Maryland

Jonathan Moscovici
Department of Mathematics
    and Statistics
McGill University
Montreal, Quebec, Canada

Mwansa Mulenga
Institute of Virology
University of Maryland School
    of Medicine
Lasaka, Zambia

Mercy Niyang
Maryland Global Initiative
    Cooperative
Abuja, Nigeria

Francesca Odhiambo
Institute of Virology
University of Maryland
Nairobi, Kenya

Suzanne J. Paone
School of Health Information
    Management
University of Pittsburgh
Pittsburgh, Pennsylvania

David E. Parkhill
Hitachi Global Center for
    Innovative Analytics
Hitachi Consulting
Denver, Colorado

Catherine Plaisant
Human-Computer Interaction Lab
Institute for Advanced Computer
    Studies
University of Maryland
College Park, Maryland

Pierre Pluye
Department of Family Medicine
McGill University
Montreal, Quebec, Canada

Kislaya Prasad
Decision, Operations, and
    Information Technologies
Robert H. Smith School of Business
University of Maryland
College Park, Maryland

Carol Repchinsky
Special Projects Pharmacist
Canadian Pharmacists Association
Ottawa, Canada

Derek Ritz
Principal Consultant
ecGroup Inc.
Ancaster, Ontario

Ryan H. Sandefer
Department of Health Informatics
    and Information Management
The College of St. Scholastica
Duluth, Minnesota

Ben Shneiderman
Human Computer Interaction Lab
Institute for Advanced Computer
    Studies
University of Maryland
College Park, Maryland

Michael Shulha
Research Manager
Electronic Medical Record Project
HFPC Montreal Jewish General
    Hospital
Montreal, Canada

Constance Shumba
Institute of Human Virology
University of Maryland School of
    Medicine
Kampala, Uganda

Kristen Stafford
Department of Epidemiology and
    Public Health
University of Maryland School
    of Medicine
Baltimore, Maryland

Gregory D. Stevens
Keck School of Medicine
University of Southern California
Alhambra, California

David L. Tang
Information Sciences
McGill University
Montreal, Canada

Charles (Chuck) Thompson
Senior Health Research
    Informaticist
RTI International
Rockville, Maryland

Dorothy Weinstein
Health Policy Consultant
Bethesda, Maryland

Introduction

Katherine Marconi and Harold Lehmann

PURPOSE

The practice of medicine and the business that encompasses it are rapidly changing. But while changes in health care delivery are widely recognized and discussed, much less is known about where health care as an industry will be 5, 10, or even 15 years from now. In the editors' lifetimes, this highly regulated market has gone through several evolutions (or as some would posit revolutions). The Accountable Care Act (ACA) has set the direction for the near future. But what happens after health care reform?

Contributing to the changes in health care delivery is the role of computing and information technology. While many writers focus on the revolution at the computerized bedside, in this book, we will be focusing on the current and future uses of the material being computed: the data and their ancillary analytics. Our authors write about how individual bits of health information can be organized into *big data* to improve the business of delivering services and to communicate to consumers. As an industry, we are just beginning to realize the potential that myriad information health deliveries hold, for health care both in the United States and globally.

Informatics has been dealing with data for years. What is new is the availability of large volumes of data, the degree to which these data are viewed as mission critical, and the scale of technologies required to make the data provide those critical missions. We call this state of affairs big data. In Chapter 8, Bruce Johnson points out, "The concept of big data is just that: a concept for the value an organization can realize from in-depth analysis of all data. The concept of big data is therefore not a database or data architecture but is more the solutions that leverage any and all data, wherever they come from. In health care, the concepts of big data are enabled only in organizations that focus on data—capture, management, and usage." However, the reader will find several overlapping definitions in this book.

The purpose of this book is to provide frameworks using cases and examples of how big data and analytics play a role in modern health care, including how public health information can inform health delivery. This book is written for health care professionals, including executives. It is not a technical book on statistics and machine-learning algorithms to extract knowledge out of data or a book exploring the intricacies of database design. It represents some of the current thinking of academic and industry researchers and leaders. It is written in a style that should interest anyone interested in health information and its use in improving patient outcomes and the business practices that lead to improved outcomes.

We stress *usage*, because without providing the right information to the people who need it, when they need it, data capture will not add value. The authors in this volume thus provide examples of how big data's management and use can improve access, reduce cost, and improve quality.

Big data and health analytics have been criticized for their unrealized potential. In some ways, the authors of these criticisms are correct. In a 2014 article that appeared in *Health IT News* (p. 1), Carl Shulman talks about how "fast, easy tech" matters. At this point, fast and easy electronic health information is rarely available. Data are collected, but the business plan of making it comprehensive and valid for a variety of purposes is missing. Some of the challenges for big data and health analytics today include the following:

- Incorporating new information, such as biomedical data, and new technologies into electronic health records (EHRs) that store big data. Text data require special algorithms, genetic data may be voluminous, and continuously monitored physiological data can be at arbitrary levels of granularity.
- The eventual movement to ICD-10-CM/PCS coding. While this coding provides a wealth of specific diagnostic information, the investment in data systems and associated business practices to handle complex codes is large. More generally, there is a potential loss of information between the raw data collected and the standard tagging required.
- Harnessing the potential of unstructured data for analysis, such as medical imaging and text.
- Building a culture of data sharing and the architecture, including interoperability, to meet health system needs, including future meaningful use requirements.

- Building data systems that meet requirements of accountable care organizations (ACOs) and other types of payment reforms.
- Producing understandable information for both providers and consumers.
- Maintaining patient privacy while aggregating data that increasingly can identify the individual, even without the Health Insurance Portability and Accountability Act (HIPAA) 18 safe-harbor data items.

The National Academy of Sciences talks about teaching students to extract value of big data. This imperative assumes we know what to teach them. For those of us in the health care industry who are involved in big data and health analytics, showing added value to the many different health professions is our challenge for health big data and analytics.

ORGANIZATION OF CHAPTERS

Our book is organized into three sections that reflect the available data and potential analytics: sources and uses of health data, business practices and workforce environments, data presentation and analysis framework. Each section shows the opportunities to improve health delivery through the analysis of data sets that may range from population information to clinical and administrative data.

Section I: Sources and Uses of Health Data

This book starts with a discussion of the types of health information that can be combined into big data. In Chapter 1, Donald Donahue discusses "the wicked problem of knowing where to look" for data. Once potential information is identified, what needs to be considered to integrate it into an accessible data source that maintains the integrity of the information? Both Donahue and Chapter 2's author, David Parkhill, provide examples of how health information becomes more useful as it is aggregated and interpreted. In Chapter 2, the theme of knowing where to look is applied to the vast amount of unstructured data, including everything from text documents to clinical images and video.

Chapter 3 is a brief overview of the challenges encountered in creating big data from disparate data sets. The analysts who authored this chapter are part of a large health system. They assist different practices within the system to identify, gather, and analyze information to improve patient care. Some of the challenges that they have experienced are proprietary data structures, lack of standard data definitions, the need for multidisciplinary staffing, and appropriate analytical tools to handle big data.

Chapters 4 through 7 focus on solving specific problems using a variety of health data. In Chapter 4, Ryan Sandefer and David Marc discuss the ecosystem of federal big data and its use in health care, including HealthData.gov. They then show how open-source tools can be used to analyze one open-source data set: the Centers for Medicare and Medicaid (CMS) hospitals' attestation data for Stage 1 of Meaningful Use. Their analysis is based on a traditional epidemiology principle: numerators (hospitals reporting Stage 1 of Meaningful Use) need denominators (the number of hospitals in a defined geographic area) for analysis. They also point out that successful big data analytics still depend on sound research methodologies.

Roland Grad and his colleagues in Chapter 5 evaluate using mHealth technologies, including email, apps, and RSS feeds, to push clinical information to physicians. In 2006 they began collecting responses from 10,000 Canadian physicians and pharmacists on the usefulness of InfoPOEMs (patient-oriented evidence that matters) to them. They also point out ways to expand their future evaluations of communicating close to real-time clinical advances to practitioners.

In Chapter 6, Gregory Stevens returns to available sources of population data. But his focus is on primary care physician practices and how community population data can be used to build models of vulnerability. In turn, these models help focus health promotion interventions for individual patients. Community health beliefs and practices do impact the health habits of patients along with the chances of changing those habits.

In the last chapter in this section, Chapter 7, Martine Etienne-Mesubi and her colleagues bring an international perspective to building and using health information systems in emerging economies. Their focus is on one disease: HIV care. But their experiences can be applied to most types of health care in the developing world. This chapter leaves us with a question: Is it more difficult to build health information and analytic systems from scratch even when resources are scarce, or is it more costly and time-consuming to rebuild an integrated EHR from a plethora of existing administrative and clinical systems?

Section II: Business Practices and Workforce Requirements

In Chapter 8, Bruce Johnson begins this section by discussing the data architecture needed for big data and health analytics. He shows how we should appreciate the complexity of big data. Organizations need to consider this complexity as they standardize data, build new technologies into their systems, and grow their analytic capacity.

The business practices surrounding big data are developing along with the technology to house and analyze it. In Chapter 9, Linda Dimitropoulos and Charles Thompson talk about the balance needed between best practices for data governance and managing and meeting user needs. Their chapter is organized using a health data governance framework adopted from the Data Governance Institute's general data framework. Chief information officers take note: the chapter walks through the challenges of and solutions to building governance structures and processes, establishing accountable stakeholders, managing risks, defining clear metrics, and assuring data security.

In Chapter 10, Matthew Dobra and his colleagues take a different tactic toward governance. They review the growing government regulations and current health practices that impact health data and the adverse consequences that may impact patient care. They end by making a series of policy and practice recommendations for the gathering, storage, and use of big data.

This section ends with an overview of workforce and training requirements needed to realize the potential of big data and analytics. In Chapter 11, Lynda Hardy reviews the two related fields: health informatics and health information management. Together they provide the skills necessary for maximizing the potential of big data. Health informatics professionals develop and work with electronic health records and data to make information accessible and useful in clinical and business decision-making. Health information managers focus more on the content of health records, including data coding and accuracy. Both groups share common skill sets (e.g., familiarity with government regulations and security requirements) and separate skill sets—the analytic depth that health informaticists should possess. She also stresses how blending the skills of these two groups with clinical insights has led to the development of relatively new fields, such as nurse and physician informaticists.

Section III: Data Presentation and Analysis Framework

Communication of patterns found in complex data is challenging. In Chapter 12, Catherine Plaisant, Ben Shneiderman, and their colleagues from the Human-Computer Interaction Laboratory at the University of Maryland show some of the creative ways that everything from individual patient information to prescription records and to the global burden of disease can be visually communicated. Using the analytics systems that they have developed, Lifeline and Eventflow, the beauty of identifying practice patterns can easily be read.

Kim Jayhan in Chapter 13 takes on population management, a popular concept today, showing how business intelligence enhances patient care. He uses case studies including simple analytics to show the potential to bring better health care for populations, improved patient experience, and reduced per capita cost—the triple aim.

Chapter 14 continues this discussion of how analytics improves decision-making in four areas: reducing health care costs, making informed treatment decisions, improving the design and selection of intervention programs, and combatting fraud and waste. Margarét Bjarnadóttier and her colleagues end their chapter by posing specific questions that need to be answered as the field of further analytics develops.

Thinking big is not a problem for the author of our last chapter. In Chapter 15, Derek Ritz presents an e-health evaluation framework based on process control theory and data analytics. Both internationally and in the United States and its states, health systems are a topic of discussion and study. What makes for an efficient and well-functioning health system? How should accessibility to health services be measured? How do consumers fit into this system and stay connected to their care?

With the information presented by these authors, the reader will leave literate in the issues of big data. We hope, though, even more, the reader will leave excited about the potential ahead and even be empowered to join in making that potential real.

REFERENCES

Data Governance Institute. 2008. Current US federal data laws addressing data privacy, security, and governance. Available at http://www.datagovernance.com/adl_data_laws_existing_federal_laws.html

National Council of the National Academies, Board on Mathematical Sciences and Their Applications. 2014. Training students to extract value from big data. April 11–12. Available at http://sites.nationalacademies.org/deps/bmsa/deps_087192

Shulman, C. 2014. Fast, easy tech matters to physicians. *Healthcare IT News*. April 10, p. 1. Available at http://www.healthcareitnews.com/news/fast-easy-tech-matters-physicians?topic=08,19

List of Abbreviations

Acronym	Definition
ACA	Affordable Care Act
ACA-LO	Application-Levels of Outcomes
ACOs	Accountable Care Organizations
ADT	Admission, Discharge, and Transfer
AeHIN	Asia E-Health Information Network
AHIM	American Health Information Management Association
AHIP	American Health Insurance Plans
AHRQ	Agency for Health Research and Quality
AIR	Additional Improvement in Reclassification
AMA	American Medical Association
AMIA	American Medical informatics Association
ANIA	American Nursing informaticists Association
ARRA	American Recovery and Reinvestment Act
ART	Antiretroviral
ASHIM	American Society of Health Information Management
BHC	Building Healthy Communities
BHNI	Bureau of National Health insurance
BI	Business intelligence
CAGR	Compound Annual Growth Rate
CAHIT	Center for the Advancement of Health IT
CAHs	Critical Access Hospitals
CARe	Center for Assistance in Research Using eRecord
CAS	Complex Adaptive Systems
CAT	Computer Axial Tomography
CBSA	Core-Based Statistical Area
CBTS	Community-Based Treatment Supporters
CCHIIM	Commission On Certification for Health informatics and Information Management
CDE	Common Data Elements
CER	Comparative Effectiveness Research
CHIB	Center for Health-Related informatics and Bioimaging
CHIDS	Center for Health Information and Decision Systems
CI	Continuous Improvement

CIA	Central Intelligence Agency
CIC	Clinical Information Channel
CMA	Canadian Medical Association
CME	Continuing Medical Information
CMMB	Catholic Medical Mission Board
CMO	Chief Medical officer
CMS	Centers for Medicare and Medicaid
CNMC	Children's National Medical Center
CPHIS	Certified Professional in Health Information Systems
CPT	Common Procedure Terms
CQI	Continuous Quality Improvement
CRAN	Comprehensive R Archive Network
CRII	Clinical Relevance of Information Index
CRS	Catholic Relief Services
CSDH	Commission On Social Determinants of Health
DALYs	Disability-Adjusted Life-Years
DARPA	Defense Advanced Research Projects Agency
DBMS	Database Management Systems
DDIU	Data Demand and Information Use
DFLE	Disability-Free Life Expectancy
DGI	Data Governance Institute
DICOM	Digital Imaging and Communications in Medicine
EBP	Evidence-Based Practice
EDM	Electronic Data Methods
EDWs	Enterprise Data Warehouses
EHR	Electronic Health Records
EMR	Electronic Medical Record
ENIAC	Electronic Numerical Integrator and Computer
EP	Eligible Professional
ER	Emergency Room
ESRD	End Stage Renal Disease
ETL	Extract, Transform, and Load
FBI	Federal Bureau of Investigation
FDA	Food and Drug Administration
FOIA	Freedom of Information Act
FWA	Fraud, Waste, and Abuse
GBD	Global Burden of Disease
GERD	Gastro-esophageal Reflux Disease
GINA	Genetic Information Non-Discrimination Act

GPA	Grade Point Average
HALE	Health-Adjusted Life Expectancy
HCOs	Health Care Organizations
HCUP	Healthcare Cost and Utilization Project
HIE	Health Information Exchange
HIMSS	Health Information and Management Systems Society
HIPAA	Health Insurance Portability and Accountability Act
HIT	Health Information Technology
HITECH	Health Information Technology for Economic and Clinical Health
HRQoL	Health-Related Quality of Life
HRSA	Health Resources and Services Administration
HSA	Health System Analysis
IAM	Information Assessment Method
ICD 9	International Classification of Diseases 9th edition
ICD 10	International Classification of Diseases 10th edition
ICS	Inhaled Corticosteroids
ICT	Information and Communication Technology
IDN	Integrated Delivery Network
IHI	Institute for Healthcare Improvement
IMA	Interchurch Medical Assistance
InfoPOEMs	Patient-Oriented Evidence That Matters
IOM	Institute of Medicine
IOS	Interorganizational Systems
IPPS	Inpatient Prospective Payment System
IT	Information Technology
IV	Intravenous
JCAHO	Joint Commission on Accreditation of Healthcare Organizations
LABAs	Long-Acting Beta-Agonists
LOINC	Logical Observation Identifiers Names and Codes
M&E	Monitoring and Evaluation
MOOCs	Massive Open Online Courses
MPI	Master Patient Index
MRIs	Magnetic Resonance Imaging
MRN	Medical Record Number
MU	Meaningful Use
NAEPP	National Asthma Education and Prevention Program
NCQA	National Committee for Quality Assurance

NICE	National Institute for Health and Care Excellence
NIH	National Institutes of Health
NLP	Natural Language Processing
NSF	National Science Foundation
NSQIP	National Surgical Quality Improvement Program
O&E	Outcomes and Evaluation
OCR	Optical Character Recognition
ODS	Operational Data Store
OGP	Open Government Partnership
ONC	Office of the National Coordinator
PACS	Picture Archiving and Communication System
PBA	Pattern-Based Analysis
PBF	Performance-Based Financing
PCMHs	Patient-Centered Medical Homes
PCORI	Patient Centered Outcomes Research Institute
PCPs	Primary Care Physicians
PDSA	Plan–Do–Study–Act
PEPFAR	President's Emergency Plan for AIDS Relief
PhD	Doctor of Philosophy
PHI	Personal Health Information
PLO	Patient-Level Outcomes
PMML	Predictive Model Markup Language
PQRS	Physician Quality Reporting System
PTCA	Percutaneous Transluminal Coronary Angioplasty
PUF	Public Use File
QALYs	Quality-Adjusted Life-Years
QI	Quality Improvement
RCT	Randomized Controlled Trial
ROC	Receiver Operating Characteristic
RWJF	Robert Wood Johnson Foundation
SABA	Short-acting Beta-agonists
SAS	Statistical Analysis System
SCA	Site Capacity Assessment
SES	Socioeconomic Status
SNOMED	Systematized Nomenclature of Human Medicine
SOPs	Standard Operating Procedures
SQL	Structured Query Language
STAs	Senior Technical Advisors
UHC	Universal Health Coverage

UMLS	Unified Medical Language System
UMSOM/IHV	University of Maryland's School of Medicine/Institute of Human Virology
UN	United Nations
UPI	Unique Patient Identifier
UPMC	University of Pittsburgh Medical Center
VAS	Visual Analog Scale
VNA	Vendor Neutral Archive
WHO	World Health Organization
YLL	Years of Life Lost

Section I

1

Little Big Data: Mastering Existing Information as a Foundation for Big Data

Donald A. Donahue, Jr.

CONTENTS

OBJECTIVES

After reading this chapter, the reader shall be able to:

- Describe what volume of health data are generated by the typical health center
- Evaluate the four types of projects and their implications for answering questions with health care data

capacity and the corresponding reduction in size of the machine. In less than 50 years, in 1995 a team at the University of Pennsylvania had replicated the functionality of ENIAC on a single silicon chip measuring 7.44 mm by 5.29 mm (Van Der Spiegel, 1996). A mere 12 years later, some 62 years after the launching of ENIAC, Apple released the first iPhone on June 29, 2007, heralding a new age in mobile computational power. The iPhone—and its Android and Blackberry cousins—offer substantial communication and computing capabilities. Roughly the size of a deck of cards, the iPhone 5 can perform 20,500,000 instructions per second compared with ENIAC's 385 multiplications per second.

This explosion in computational power spawned a corresponding growth in data generation. This led, in turn, to the emergence of the concept of big data. But what is big data? These data come from everywhere: sensors used to gather climate information, posts to social media sites, digital pictures and videos, purchase transaction records, and cell phone GPS signals, to name a few. We create 2.5 quintillion bytes of data every day. Of all the data in the world today, 90% has been created in the last two years (IBM).

The ability to store and use large amounts of data has historically been limited by the size and cost of hardware, limitations in storage capacity, and staff and maintenance requirements. Increased connectivity, advances in storage capabilities, and market dynamics have fostered the growth of network-based services, more commonly referred to as the cloud (Carroll, Kotzé, and van der Merwe, 2012). Microsoft Research Executive Tony Hey describes the potential of cloud computing as "the large cloud/utility computing provides can have relatively very small ownership and operational costs due to the huge scale of deployment and automation. Simple Web services interface to store and retrieve any amount of data from anywhere on the Web" (n.d.). The unprecedented growth in access can, however, present an overwhelming amount of data, exceeding the ability to effectively use it. Hey goes on to point out that there is a science to retrieving meaningful data and interpreting it.

The potential for an overwhelming data flow is such that a term has evolved to describe the phenomenon: the data deluge. The data deluge refers to the situation where the sheer volume of new data being generated is overwhelming the capacity of institutions to manage it and researchers to make use of it (President's Council of Advisors on Science and Technology, 2007). The rush toward increased volume is likely to exacerbate the already disjointed and dysfunctional array of information sources that populate the health care landscape. While technology can be an efficiency facilitator, it can also be an overwhelming force.

THE HEALTH CARE DATA MONSTER

Health care generates a tremendous amount of structured data. A 1,000-bed facility, where each patient record potentially could contain as many as 10,000 characters, could produce ~1.2 GB per year of structured data in individual patient records alone. Information in these records is readily identifiable and directly supports analysis, allowing examination of such management indicators as average length of stay, patients per bed per year, and number of readmissions within 30 days.

The vast amount of data created—as much as 80%—is unstructured (text, voice annotations, images). The challenge becomes how to use that unstructured data toward a beneficial purpose. We find ourselves at a technological crossroads. A massive influx of new data offers advanced analytical potential, yet we do not effectively use the data already on hand.

The concept of big data impacts here. Structured data size for individual providers is not a major problem in this context. Available analytical tools can identify trends and issues within the limited 20% world of structured data. The key challenge is data sourcing, data extraction, data consolidation, data cleaning, and data transformation. How can we combine the structured with the unstructured to produce a utilitarian foundation?

Establishing such utility is increasingly central for health care. Two landmark reports from the Institute of Medicine—*To Err Is Human: Building a Safer Health System* (IOM, 2000) and *Crossing the Quality Chasm: A New Health System for the 21st Century* (IOM, 2001)—highlighted both the need for improvement and the role information technology can serve. The government's focus on comparative effectiveness, quality, cost containment, and outcomes being driven by the Health Information Technology for Economic and Clinical Health (HITECH) Act of 2009 and reinforced by the Patient Protection and Affordable Care Act (ACA) of 2010 initially encouraged the adoption of technology and later penalized absence of such adoption. The ability to create efficiencies, identify outliers, and measure performance is increasingly becoming a core management tool for health care (Agency for Healthcare Research and Quality, 2007; Steinberg, 2003; U.S. Department of Health and Human Services, 2014).

THE WICKED PROBLEM OF KNOWING WHERE TO LOOK

The challenge for health care is to identify where actionable data reside, to extract them, and to make use of them. Rittel and Webber (1973) and Churchman (1967) "defined a class of problems that are ill formatted, employ confusing information, many clients and decision makers, conflicting values and resolutions that have 'thoroughly confusing' ramifications, which they call 'wicked problems'" (Tomasino, 2011, p. 1353). "The hospital—altogether the most complex human organization ever devised" (Drucker, 2006, p. 54)—is an intricate matrix organization composed of multiple autonomous and interdependent cohorts (ibid.). This complexity is multiplied when the broader spectrum of health care—outpatient clinics, private provider offices, emergency medical services, long-term care, pharmacies, researchers, insurers, and others—is considered. Each of these entities may have its own information technology (IT) system, data repository, and terminology. This can result in confusing information, many clients and decision-makers, and conflicting values and resolutions, the very essence of a wicked problem.

The health care landscape is constantly shifting. The dynamic of conflicting perspectives and the need to establish internal institutional relationships generate interorganizational systems (IOS). IOS, in turn, organize as complex adaptive systems (CAS) (Waldrop, 1992). Unlike a production line, where a product follows a prescribed linear path to completion, an encounter with the health care system can vary and likely will based on myriad factors such as diagnosis, location (*Dartmouth Atlas of Health Care*, 2014), payer–provider contractual agreements, and provider referral patterns. That these CAS are multifaceted and fluid makes institutional data analysis challenging, and extant data sources often provide only apples-to-oranges comparisons.

The realm of project management offers a framework for examining the analytical needs of a health care organization. Turner and Cochrane (1993) defined four types of projects:

Type 1: Goals and methods of achieving the project are well-defined.
Type 2: Goals are well-defined but methods are not.
Type 3: Goals are not well defined but methods are.
Type 4: Neither goals nor methods are well-defined.

Health care data are contained in multiple, often unconnected systems. Hospital information technology can include discrete systems for scheduling, individual medical records, radiology, imaging, pharmacy, laboratory, blood bank, pathology, the emergency department, a master patient index, finance, billing, human resources, and supplies. Given the individuality of each patient, variations in practice, and the disparate sources of data, an analytical need can be any type project. How can we manage an enterprise when the goals and methods routinely vary?

THE CHALLENGE AT HAND

Current HIT systems generate myriad reports. Typically, these represent performance within a functional realm, such as financial performance or clinical operations metrics. The result is these reports can be overwhelming. In the words of health care consultant Quint Studer (2013), "There are so many areas to oversee, decisions to make and problems to solve. If you aren't careful, you'll spend your whole day responding and reacting instead of laser-focusing on the issues that drive results ... days turn into weeks that turn into months that turn into years." With countless systems generating multiple management reports, the health care executive can be awash in data but wanting for actionable insights. Consider a case study in system performance. Who are my poorly performing providers in terms of costs versus patient satisfaction and why? The source data contain approximately four million records, collected over a period of five years from more than 100 health care providers.* Data descriptors include 183 attributes, such as the following:

- Person specific information such as gender, age, and ethnicity
- Encounter information such as:
  - Provider ID
  - Multiple diagnoses and codes
  - Multiple procedures and codes
  - Length of stay, total costs, disposition, and medical coverage type
- Patient satisfaction quality indicator

A typical management report will appear in tabular form (Figure 1.1). Even though this representation is a comprehensive depiction of a broad

---

* The data for this example are drawn from actual deidentified medical records.

Filter: Data is filtered +

Attributes: **36** Records: **144,655** | 🔲 ✦ Explore | 🖾⟲

No.	Name	States		State	Records	Total Cost (Average)	Quality (Average)	˅ Provider
1	Patient ID	Continuous		190555.0	6,752 (4.7%)	171,044.25		4.31
2	Provider ID	111		190429.0	5,781 (4%)	0		2.74
3	Type of Care	6		190525.0	4,768 (3.3%)	63,215.82		4.03
4	Patient Age	2 + Continuous		190148.0	4,471 (3.1%)	65,032.14		3.99
5	Age Range (20)	20		190422.0	4,469 (3.1%)	61,354.54		3.94
6	Age Range (5)	6		191228.0	4,072 (2.8%)	44,506.03		3.74
7	Gender	5		190470.0	3,886 (2.7%)	66,988.65		4.03
8	Ethnicity	4		190323.0	3,773 (2.6%)	76,936.66		4.13
9	Race	7		190034.0	3,688 (2.5%)	33,530.38		3.62
10	Patient Zip Code	2505		190400.0	3,656 (2.5%)	59,053.33		4.04
11	Patient County	52		190392.0	3,205 (2.2%)	87,466.72		4.23
12	Length Of Stay	2		190529.0	3,080 (2.1%)	46,870.22		3.83
13	Admission Quarter	5		190796.0	3,059 (2.1%)	161,008		4.22
14	Admission Year	13		191227.0	3,057 (2.1%)	41,059.8		3.72
15	Admission Source Site	10		190631.0	2,729 (1.9%)	87,398.29		4.18
16	Admission Source License	4		190522.0	2,679 (1.9%)	77,091.14		4.11
17	Admission Source Route	3		190758.0	2,676 (1.8%)	116,745.58		4.28
18	Type of Admission	5		190078.0	2,661 (1.8%)	88,020.96		4.2
19	Disposition	14		190243.0	2,586 (1.8%)	62,351.34		4.04
20	Do Not Resuscitate	3		190385.0	2,370 (1.6%)	102,576.01		4.23
21	Payment Category	10		190568.0	2,369 (1.6%)	84,529.19		4.19
22	Coverage Type	4		191231.0	2,329 (1.6%)	21,092.22		3.53
23	Licensed Payment Plan	54		190754.0	2,327 (1.6%)	53,210.85		3.94
24	Total Cost	3		190630.0	2,281 (1.6%)	104,781.33		4.2
25	Primary External Cause of Injury Ad...	797		190413.0	2,212 (1.5%)	44,339.42		3.83
26	Additional External Cause of Injury 1...	510		190517.0	2,197 (1.5%)	90,213.7		4.19
27	Additional External Cause of Injury 2...	479						
28	Additional External Cause of Injury 3...	279						
29	Additional External Cause of Injury 4...	192						
30	Major Diagnostic Category	26						
31	Medicare Severity Diagnosis Related...	Continuous						
32	Principal Diagnosis (ICD-9-CM)	197 + Continuous						
33	Condition Present On Admission - Pr...	6						
34	Principal Procedure for Treatment (...	1 + Continuous						
35	Days Until Principal Procedure	192						
36	Other Diagnosis 1 (ICD-9-CM)	555 + Continuous						

FIGURE 1.1
Representative data report for providers versus cost and quality, circulatory system disorders.

FIGURE 1.2
The landscape of analytics.

array of indicators, it does not readily provide actionable information. It leaves the user to ponder: Are there insights in the data? Can I understand why there is a problem? Can I predict what could happen down the road? Can analytics point to solutions that I can track over time?

Insights can be uncovered via analytical thinking. "Analytical thinking is a structured approach to answering questions and making decisions based on facts and data" (Hanrahan, 2012):

- First, figure out that I have a problem and then *clearly* define it.
- Get the right data to help come up with answers; check, verify, clean, and normalize.
- Locate specific problematic areas within the data.
- Prioritize these problem areas.
- Explore relationships and patterns in the data.
- Drill down to identify solutions.
- Confirm hypotheses and analyze errors.
- Share findings with others.
- Determine how solving the problem will affect me going forward.
- Decide and act (Figure 1.2).

HIDING IN PLAIN SIGHT

There are multiple, well-established analytical programs, many dating back to the 1960s. General-purpose solutions (tools and platforms) include such recognizable applications as Excel, SAS, SPSS, Cognos, Tableau, and QLikView.

New offerings emerge on a regular basis that facilitate data mining, business intelligence, statistics/advanced analytics, prediction/forecasting, and visual exploration. Specialized solutions offer predictive applications, forecasting, scheduling, and process optimization functionalities. All have relevance in health care. The challenge is to decide which one is the optimal application. That decision should be based on the nature of the issue. The relative merits of each product are beyond the scope of this chapter.

Decision-making can be divided into three broad, progressively active categories: descriptive, predictive, and prescriptive (Bell, Raiffa, and Tversky, 1998). In health care, the information that supports descriptive deliberations includes patient population management, clinical quality and efficacy, outliers for providers or patients, and coding errors and fraud. These effectively measure or reflect events that have already occurred. Predictive analysis can project issues such as revenues in 30, 60, and 90 days; readmissions (e.g., patient with congestive heart failure [CHF] will be readmitted to the hospital within 30 to 90 days); and patient groups for risk adjustment. Prescriptive actions influence future outcomes and include patient flow management, accurate costing, and asset management. The logical utility is that it is better to influence results than to react to past events.

Let us return to the previously mentioned case study. Health care is increasingly under pressure to control costs and improve quality. Industry internal initiatives such as the IOM reports, national policy exemplified by ACA, and market competitive forces demand greater insights into the forces that drive health care outcomes. Assume we wish to identify providers with substandard outcomes in terms of cost versus patient satisfaction, with a focus on circulatory system disorders. In all probability, the relevant indicators reside in multiple IT systems. The aggregate data set includes 732 million descriptors. Defining the applicable attributes for analysis represents a type-2 project; the goals are well defined (identifying poorly performing providers), but the methods are not. What might be the indicators of poor performance? On what hypothesis might analysis be based?

> It is a capital mistake to theorize before one has data. Insensibly one begins to twist facts to suit theories, instead of theories to suit facts.
>
> **Sir Arthur Conan Doyle**
> *Sherlock Holmes, A Scandal in Bohemia*

Quality pioneer Avedis Donabedian called for a multitiered approach to sampling, drawing from a broad range of attributes (1988). This might suggest examining the entirety of available facts. In this context, we deal only with extant data, not the vast potential being unleashed by technological advancement—and not yet available. The sheer volume of existing facts is overwhelming. The goal is not to acquire more data but to identify relevant data. This can be done by identifying certain patterns within the available information.

The first task is to aggregate the data. Extract, transform, and load (ETL) processes extract data from outside sources, transform it to fit operational needs, and load it into the end target (database, operational data store, or data warehouse) (Golfarelli and Rizzi, 2009). The range of target formats is broad, ranging from a single file on a laptop to sophisticated corporate-wide repositories (Inmon, 2005). For the purpose of this example, a single, comma delimited* file was created from the various source systems.

This facilitates creation of a single file within which to explore. It does not, however, provide a starting point or methodology to identify outliers. The question of what attributes typify a high-cost, low-satisfaction provider remains unanswered. A method of attributional analysis could identify these incidents. The emerging technology of pattern-based analysis (PBA) provides that tool.

PBA is an analytic methodology that identifies key multivariate correlations or *patterns* in the data. A pattern is a group of low-dimensional data records from a high-dimensional data set. Examples include frequent patterns (clustering), infrequent patterns (anomaly detection), and sequential patterns (time series). Initially developed for the U.S. Navy as a means to track shipboard travel of communicable diseases, PBA has evolved to provide insight within data to guide further exploration and analysis and to facilitate both automated hypothesis generation and domain-driven hypothesis testing.

The analysis began with selection of a reference descriptor. As the focus was to compare cost with quality—characterized by patient satisfaction, measured from 1 (lowest) to 5 (highest)—total cost was selected as the baseline attribute signified within the analytical program as the target. An examination of the relationship between total costs and all other attributes identified the greatest correlation between cost and quality.

---

* A type of data format in which each piece of data is separated by a comma. This is a common format for transferring data from one application to another because most database systems are able to import and export comma-delimited data.

While this may seem intuitive, the nature of that correlation must be examined to understand its relevance.

PBA allows visualization of relationships. By examining the distribution of costs against satisfaction ratings, it is possible to identify areas of concern. Reviewing these relationships (Figure 1.3), it becomes apparent that the majority of satisfactions scores lie in the 4–5 range, even as some of those encounters incurred extremely high costs. What is troublesome, however, is the cluster of relatively high-cost events that produced the lowest satisfaction score of 1, visible in the lower-left hand corner of Figure 1.4. Identifying the underlying reason for this disparity—high cost and low satisfaction—offers the opportunity for process enhancement and improved outcomes.

Further visualization, via cascading analytics within PBA, allows examination of patterns for these events (Figure 1.5). By exploring the collections of patterns associated with the greatest cost, low patient satisfaction points, the two top attributes are identified. Some 48 patients experienced 10 or more procedures, the top pattern. The second pattern identifies that 98 patients received two to four procedures under Medicare.

The ability to drill down, applying progressive examination of the underlying patterns for any given attribute, allows more detailed investigation. Having identified a cluster of patients associated with the two top

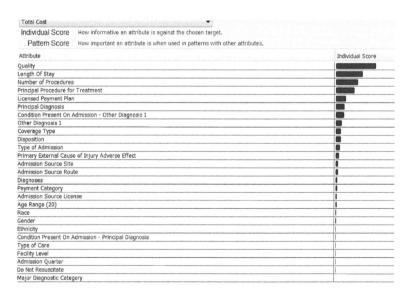

FIGURE 1.3
Analysis of patterns: Most important attributes against cost.

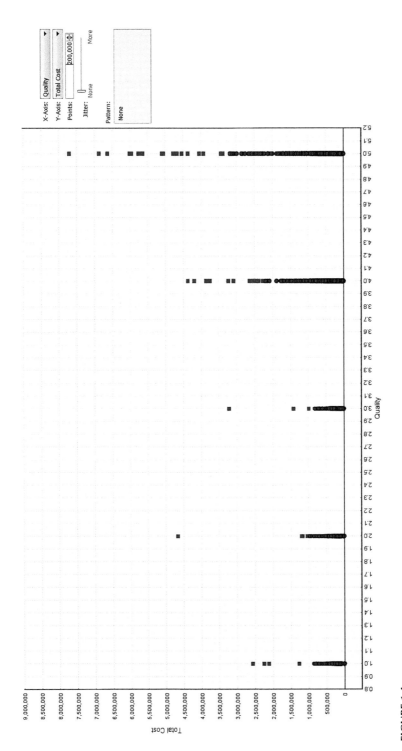

FIGURE 1.4
Additional exploration—visualizing (cost, quality) outliers.

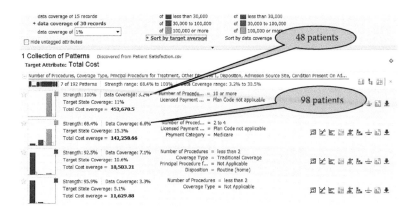

FIGURE 1.5
Pattern-based discovery—see high-cost, low-quality patterns.

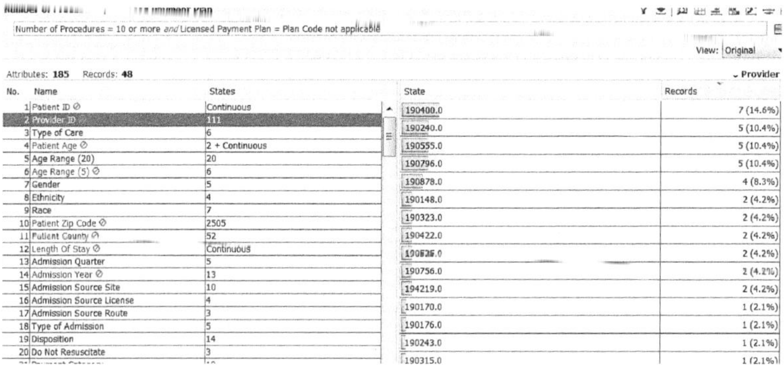

FIGURE 1.6
Casting a tighter net—provider ID distribution for top pattern.

patterns, it might be instructive to ascertain which providers generated these substandard outcomes. This window (Figure 1.6) identifies the top 4 providers (of 111) that account for 46% of poor outcomes within the pattern.

This identifies a pattern of substandard performance among a small group of providers. Any corrective actions would require specific knowledge of the source of that substandard performance. What are the key procedures involved in these outcomes? Continuing the drill-down process, it is possible to identify the distribution of procedures among these seemingly poorly performing providers. We wish to examine the principal procedure for treatment. The PBA program allows isolation of that information as it has identified the practice pattern of the providers being examined. The resultant screen shot (Figure 1.7) dramatically

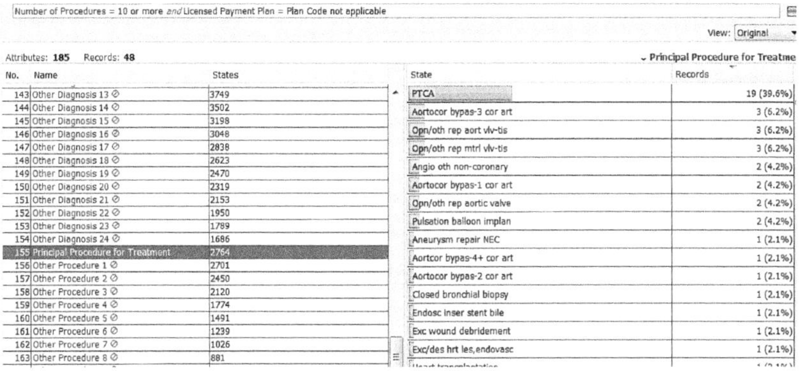

No.	Name	States
143	Other Diagnosis 13	3749
144	Other Diagnosis 14	3502
145	Other Diagnosis 15	3198
146	Other Diagnosis 16	3048
147	Other Diagnosis 17	2838
148	Other Diagnosis 18	2623
149	Other Diagnosis 19	2470
150	Other Diagnosis 20	2319
151	Other Diagnosis 21	2153
152	Other Diagnosis 22	1950
153	Other Diagnosis 23	1789
154	Other Diagnosis 24	1686
155	Principal Procedure for Treatment	2764
156	Other Procedure 1	2701
157	Other Procedure 2	2450
158	Other Procedure 3	2120
159	Other Procedure 4	1774
160	Other Procedure 5	1491
161	Other Procedure 6	1239
162	Other Procedure 7	1026
163	Other Procedure 8	881

State	Records
PTCA	19 (39.6%)
Aortocor bypas-3 cor art	3 (6.2%)
Opn/oth rep aort vlv-tis	3 (6.2%)
Opn/oth rep mtrl vlv-tis	3 (6.2%)
Angio oth non-coronary	2 (4.2%)
Aortocor bypas-1 cor art	2 (4.2%)
Opn/oth rep aortic valve	2 (4.2%)
Pulsation balloon implan	2 (4.2%)
Aneurysm repair NEC	1 (2.1%)
Aortcor bypas-4+ cor art	1 (2.1%)
Aortocor bypas-2 cor art	1 (2.1%)
Closed bronchial biopsy	1 (2.1%)
Endosc inser stent bile	1 (2.1%)
Exc wound debridement	1 (2.1%)
Exc/des hrt les,endovasc	1 (2.1%)

FIGURE 1.7
Principal procedure distribution for top pattern.

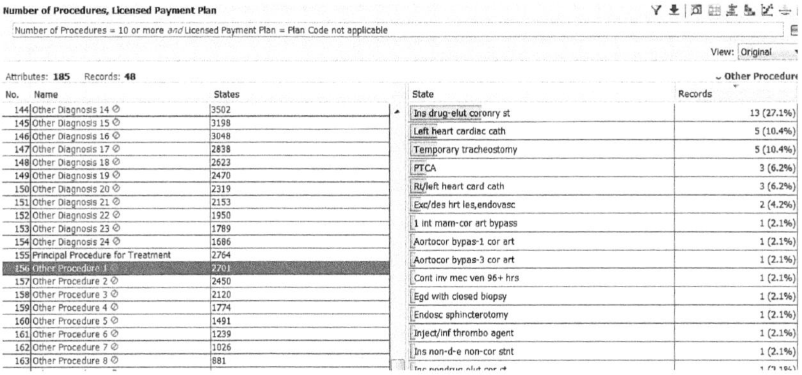

No.	Name	States
144	Other Diagnosis 14	3502
145	Other Diagnosis 15	3198
146	Other Diagnosis 16	3048
147	Other Diagnosis 17	2838
148	Other Diagnosis 18	2623
149	Other Diagnosis 19	2470
150	Other Diagnosis 20	2319
151	Other Diagnosis 21	2153
152	Other Diagnosis 22	1950
153	Other Diagnosis 23	1789
154	Other Diagnosis 24	1686
155	Principal Procedure for Treatment	2764
156	Other Procedure 1	2701
157	Other Procedure 2	2450
158	Other Procedure 3	2120
159	Other Procedure 4	1774
160	Other Procedure 5	1491
161	Other Procedure 6	1239
162	Other Procedure 7	1026
163	Other Procedure 8	881

State	Records
Ins drug-elut coronry st	13 (27.1%)
Left heart cardiac cath	5 (10.4%)
Temporary tracheostomy	5 (10.4%)
PTCA	3 (6.2%)
Rt/left heart card cath	3 (6.2%)
Exc/des hrt les,endovasc	2 (4.2%)
1 int mam-cor art bypass	1 (2.1%)
Aortocor bypas-1 cor art	1 (2.1%)
Aortocor bypas-3 cor art	1 (2.1%)
Cont inv mec ven 96+ hrs	1 (2.1%)
Egd with closed biopsy	1 (2.1%)
Endosc sphincterotomy	1 (2.1%)
Inject/inf thrombo agent	1 (2.1%)
Ins non-d-e non-cor stnt	1 (2.1%)

FIGURE 1.8
Secondary procedure distribution for top pattern.

demonstrates that 4 of 10 of the procedures performed by these providers are percutaneous transluminal coronary angioplasty (PTCA). A remarkable trend has been identified among these four providers.

Having identified a pattern within procedures performed, it might be beneficial to examine secondary procedures, as coronary cases are typically complex and this particular group of patients received 10 or more procedures. Viewing the highlighted Principal Procedures line, it is easy to see on the line below that a similar number of secondary procedures were performed. By highlighting the secondary procedures line, it can be seen that "Ins drug-elut coronary stent" (Insert drug-eluting coronary stent) is dominant (Figure 1.8). This makes sense in that the two procedures (the primary and the secondary) are commonly performed in tandem.

By identifying the cascading patterns in the available data, a cluster of high-cost–low-satisfaction encounters has been identified. This establishes a hypothesis that a specific group of providers is contributing to high cost and low satisfaction within a particular grouping of patients. Closer examination of the patient data for this specific subpopulation may be further enlightening.

Having identified PTCA as the outlier cost issue, a review of the patient distribution for this procedure would prove instructive. Here again is where pattern discovery can be illuminating. By examining patient characteristics (Figure 1.9), it can be seen that the average cost for the top pattern, 65yrs+ PTCA female, is $444.570, greater than average cost for males in this same age bracket and procedure, $344.289. Armed with this insight, it becomes possible to proactively monitor this subpopulation as they enter the system with high-cost providers to potentially reduce costs and increase patient satisfaction.

Discovery of the latent patterns within the data has revealed an actionable attribute. There is real potential to reduce costs and increase satisfaction given the considerable disparity of costs between two groups receiving the same procedure. Considering the immense complexity within a data field containing hundreds of millions of elements reflecting dozens of categories, additional exploration is possible; the extent is limited only by the intent of the analyst.

Curiosity might lead one to examine the eventual outcome of these encounters. Investigation of the disposition of these cases produces an intriguing revelation. Conventional wisdom dictates that providing ongoing

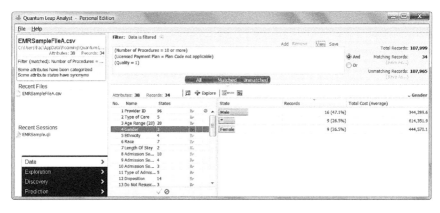

FIGURE 1.9
Patient data for more specific subpopulation—may suggest options.

Number of Procedures = 10 or more *and* Licensed Payment Plan ≈ Plan Code not applicable

View: Original ▼

Attributes: **185**   Records: **48**

▼ Disposition

No.	Name	States		State	Records	Total Cost (Average)
1	Patient ID ◇	Continuous		Skilled Nursing/Intermediate Care (SN/IC) within the admitting hospital	2 (4.2%)	282,779.5
2	Provider... ◇	111		Routine (home)	18 (37.5%)	309,720.72
3	Type of Care	6		Skilled Nursing/Intermediate Care(SN/IC) at another facility	9 (18.8%)	403,278.56
4	Patient ... ◇	2 + Contin...		Home Health Service	11 (22.9%)	499,862
5	Age Range...	20		Acute Care at another hospital	3 (6.2%)	630,256.67
6	Age Ran... ◇	6		Other Care (not SN/IC at another hospital)	1 (2.1%)	821,889
7	Gender	5		Died	4 (8.3%)	936,751
8	Ethnicity	4		Acute Care within the admitting hospital	0	
9	Race	7		Invalid/Blank	0	
10	Patient ... ◇	2505		Left Against Medical Advice	0	
11	Patient ... ◇	52		Other	0	
12	Length ... ◇	Continuous		Other Care within the admitting hospital	0	
13	Admission ...	5		Prison/Jail	0	
14	Admissi... ◇	13		Resident Care Facility	0	
15	Admission ...	10				
16	Admission ...	4				
17	Admission	3				
18	Type of Ad...	5				
19	Disposition	14				
20	Do Not Res...	3				
21	Payment C...	10				

FIGURE 1.10
Influencing costs—impact of discharge disposition.

services is least expensive in a home health service model. Analysis of the patterns for these high-cost patients (Figure 1.10) reveals that several alternative treatment venues are less expensive than the home health option, some considerably so. Comparison of the first four lines shows a remarkable disparity between the costs of the available options. While not a definitive descriptor—closer examination of representative cases is warranted—this is a strong indicator that a counterintuitive approach to managing these patients may be optimal.

THE UTILITY OF EXISTING DATA

Emerging technologies offer the ability to uncover actionable information within extant data. The case examined involved identification of outliers that adversely impacted health care operations. In this instance, traditional examination of the numerous management reports and data sets—data slicing and dicing—did not reveal any insights. Exploration identified an unusual and nonoptimal (Quality, Cost) relationship for the lowest satisfaction rating, Quality Level 1. Pattern-based discovery identified two dominant outlier patterns that explain this relationship. Drilling down into the top pattern provided a view into the dominant providers, principal and secondary procedures, and the underlying data that provide insight into the role of additional procedures and other factors.

With this added insight, the health care system can now monitor 65yrs+ females undergoing PTCA with high-cost providers to potentially reduce costs and improve patient satisfaction. It can also conduct what-if analysis on discharge dispositions, suggesting an option of transferring patients to other treatment venues to reduce costs.

Fidelity of data exploration can be increased through application of another emerging capability, semantic technology. Semantic technologies provide an abstraction layer above existing IT technologies that enable bridging and interconnection of data, content, and processes (Pollock and Hodgson, 2004). In a sense, this offers a universal translator to correlate disparate terms. Consider, for example, a search for issues related to the knee. Knee injuries are a common complaint. "In 2003, patients made approximately 19.4 million visits to physicians' offices because of knee problems. It was the most common reason for visiting an orthopaedic surgeon" (American College of Orthopaedic Surgeons, 2007). Unfortunately, a search for a specific term or diagnosis can miss relevant annotations. Knee problems can be recorded as knee pain, patella, chondromalatia, bursitis, ACL, MCL, PCL, anterior cruciate ligament, meniscus tear, or torn cartilage. In fact, the list of terminology sources in health care is itself dizzying. A program used in the Military Health System in a project to enhance data interoperability itself drew from a dozen sources (Figure 1.11).

Semantic technology correlates these disparate terms so that a search on one will reveal all. Given the wide variety of terminology in medicine, this increases the accuracy of analysis.

CPT – Current Procedural Terminology, medical nomenclature used to report medical procedures and services

ICD9/10 – The International Classification of Diseases

LIONC – universal code system for identifying laboratory and clinical observations

MedDRA – the Medical Dictionary for Regulatory Activities

MEDCIN – terminology around EMRs and point-of-care tools

Medi-Span – Master Drug Data Base, Medi-Span Electronic Drug File™

NCBI – curated classification and nomenclature for all of the organisms in the public sequence databases.

NDDF – National Drug Data File

NLP – Natural Language Processing

RxNorm – normalized names for clinical drugs

SNOMED CT – SNOMED Clinical Terms, the most comprehensive, multilingual clinical healthcare terminology in the world

UMLS – National Library of Medicine's Unified Medical Language System

---

FIGURE 1.11
Sources of medical terminologies. (Courtesy of KnowMED, Inc.)

INTO THE FUTURE

The ability to use existing data in no way diminishes the promise of rapidly advancing technology. IBM's highly touted Watson supercomputer is being developed as a clinical decision support system. In February 2013, IBM announced that Watson software system's first commercial application would be for utilization management decisions in lung cancer treatment at Memorial Sloan-Kettering Cancer Center in conjunction with WellPoint (IBM). Initial results have been impressive. A full 90% of nurses in the field who use Watson now follow its guidance.

Equally impressive is the capital expenditure needed to operate Watson. Watson is made up of a cluster of 90 IBM Power 750 servers (plus additional input-output [I/O], network and cluster controller nodes in 10 racks) with a total of 2,880 POWER7 processor cores and 16 terabytes of RAM. The hardware cost is in the millions (IBM). It is likely that this power will one day become a common utility in health care. Until then, health care organizations can leverage the power of the data already on hand.

The concept of big data can be both daunting and exhilarating, but more is not necessarily better. Health systems, payers, and public health already possess a trove of information—albeit in disparate and disconnected repositories—from which to garner tremendous insights. Emerging analytical capabilities hold great potential for leveraging both the growing HIT sector and existing data.

The rush toward increased volume is likely to exacerbate the already disjointed and dysfunctional array of information sources that populate the health care landscape. While technology can be an efficiency facilitator, it can also be an overwhelming force. Absent foundational understanding, the cloud is simply fog at a high elevation.

> Don't wait for what you don't have. Use what you have, begin now and what you don't even expect will come alongside with excess of what you expect. Go, make it happen.
>
> **Israelmore Ayivor**

REFERENCES

Agency for Healthcare Research and Quality. 2007. *Evaluation of the Use of AHRQ and Other Quality Indicators*. December. Rockville, MD. Available at http://www.ahrq.gov/research/findings/final-reports/qualityindicators/qualityindicators.pdf

American College of Orthopaedic Surgeons. 2007. Common Knee Injuries. Available at http://orthoinfo.aaos.org/topic.cfm?topic = a00325

Bell, David E., Howard Raiffa, and Amos Tversky (Eds.). 1998. *Decision Making: Descriptive, Normative, and Prescriptive Interactions*. New York: Cambridge University Press.

Carroll, Mariana, Paula Kotzé, and Alta van der Merwe. 2012. Securing Virtual and Cloud Environments. In I. Ivanov et al., *Cloud Computing and Services Science, Service Science: Research and Innovations in the Service Economy*. New York: Springer Science+Business Media.

Churchman, C. West. 1967. Guest Editorial: Wicked Problems. *Management Science*, 14(4): B141–B142.

Dartmouth Atlas of Health care. 2014. Available at http://www.dartmouthatlas.org/

Donabedian, Avedis. 1988. The Quality of Care. How Can It Be Assessed? *JAMA* 260(12): 1743–1748.

Donahue, Donald A., Jr. 2011. BioWatch and the Brown Cap. *Journal of Homeland Security and Emergency Management* 8(1): Article 5. Available at http://www.bepress.com/jhsem/vol8/iss1/5, DOI: 10.2202/1547-7355.1823

Drucker, Peter F. 2006. *Classic Drucker*. Cambridge, MA: Harvard Business School Publishing Corp.

Gans, Herbert J. 1967. *The Levittowners. Ways of Life and Politics in a New Suburban Community*. New York: Columbia University Press.

Golfarelli, Matteo, and Stefano Rizzi. 2009. *Data Warehouse Design: Modern Principles and Methodologies*. New York: McGraw-Hill.

Hanrahan, Pat. 2012. Analytic Database Technologies for a New Kind of User—The Data Enthusiast. Paper presented at the ACM SIGMOD/PODS Conference, Scottsdale, AZ, May.

Hey, Tony. n.d. *eScience, Semantic Computing and the Cloud*. Available at http://computerlectures.pnnl.gov/pdf/hey_presentation.pdf

Inmon, William. 2005. *Building the Data Warehouse*. New Jersey: John Wiley and Sons.

Institute of Medicine (IOM). 2000. *To Err Is Human: Building a Safer Health System*. L. T. Kohn, J. M. Corrigan, and M. S. Donaldson, eds. Washington, DC: National Academy Press.

Institute of Medicine (IOM). 2001. *Crossing the Quality Chasm: A New Health System for the 21st Century*. Washington, DC: National Academy Press.

Kayyali, Basel, David Knott, and Steve Van Kuiken. 2013. The Big-Data Revolution in US Health Care: Accelerating Value and Innovation. April. Available at http://www.mckinsey.com/insights/health_systems_and_services/the_big-data_revolution_in_us_health_care

Pollock, Jeffrey T., and Ralph Hodgson. 2004. *Adaptive Information: Improving Business through Semantic Interoperability, Grid Computing, and Enterprise Integration*. New Jersey: J. Wiley and Sons.

President's Council of Advisors on Science and Technology. 2007. *Leadership under Challenge: Information Technology R&D in a Competitive World An Assessment of the Federal Networking and Information Technology*. R&D Program 35.

Steinberg, Earl P. 2003. Improving the Quality of Care—Can We Practice What We Preach? *New England Journal of Medicine* 348(26): 2681–83.

Studer, Quint. 2013. The Hospital CEO's Ultimate Dashboard: What to Check Daily, Quarterly and Yearly. July 1. *Becker's Hospital Review*. Available at http://www.beckershospitalreview.com/hospital-management-administration/the-hospital-ceo-s-ultimate-dashboard-what-to-check-daily-quarterly-and-yearly.html

Tomasino, Arthur P. 2011. Public Safety Networks as a Type of Complex Adaptive System. Paper presented at the International Conference on Complex Systems, Boston, MA, June 26–July 1, p. 1353. Available at http://necsi.edu/events/iccs2011/papers/77.pdf

Turner, J. Rodney. 1992. *The Handbook of Project Based Management: Improving the Processes for Achieving Your Strategic Objectives.* New York: McGraw-Hill.

Turner, J. Rodney, and Robert A. Cochrane. 1993. Goals-and-Methods Matrix: Coping with Projects with Ill Defined Goals and/or Methods of Achieving Them. *International Journal of Project Management* 11(2): 93–102.

Van Der Spiegel, Jan. 1996. ENIAC-on-a-Chip PENNPRINTOUT. March. Available at http://www.seas.upenn.edu/~jan/eniacproj.html

Waldrop, M. Mitchell. 1992. *Complexity: The Emerging Science at the Edge of Chaos.* New York: Simon and Schuster.

Weik, Martin H. 1961. The ENAIC Story. *Journal of the American Ordnance Association.* Available at http://ftp.arl.mil/~mike/comphist/eniac-story.html

2

Managing Unstructured Data in a Health Care Setting

David E. Parkhill

CONTENTS

OBJECTIVES

After reading this chapter, the reader shall be able to:

- Describe what data are considered unstructured
- Understand techniques for extracting information out of unstructured data
- Describe analytic methods used with unstructured data
- Distinguish between text- and natural-language processing
- Articulate differences between text- and image-based searching

ABSTRACT

Paper and electronic medical records are filled with physicians' comments, interpretations of patient tests, nursing observations, and images. These notes are important to interpreting diagnoses and treatments, but they provide challenges when creating and performing analytics in electronic medical records. Taking the many forms of unstructured data, tagging and indexing them, and providing accessible analytics is a necessity if electronic health records (EHRs) are to save time for medical teams and facilitate care and treatment. In this chapter, an overview is provided of the emerging technologies for unstructured data analysis.

INTRODUCTION

Unstructured data are generally defined as data for which it is difficult or impossible to create a typical database schema. Such data include text-based documents; images such as photographs, x-rays, or other such medical scans; and video. In contrast, structured data can be organized in a meaningful way by imposition of a data schema, typically a relational structure of tables with columns that define the data type and semantics and rows that contain the individual data records. In areas other than health care, such as financial services, the vast majority of data are structured. A customer record of a financial institution would consist of fields such as Customer Name, Address, Account Number, Account Balance, and Transactions. All of these data are typically stored in a relational database, which enables ease of updating, querying and aggregating the data to provide operational information, and so-called business intelligence to the financial institution.

In the medical arena, structured data also exist, and there is a growing amount of such data with the implementation of electronic medical record (EMR) and EHR systems. EMR implementations are being driven by the Meaningful Use incentives provided by the U.S. government, while the EHR systems are motivated by individuals desiring to keep their own record of conditions and treatments. Much of the data stored by an EMR are structured, though it is not always stored in a strict relational format, as the Epic EMR™ uses what the company calls an *extended relational* data store. Concurrently, there is also an ever-increasing amount of electronic data being created that are not structured. The unstructured kinds of data of interest in health care are text-based documents such as physician encounter notes, progress notes, and test results as well as medical imaging studies including magnetic resonance imaging (MRIs), computer axial tomography (CAT) scans, and the common x-ray. It is estimated that 80% of the data created in a typical health care provider environment are unstructured data of one form or another (Terry, 2013).

With the pressures that the industry faces to improve patient outcomes and reduce cost, unstructured data have become an important focus of analytics in both the provider and health plan communities. The information contained in physician notes, progress notes, and radiology reports provides a comprehensive view of the treatment of a particular patient. The aggregation of such documents across a larger population of patients provides the foundation for analysis of quality of care, treatment protocols, patient outcomes, drug effectiveness, and the effectiveness and durability of medical devices. However, until these documents are classified and analyzed in a manner that enables analytics to be performed, the relevant information remains locked inside of them.

There is also a need for health care providers to be able to easily obtain a complete, or 360°, view of a patient. This is not easily accomplished when portions of a patient's record are structured data in an EMR and other relevant information is simply attached to the record as a fax image, PDF document, or a reference to an image in a picture archiving and communication system (PACS). This need for a comprehensive view of the patient leads to the requirement that unstructured data be organized, classified, and indexed in a manner that enables such a view to be created.

This chapter explores the types of unstructured data found in a typical health care environment and examines the techniques that can be used to analyze, classify, and use these data types and sources. The intent of the chapter is to provide an overview of use cases and techniques for application in the integration of unstructured data in the health care field. Certain concepts and approaches from natural language processing (NLP), text analytics, and text search are included in the discussion but are not explored in depth.

UNSTRUCTURED DATA IN DETAIL

There are many forms of unstructured data in the health care arena. As noted already, these forms include text documents such as encounter notes, progress notes, radiology reports, and lab reports. A sample encounter note is shown in Figure 2.1.

Encounter Notes

Note that there is substantial semantic content in the encounter note, and much of it is actually data that could be considered structured data, were if it was extracted and formatted in a manner that allows it to be stored in a database. For example, the patient ID, the number "377784364," appears twice in the record and in the second occurrence is tagged with the text tag "Patient ID." Also, the patient name "Alex Nayberg" is indicated as well as the patient gender, "M". Both the procedures performed and the diagnoses are indicated, as "annual eye exam" and "1. Diabetes Mellitus (sic) 2. Diverticulosis. 3. Hypertension," respectively. This information is

377784364
Alex Nayberg
M
Encounter Note:

DATE OF VISIT: 8/22/2012 Patient I D: 377784364

ENCOUNTER DIAGNOSES: 1. Diabetes Mellitus. 2. Diverticulosis. 3. Hypertension.

1 PROCEDURE: annual eye examination Patient's retinal changes occurring in diabetes mellitus, marked by microaneury

FIGURE 2.1
Sample encounter note.

immediately and obviously meaningful to a human reader but is simply a collection of characters to an unsophisticated software analytics program.

In some EMR systems, this information would be added to the patient record as structured data, with the procedure indicated in a procedure field and the diagnoses entered in a set of diagnosis fields. However, in other situations, this document would simply be attached to the electronic record of the patient as is, either in a plain text, Word, or PDF electronic format. As such, it is virtually useless for anything other than human analysis. This situation is exacerbated in circumstances where a third-party provider, such as a radiologist, is analyzing an image and then verbally dictating a report that is converted to a text document (Nuance Communications, Inc., 2013). Such a document is frequently then delivered to the primary care physician, either as an electronic text document, paper document, or, in the worst case, a fax document. In this situation, the document is likely attached to the patient record as is or is scanned into the record as an image, again making it useless for anything other than human reading.

An analogous situation exists for information such as blood test results. A sample lab report is shown in Figure 2.2. To a human reader, it is obvious who the patient is and what the blood test results are, along with the expected ranges for the various tests requested. However, in this form, the information is no more useful than that in the aforementioned encounter note.

Medical Images

If we include medical images, the problem becomes even more acute, in that the images usually don't have any text associated with them—they are essentially pictures, and the same limits that apply to pictures of the world around us apply to medical images. A sample image of a knee x-ray is shown in Figure 2.3. Fundamentally, unless we bring prior knowledge of the subject of the picture or image we don't have any idea of what we're looking at or, in the case of a medical image, what we might be looking for.

In this case, it is possible to apply image analysis software to the pixels that comprise the image and recognize that it is, in fact, a pair of knees. The information that is much more difficult, if not currently impossible, for a software program to discern is that the x-ray was taken to assess the condition of the cartilage in the knee and that the cartilage is in fact worn down to less than half of its normal thickness on the right side of the right knee. An excerpt of a radiologist's report for an MRI of this same knee is shown in Figure 2.4. This is a fax image that is typical of many

Patient Name:	Alex Nayberg
Practice:	Family Doctors
Current Provider:	D. Smith, MD
Encounter Date:	10/27/2011 6:54 AM
Primary Care Physician:	

Lab Result Report
All lab results received within the past 30 days

Lab Results

Comp Metabolic Panel w/GFR: 10/21/2011 09:45

Description	Result	Flags	Range
A/G Ratio	1.5		0.8–2.0
Albumin	4.2		3.4–5.3
Alkaline Phosphatase	65		20–125
ALT	30		20–66
Anion Gap	13		6–18
AST	12		7–37
Bilirubin, Total	0.3		0.2–1.5
BUN	19		7–25
BUN/Creatinine Ratio	21.0		6–25
Calcium	9.6		8.5–10.4
Chloride	108		98–110
CO_2	25		21–33 .
Creatinine	0.90		0.5–1.4
Estimated GFR (Calc)	> 60		
Globulin	2.8		2.2–4.2
Glucose	80		70–99
Potassium	4.2		3.5–5.3
Protein, Total	7.0		6.0–8.3
Sodium	142		135–146

Comments :
Estimated GFR (Calc): (NOTE)
units = mL/min/1.73 m^2
If African American multiply rate times 1.2
Testing Performed: St Anthony Hospital Central 4231 West 16th Ave,
Denver, CO 80204

Thyroid Stimulating Hormone 3rd Gen10/21/2011 09:45

Description	Result	Flags	Range
Thyroid Stimulating Hormone 3r	1.950		0.30–5.00

FIGURE 2.2
Sample blood test results.

such reports, with poor resolution that presents difficulty for the person attempting to read it. To convert it to a text document, optical character recognition (OCR) software can be used to convert the image form of the document into a text document, which can then be analyzed with the following techniques discussed.

In all of these cases, there are data that could be structured data but that aren't represented as such. Common to all of them is the identification

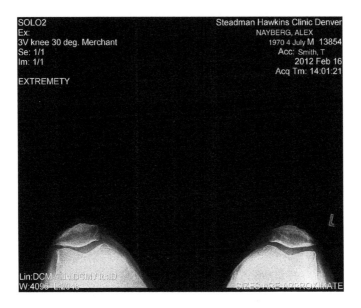

FIGURE 2.3
Knee x-ray.

of the patient, either by name or medical record number (MRN). For the encounter note and x-ray/MRI report, there are diagnoses that represent clearly defined medical terms and that correspond to elements of the ICD-9 or ICD-10 taxonomies. The techniques for unlocking the unstructured data in each of these formats are explored in the next section.

METADATA, TAGGING, AND INDEXING

The fundamental techniques required to create useful analytic information from unstructured data are the concepts of metadata, tagging, and indexing. Metadata and tagging are explained first as they enable the implementation of the third concept, indexing.

Metadata

Metadata are essentially data about data. A simple example of this is the name and data type of a column in a relational database. For example, a column name of Medical Record Number with a data type of integer denotes that the information in the column is what we would understand

Advanced Medical Imaging

Patient Name: NAYBERG, ALEX
DOB: July 4, 1970
Study Date: 10/25/2011 1:30:00 PM
HISTORY:
Anterior right, knee pain for 3 weeks with associated swelling. No known
history of trauma.

COMPARISON:
None.

TECHNIQUE:
Multiplanar multisequence MRT of the right knee without contrast.

FINDINGS:
There is minor increased signal noted in the anterior horn of the
lateral meniscus without a discrete linear surfacing component. The
body and posterior horn of the lateral meniscus are unremarkable. There
is minor ill-defined increased signal in the body and posterior horn of
the medial meniscus as well, again without a discrete linear surfacing
element.

There is moderate chondral loss over the weight bearing surface of the
medial femoral condyle. There are minor medial femorotibial compartment
osteophytes. There may be a near full thickness chondral fissure in the
posterior articulating cortex of the medial femoral condyle as well.
There appears to be chondral loss related to the lateral femorotibial
compartment as well, but this appears less significant. There is full
thickness chondral loss over the lateral patellar facet with moderate
chondral fissuring and cartilage loss over the medial facet and patellar
apex. There is subchondral cystic change in the patella. There are
ill defined regions of increased I2 weighted signal identified in the
anterolateral femoral condyle and apposed patella. There is
patellofemoral osteophyte formation as well.

FIGURE 2.4
Fax image of a radiology report.

to be a numeric MRN. Extending this concept to the encounter note of
Figure 2.1, the text "PatientID" is also a form of metadata, indicating that
there is a notion of a unique character string or number that identifies a
specific patient. The concept of a patient ID is often specific to the provider organization or health plan that acts as the insurer for the patient.
To aggregate patient records across provider networks and across provider
and health plans, the concept of a master patient index (MPI) is likely also
required. This MPI would also be a metadata concept, one that is similar
to PatientID but with a very different context and meaning.

Tags

The notion of a tag can be thought of as a label that might be applied to
something to indicate what it is. Tags correspond to the specific metadata

TABLE 2.1

Document Types and Relevant Metadata and Tags

Document	Possible Metadata Concepts	Corresponding Tags
Encounter note	Master Patient ID, Document type, MRN, Patient Name, diagnoses, procedure	*MPI:* 123456 *Document type:* Progress note *Patient Name:* Nayberg, Alex *MRN:* 377784364 *Diagnosis Tag 1:* Diabetes Mellitus *Diagnosis Tag 2:* Diverticulosis *Diagnosis Tag 3:* Hypertension
Blood test results	Master Patient ID, Document type, MRN, patient name, test type	*MPI:* 123456 *Document type:* Blood test result *Patient Name:* Alex Nyberg Test type: CBC
X-ray	Master Patient ID, Document type, Patient Name Image type, MRN, Subject	*MPI:* 123456 *Document type:* Image *Patient Name:* Nayberg, Alex *Image type:* X-ray *MRN:* 13854 *Subject:* Knee

concepts identified for the item in question. The knee x-ray above might have the metadata notion of "subject" associated with it, indicating that the image is an x-ray of something, and "knee" would be the tag assigned to the subject metadata tag of the image.

Relating the notion of metadata to the previous examples, the documents previously discussed could have the metadata and tags shown in Table 2.1.

Indexing

In its simplest form, the concept of indexing consists of identifying and maintaining a list of pointers or references to all documents with specific tags. Using our previous examples, an index on MPI would include the encounter note, blood test, and x-ray documents. An index on "Images" would include only the x-ray. Note that the use of the MPI resolves the ambiguities that are introduced by the two different forms of the patient name as well as the differences in the medical record numbers. Essentially, an index enables direct and rapid access to a set of documents with a given tag.

Consider the possibility that all encounter notes that contain the words "diabetes mellitus" were indexed. Such an index would enable immediate access to and identification of all patients with diabetes. An index on the term "retinopathy" would allow for the same sort of identification and access. By combining the access enabled by this pair of indices, one could then explore the question of which patients in a provider network have both diabetes and retinopathy. The processes and tools to create such indices and the implications of being able to create electronic queries of this sort are explored in the next section.

ANALYSIS OF UNSTRUCTURED DATA

To create indices on unstructured data, a mechanism must exist for software to analyze and understand the content. The approaches for doing this divide along the lines of the types of data under consideration, typically text and images.

Image Metadata and Tagging

In the case of medical images, obtaining metadata and tags is typically fairly straightforward. When an imaging study is performed at least with digital imaging equipment, the relevant metadata are electronically recorded by the technician performing the study. They are normally attached to the image in a machine-readable format and stored with the image in a picture archiving system. It also appears when the images are viewed, as in the images shown in Figure 2.3. Even if the metadata are not readily available, the text character form of it on the images can be analyzed with OCR software with a high degree of accuracy. From there, it is an easy problem to solve—the text following the words "Patient Name" is extremely likely to be the patient name. Analysis of this sort is a simple case of what's required for the analysis of text-based documents.

Text Analytics and Natural Language Processing (NLP)

Text analytics is the broad field of techniques that apply software algorithms to attempt to understand the content of written language. NLP is considered to be a subset of the broad category of text analytics (Fenton, 2012). The goal of NLP is to fully understand the meaning of a phrase, sentence, or paragraph, in the extreme case to the point where it could be translated into another language. As there is not common agreement on the precise use of terms in this field, for purposes here the term *search text analytics* will be used to refer to techniques that do not extend to attempting to understand the full meaning of a text. Search text analytics has a more modest, though useful, goal of understanding the topic of written language and the general semantics associated with it, but more for the purpose of indexing rather than translation. Text analytics is used for search purposes such as Internet searching or file-system–based searching in content and document management systems such as Microsoft's SharePoint. In general, text analytics can be considered a subset of NLP. Both approaches have legitimate applications to unstructured data in health care and are discussed in the following section, with search text analytics considered first.

SEARCH TEXT ANALYTICS DECONSTRUCTED

Search text analytics approaches consist of scanning text to find individual words, phrases, or combinations of words that may be of significance. The first step in such analysis is known as lexical analysis, which is the decomposition of sentences or sentence fragments into individual words or phrases. Software to perform this type of decomposition has been available since the time of the early text editors and word processing programs. These tools, along with additional capabilities, have been integrated into open-source software toolkits such as Unstructured Information Management Architecture (OASIS, 2009), the OpenNLP framework (Walenz, 2009), and the Natural Language Toolkit (NLTK; Bird, Klein, and Loper, 2009).

Once individual words have been identified in text, the next step is to decide which words are of interest. A typical approach is to create a lexicon of words or phrases that are relevant to the application at hand.

Diabetes Mellitus Encounter Notes

To illustrate the use of a lexicon on a small scale, consider a problem where the objective is to find all encounter notes that might relate to diabetic patients: the words "diabetes" and "mellitus" would be of primary interest, as would the phrase "diabetes mellitus." Additional words of interest in this case would be "retinopathy" and "nephropathy," as they can refer secondary symptoms or conditions found in advanced stage diabetes. Having defined these terms as a basic lexicon, a simplistic approach is to analyze all encounter notes, tag the documents in which they each occur, and create an index for each of these terms that points to all documents in which they occur. This approach provides ready access to all of the relevant documents, which could be useful in and of itself. However, any interpretation of the document contents, such as obtaining a simple count of the total number of diabetic patients, would not likely be accurate using only this five-word lexicon, in that the count would also include patients with nondiabetes-related retinopathy and nephropathy.

A more sophisticated approach is therefore required. The next level of text analytics involves creating rules regarding when certain words occur together or when a set of words all appear in the same document. Such a set of rules is called a rule base, and the rule base is used to search the contents of each document to ascertain which rules are valid with respect to a given document. A rule base for the diabetes example might contain a rule expressing the requirement that a document with the word "retinopathy" must also contain one of the words "diabetes," "nephropathy," or "mellitus" to be considered a document of interest. This would include all encounter notes that might have relevance to diabetes but would exclude those than mention only retinopathy with no other diabetes related indications. In this fashion, it is possible to construct a rule base that can identify encounter notes that have some direct relevance to a diabetes diagnosis.

Extending the technique further, it is also possible to construct a rule base that identifies potential diabetic candidates. If a document were to have the terms "nephropathy," "renal failure," and "retinopathy" but no mention of diabetes, such a document could be tagged as a potential diabetes-related document, given that the three terms all describe conditions that are related to or are coincident with diabetes. The use case for this rule is to find patients who may have diabetes but who have not been diagnosed directly as such. Absent an explicit diagnosis, the patient is probably not on a diabetes treatment protocol, and the condition is unlikely to be being treated.

Health Care–Specific Lexicons

To construct a rule base such as the one described, it is helpful to have a set of terms readily available to include as components of the rule base. In the health care field, the Medical Subject Headings (MeSH; Nelson, 2009) and the Unified Medical Language System (UMLS; Bodenreider, Willis, and Hole, 2004; Hole et al., 2000) provide comprehensives health care–specific lexicons. Using a lexicon as a foundation leads to knowledge modeling and classification techniques, semantic modeling, and taxonomy creation. Briefly, the goal of semantic modeling is to create a knowledge base that represents a particular domain of human knowledge that enables reasoning to be performed and inferences to be made on specific instances of information in the domain. SNOMED and LOINC are examples of ontologies in the medical domain. A taxonomy is a classification system that identifies specific items or specific conditions. The ICD-9 and ICD-10 coding systems and Common Procedure Terms (CPT; AMA, 2014) codes are taxonomies relevant to health care. Having the ability to leverage an existing lexicon or taxonomy in the development of a text analysis rule base makes it much easier to identify the terms relevant for the rule base. The availability of an existing ontology can supply predefined rules that may apply to the problem under consideration.

Applying Text Analytics to Diabetic Patient Records

Figure 2.5 shows an example of how text analytics can be used to create a useful application that analyzes encounter notes and identifies potentially undiagnosed diabetes patients in a fictional health care system.

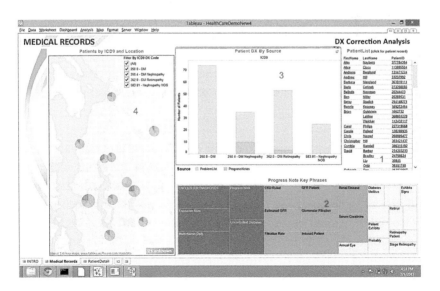

FIGURE 2.5
Diabetes diagnosis correction dashboard.

The aforementioned techniques were applied to a collection of patient records that consisted of unstructured data in the form of encounter notes.

The figure is a screen shot of an analytics dashboard of the application. There are four panels of the dashboard, and they are labeled 1 through 4 in the figure. The content of each panel is as follows:

1. This panel is a set of structured data, representing patient names and PatientID fields from an EMR. This data can be clicked on to drill down to a more detailed level from the patient record, including encounter notes and image scans. The encounter note of Figure 2.1 is one such data item.
2. Panel 2 consists of a set of terms that were used to analyze the encounter notes. When drilling down into a specific record, this panel changes to indicate which terms were found in the record under examination.
3. The third panel is a bar graph of specific diagnosis codes and terms that were found across the population of the patients. The left-most diagnosis is diabetes mellitus, ICD-9 code 250.0, and the next one is diabetes nephropathy, IDC-9 code 250.4. The darker bars represent the number of records in which the diagnosis term was explicitly found, while the lighter bars represent the number of records for which that diagnosis was inferred from the encounter note.
4. The map on the left is a geographic indication of which clinics in the provider system the individual patients primarily visit. Drilling down on any of the specific pie chart segments will change the other panels to reflect which specific patients are associated with those clinic locations.

Though this example is specific to the clinical aspects of diabetes-related conditions, the approach is also valid for analyzing questions such as the institutional costs associated with those patients with both the explicit and inferred diagnoses. By using the text analytics to find such patients, the complete patient record for all such patients can then be identified and aggregated, and, in combination with information from the provider's billing system, a determination of the annual cost of dealing with the undiagnosed patients can be calculated. This sort of analysis would be of particular interest to those organizations that have committed to the accountable care model of the Affordable Care Act. As an accountable care organization (ACO) receives a fixed fee for patient care rather than receiving fees for every patient visit or specific service provided, the identification and elimination of avoidable conditions and their corresponding treatments is imperative.

The general application of these text analysis techniques is to provide an automated approach to analyzing data to answer specific questions whose answers can be found only in unstructured text data and to lay the foundation for more advanced analytics across the health care enterprise.

Natural Language Processing

NLP involves much deeper analysis of unstructured text than search text analytics. The goal of NLP is to actually understand the meaning of the text. In the example application discussed previously, the inferred diabetes diagnoses were tentative—the patient records were flagged and presented to a human user for further analysis and verification of the inference. The goal of an NLP approach would be to get much closer to a definitive conclusion.

NLP techniques include the approaches of lexical analysis and tagging used in search text analytics as a foundation, along with a number of others, which are briefly discussed here. A comprehensive treatment of the topic can be found in Jurafsky and Martin (2008), wherein the authors address both analysis of written text and speech recognition.

Conceptually, the NLP problem breaks down into to basic problems that require solutions: determining the structure of the text and then determining the meaning of the text, based on not only the individual words but also what the words mean in the context of the other words. The mechanisms for understanding the structure of the text include:

- Structure analysis: determining the individual words and the identifying the part of speech that the word represents
- Grammatical synthesis: synthesizing the structure of a sentence or phrase
- Concept identification: identifying single word or compound word concepts from the structure of the text
- Application of semantic modifiers (e.g., negation) and disambiguation (e.g., understanding "treasury bonds" versus "chemical bonds") (Pereira, 2002)

Jurafsky and Martin (2008) apply a slightly different perspective on the essential components of language understanding, decomposing the problem into these steps:

- Morphology: knowledge of the meaningful components of words
- Syntax: knowledge of the structural relationships between words
- Semantics: knowledge of meaning
- Pragmatics: knowledge of the relationship of meaning to the goals and intentions of the speaker
- Discourse: knowledge about linguistic units larger than a single utterance

Other than the syntactic analysis of the text that identifies the individual words, all of these actions require application of advanced techniques in linguistics, computer science, and probability theory. Linguistic techniques are used to determine the potential structures of a text, while computer science and probability theory are applied to determine the most likely meaning of the text. Consider the use of the word "bond." It can have several meanings, and its meaning in this case is derived from the word that precedes it. The word "treasury" leads to the conclusion that the bond is a financial instrument that is an interest-paying debt obligation, while the word "chemical" preceding it leads to a conclusion that it is an electromagnetic attraction between two atomic particles. Knowing which is correct is not a simple matter for a software program; a program would depend on a probability function to know which is the most likely meaning. The problem becomes even more difficult without the modifying words, as then the meanings of other nearby words and even the general topic of the text document become important to understanding meaning. Jurafsky and Martin (2008) note five commonly applied general classes of what they call models and algorithms: state machines, rule systems, logic, probability models, and vector-space models. These topics are mentioned here to provide a sense of the complexity of the analysis techniques used in NLP; however, detailed discussion of them is beyond the scope of this chapter.

Sentiment Analysis and Predictive Analytics

With the previously noted techniques as a foundation, more advanced applications such as sentiment analysis and predictive analytics can be applied. These areas lead more deeply into the field of probability and statistics, extend into machine learning, and represent significant additional areas of application in health care. Sentiment analysis can be applied to assess a patient's mind-set and its impact on treatment outcomes or on patient satisfaction and quality surveys. Applications of predictive analytics include projections of readmission rates impacted by postdischarge follow-up techniques and projections of successful treatment outcomes given a set of treatments and are being considered as an alternative to extensive clinical trials of new drug therapies.

IMAGE MANAGEMENT AND ANALYSIS

Image management and analysis and the related technology approaches are not as technologically advanced as those for text analytics but have recently emerged as an area of growing interest for both additional research and clinical application (Hsu, Markey, and Wang, 2013). As mentioned already, the metadata for images are fairly easy to acquire, but moving beyond patient name, date of study, and other such items is considerably more difficult than text analytics. This section will address current approaches for managing images and briefly touch on techniques for performing image analysis.

Though most medical imaging systems now create digital records, the access to these records is often exclusively through the PACS facility provided by the vendor of the imaging equipment. This means that searching for and analyzing an image is limited to using the so-called viewer software that the vendor provides for viewing their image format. In recent years, the Digital Imaging and Communications in Medicine (DICOM) standard has enabled vendor independent viewers to be created and has also enabled the concept of a vendor neutral archive (VNA) for image storage. The VNA enables storage of images from the imaging machines of various types and multiple vendors, allowing, for example, a patient's x-rays, MRIs, and CAT scans to all be stored and managed in one system. Conceptually, this allows the images to all be tagged with the same patient identifier and an index to be built for all images of a given patient, regardless of the image type or the vendor of the imaging equipment. Integration of images in this way allows a clinician immediate access to all of a patient's imaging studies and also provides a way for the images to be integrated with or linked to the patient's EMR. This then leads to the ability to provide the clinician with the 360° view of the patient mentioned earlier, as illustrated in Figure 2.6.

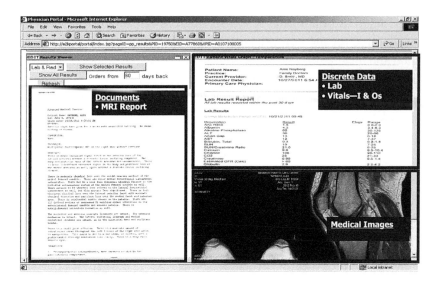

FIGURE 2.6
360° view of the patient.

In addition to the techniques of image tagging and indexing, image searching techniques are emerging that enable images to be searched by visual content, collectively known as computer-based image retrieval (CBIR; Hsu et al., 2013). Rather than specifying a patient name or MRN to retrieve an image, the image itself can be analyzed using either an image search pattern such as the aforementioned knee x-ray or a natural language description of the desired pattern, with one or more corresponding sample images. As with the analysis of natural language, significant variation will occur in the images of similar objects, and improved accuracy in recognition will come through machine learning techniques.

Though image analysis is in the very early stages of exploration and research, it is also being used for diagnostic purposes. Liu et al. (2013) describe a system for using imaging with genomic and clinical data sources as part of a diagnosis system for glaucoma diagnosis.

CONCLUSION

Though the analytic use of unstructured data in health care is more feasible than it has ever been, it is still what should be classified as an emerging technology. However, given the cost and financial pressures that health care organizations face worldwide, there will be increased interest in leveraging both structured and unstructured data to improve patient outcomes and manage costs. This level of interest will undoubtedly drive the evolution of the relevant technologies along at a faster pace, similar to the manner in which Internet search has driven the technology forward in the past decade. As with any new technology, there will be an adventure of discovery in this field, with some technologies creating disappointment and some creating unexpected and unparalleled success.

REFERENCES

American Medical Association (AMA). 2014. *CPT 2014,* professional ed. American Medical Association.

Bird, Steven, Ewan Klein, and Edward Loper. 2009. *Natural Language Processing with Python.* O'Reilly Media.

Bodenreider, Olivier, Jan Willis, and William Hole. 2004. The Unified Medical Language System: What Is It and How to Use It? Paper presented at MEDINFO, September 8, San Francisco, CA.

Fenton, Rick A. 2012. Primer on Text Analytics in Healthcare. *Healthcare Information Management & Communications Canada* 26(2): 1–3.

Hole, William T., Betsy L. Humphreys, Suresh Srinivasan, and Laura A. Roth. 2000. Customizing the UMLS Metathesaurus for Your Applications. *Proceedings of the AMIA Symposium.*

Hsu, William, Mia K. Markey, and May D. Wang. 2013. Biomedical Imaging Informatics in the Era of Precision Medicine: Progress, Challenges and Opportunities. *Journal of American Medical Informatics Association* 20(6): 1–2.

Jurafsky, Daniel, and James H. Martin. 2008. *Speech and Language Processing,* 2d ed. Upper Saddle River, NJ: Pearson Prentice Hall.

Liu, J., Z. Zhang, D.W.K. Wong, et al. 2013. Automatic Glaucoma Diagnosis through Medical Imaging Informatics. *Journal of American Medical Informatics Association* 20(6): 1–7.

Nelson, Stuart J. 2009. Medical Terminologies that Work: The Example of MeSH. In *Proceedings of the 10th International Symposium on Pervasive Systems, Algorithms, and Networks* (ISPAN 2009), December 14–16, 2009, Kaohsiung, Taiwan, pp. 380–384.

Nuance Communications, Inc. 2014. PowerScribe 360. Available at http://www.nuance.com/products/powerscribe360/index.htm

OASIS. 2009. Unstructured Information Management Architecture. Available at https://www.oasis-open.org/committees/tc_home.php?wg_abbrev = uima.

Pereira, Fernando. 2002. Machine Learning in Natural Language Processing. *University of Pennsylvania,* NASSLLI, June.

Terry, Ken. 2013. Analytics: The Nervous System of IT-Enabled Healthcare. *Institute for Health Technology Transformation.* Available at http://ihealthtran.com/iHT2analyticsreport.pdf

Walenz, Brett. 2009. OpenNLP Tutorial. University of Omaha. Available at http://kewi.unomaha.edu/resources/OpenNLPTutorial.pdf

3

Experiences with Linking Data Systems for Analyzing Large Data

Dilhari DeAlmeida, Suzanne J. Paone, and John A. Kellum

CONTENTS

OBJECTIVES

After reading this chapter, the reader shall be able to:

- Explain the need for multidisciplinary staffing for linking data within the health care system
- Explain the impact of data field customization on the effort to link data
- Describe typical challenges in using best of breed systems for linking data

ABSTRACT

This chapter highlights the experiences of a group of researchers and analysts in collaborating and working with different entities within a large hospital facility to develop a complete data set for analysis. Some of the lessons learned include the realization that a number of different data elements that are needed in providing continuous patient care live in a multitude of different systems and the struggles that we had to go through to identify the elements needed from these systems.

INTRODUCTION

The evolution of transactional information systems in non–health care sectors of the U.S. economy has spanned decades and has allowed those industries to drive business decisions through the use of progressively evolving data warehousing and analytics technologies. For example, it has become commonplace for financial services organizations to build complex customer notification and fraud management systems using large amounts of data processed on a regular basis through channels such as credit card and retail transactional platforms (Cooper et al., 2000). With evolving cost and quality pressures in the health care industry and the availability of genomic science contributions that allow clinicians to personalize treatments, the health care industry is faced with similar challenges of leveraging legacy information system investments and current data warehousing and analytics technologies to guide industry transformation. The advent of accountable care models and increasingly sophisticated managed care products from insurers warrant large stores of meaningful health-related data that is assessable through user-friendly platforms similar to those used to successfully manage businesses in other sectors of the world economy (Folland, Goodman, and Stano, 2013). Increasingly, health data will be exposed to computer programs that will manipulate it for use in both organizational forecasting and personalized care profiles and robust clinical research.

THE TRANSFORMATION OF HEALTH DATA

The implementation of transactional information systems in health care began in the late 1980s through the automation of specific functions. Laboratory testing, radiology examinations, and pharmacy management functions based on coding systems could be transformed into structured data. Subsequently, the 1990s and early 2000s saw the proliferation of early clinical information system repositories with data models specifically designed to support specific hospital transactions such as the management of test results and orders for routine and limited clinical treatments. During this same period, systems in physician offices evolved to process office visits and support professional billing. The majority of these information systems were supplied by emerging software companies using myriad proprietary and industry standard programming languages and database software (Wager, Lee, and Glaser, 2009).

This transactional automation trend continues today fueled by federal regulatory programs aimed at enhancing the deployment of electronic health records. In the management of health care, while transactional databases are useful for time-sensitive processing of specific clinical and financial functions they present unique technical limitations when attempting to use data effectively for reporting and advanced analytics on a large scale (Kappelman and Zachman, 2013). These issues include proprietary data structures, undocumented data definitions, lack of standards in data definitions, ambiguous goals related to data warehouse projects, and lack of collaborative leadership models to direct analytics efforts. The result of decades of transactional health care automation is a collection of proprietary, vendor-based information systems with highly customized site-by-site software implementations at hospitals, physician offices, and clinics across the United States. Complex implementations of these systems drive increased budgets for health care provider entities in the forms of staff costs, software licensing costs, and costs associated with proprietary systems interfaces that move data between disparate platforms.

THE NEED FOR MULTIDISCIPLINARY STAFFING

These platforms are supported by specialized staffs of information technology (IT) professionals, some of whom have moved from non–health care sectors to health care and others who originated as health care workers and then migrated toward careers in health information technology. During this same period disciplines in biomedical informatics evolved from academic medical centers with medical professionals such as physicians, nurses, and pharmacists pursuing the study of data, standards, and decision support capabilities in these systems. Academic research centers continue to lead this progression of standards to accomplish key aspects of analytics such as ensuring standards to execute semantic operability between disparate information systems platforms (Ogunyemi et al., 2013).

To execute effective analytics strategies through the use of legacy information systems combined with current data warehouse technologies and data analytics, health care entities must create organizational structures that support a climate of multidisciplinary collaboration between disciplines. Teams of professionals in information technology, biomedical informatics, practicing clinical disciplines, health information management, and financial services are needed to design and implement effective strategies in health care analytics. This approach ensures that both technical and nontechnical issues are balanced in the design of key features of data warehousing such as the mapping and translation of data elements. Likewise, because new models of care such as accountable care organizations (ACOs) may require the analysis of both clinical and financial information, there is a need to include professionals who span the clinical and financial health care management domains.

Multidisciplinary models are needed because translating historical aspects of both clinical and financial knowledge into stores of data that can be queried using data warehouse tools is a complex undertaking for any health services organization (Oborn, Banett, and Racki, 2003). Knowledge models must be developed by interdisciplinary teams to design and build effective translations that create user-friendly data stores and query mechanisms. For example, it is impossible to study panels of patients with diabetes when individual systems' coded definitions of diabetes complications do not follow a common standard. Technologies that map and warehouse data to support advanced queries and statistical analysis are rendered inadequate if groups of clinicians do not consistently code diabetes complications and do so in a standard and reproducible way.

Practicing providers as well as leaders in clinical research must be included in these discussions to ensure capture of relevant patient population characteristics. Likewise, financial and care management professionals must be included in this planning to determine the level of granularity and eventual analysis needed to meet regulatory and quality challenges in managing this population. Health information management professionals can work to determine effective coding methods and assist in developing meaningful data warehouse mapping strategies. Last, information technology professionals are needed to translate these mapping requirements to new data warehouse schemes and structures and programs that execute effective semantic operability between disparate legacy systems. Although national standards may already be established on diagnosing certain conditions, every facility may have their own interpretation and adoption of those standards. Therefore, when working with multiple systems at the same time, it is crucial to have established mapping techniques and dictionaries to avoid any confusion and misinterpretations.

THE CENTER FOR ASSISTANCE IN RESEARCH INVOLVING THE eRECORD

The University of Pittsburgh and the Medical Center (UPMC) operate a collaborative organization called the Center for Assistance in Research involving the eRecord (CARe) that is designed to facilitate compliant research access to the medical center's vast array of information systems that comprise the electronic health record. UPMC operates more than 20 academic, community, and specialty hospitals and 400 outpatient sites, with multiple different integrated health care systems. CARe started in 2010 and is one organizational configuration that a university–medical center partnership can use to facilitate the accumulating health data among the different disciplines. CARe includes analysts who are trained to work with research teams to validate requirements for research data extracts and work with a plethora of IT teams who represent different information technology platforms that house electronic health record (EHR) data. Researchers come to CARe to gain compliant and streamlined access to EHR data extracts and also to receive assistance in mapping these disparate data elements into cogent sets of research information.

By way of example, we will describe our experience at the University of Pittsburgh/UPMC with incorporating and working with multiple data sets using two different project scenarios. For the purposes of this chapter, they will be named *Scenario A (Project A)* and *Scenario B (Project B)*.

> *Scenario A*: Project A is a multiyear, multicenter project using three different systems: a custom medical archival system, a Heath IT vendor platform, and a disease-specific specialty platform (Figure 3.1). All these systems consist of the basic information needed to capture patient information but at the same time have unique features depending on the condition. For example, the custom medical archival system houses clinical and financial information, and the disease-specific specialty platform incorporates the disease-specific clinical indicators and attributes.
>
> *Scenario B*: Project B is an evaluation of a chronic condition using data from a custom archival system and a Heath IT ambulatory EHR vendor (Figure 3.2).

The terminology and logic used for data structure and types are different in most of the systems. For example, as depicted in Figure 3.3, the interdisciplinary team configuration would be crucial for a successful implementation of the project. Some key elements would include early knowledge and awareness on some of the following were crucial for a

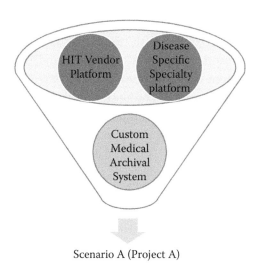

Scenario A (Project A)

FIGURE 3.1
The utilization and use of the systems involved for Project A.

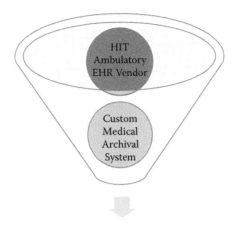

Scenario B (Project B)

FIGURE 3.2
The utilization and use of the systems involved for Project B.

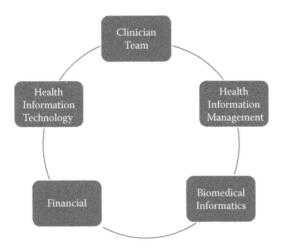

FIGURE 3.3
Example of a collaborative approach using an interdisciplinary team.

successful integration: defining data variables, identifying the constraints, identifying data sources including primary (and all possible secondary) required document specifications, creating the appropriate definitions and validation methodology, creating business rules around the project, and establishing personal health information (PHI) and deidentification requirements.

Challenges

Both of these scenarios represented unique challenges because of the multiple transactional platforms involved. They required a best of breed information strategy. Best of breed information strategies are common in the health care industry due to the nature in which provider organizations evolved in their markets and the limitations and capabilities of clinical systems vendors in the past two decades. While some form of interface capabilities typically bind these systems at provider sites for purposes of clinical workflows and transaction processing, this legacy of disparate, interfaced systems creates challenges when attempting to both extract and assimilate data across platforms.

In these two projects, we experienced the following challenges:

- Accurate and adequate documentation was missing from a number of the needed data elements. In many cases there were no data dictionaries for legacy systems data. Historically, clinical system vendors had few constraints on how some data fields were customized within customer sites. We see practices where numeric indicators are put in front of data field alpha contents to designate special billing sites and so forth. Prior to the migration to fully relational databases in health care vendor package platforms, this level of data field customization was a common method to accommodate the specific operational idiosyncrasies of workflows that had little standardization.
- Much of this disparate transactional system history and complexity is because these historical transactional information systems were primarily designed for one purpose: billing. Both data structures and business logic layers were developed initially to efficiently process claims in the inpatient, outpatient, and ancillary environments.
- Multiple analyst resources are needed due to the proprietary nature of legacy systems in terms of both data understanding and tools to access data. For example, a HIT vendor might have its own proprietary tools, which would need a unique skill set for extraction. This would lead to increased cost and complexity, for example because of a number of resources in the form of persons skilled in these platforms and additional software licensing. Both technical and organizational complexities exist due to this legacy of disparate transaction information systems.

- Multiple stakeholders exist, and there needs to be collaboration among groups to rationalize disparate data from these source systems such as HIM interpretations, clinicians, and technologists (Figure 3.3). In Project A, the project data elements that were required to meet the grant specifications were distributed in both the inpatient EMR and the disease-specific specialty platform using different field labels, meanings, and standards for time stamps. A group consisting of analysts from the EMR inpatient nursing informatics professional and the medical leadership worked to analyze these two disparate sources of data and to map them into a common requirements document.

Subsequently, health information management experts in coding and clinical standards reviewed these data to analyze each component and to ensure that the proper standards were followed. In Project B, the data came from multiple systems as well, and a team of experts from multiple disciplines worked together to resolve some of the challenges. Overall, given these challenges in the two projects we described, we were able to identify and bring to attention some of the key areas to look for when conducting projects spanning multiple different systems. We resolved missing documentation, created data dictionaries, and were able to effectively budget personnel time as a result of working through these challenges.

Future Implications

Historical paradigms and training programs in health care disciplines focus primarily on discipline-specific understanding of data, operations, and research, thus resulting in stovepipes of health care knowledge that are represented in the data models of legacy EHR platforms. To this end we see duplicate documentation streams in legacy systems for individual professionals like nurses, therapists, and physicians. Moreover, we may even see encounter-delimited data presentation such that the entire EHR may not be easily accessed from any specific dashboard.

"Fit-for-purpose" information systems discourage interoperability and collaboration and presume that specific data will be used in specific ways. This presumption denies the reality of modern information technology and hampers both clinical and research practice. A patient whose medical history includes asthma but whose pharmacy record shows no prescriptions for asthma medications in the last five years will be viewed very different from a patient with no such history in medical record but a consistent record of prescriptions being filled.

Research, in its most general embodiment, also cannot be confided to narrow presentations of data. In evolving analytics models, points of patient therapeutic progress are viewed through holistic progress metrics at any point in time, requiring these various data streams to be mapped into one or more measures that represent an amalgam of any patient's progress relative to the progress of like patients in a population. This shift in thinking requires that leaders encourage cross-disciplinary thinking and reward these patterns of behavior in evolving health care organizational models.

As more data mining tools become available, these resources will be needed to do more generalizable mapping of these systems into programs that will automatically map data for these kinds of requests. When such data mining tools become available, multiple stakeholders will desire to use data more efficiently to build generalizable data-mapping functions that can be used repeatedly for both clinical care and research. While currently manual, storing disparate system research queries will enable the design and building of more efficient libraries of queries once data-mining tools are implemented in the provider site.

Methodology for analyzing data once we have successfully retrieved the needed data set would vary depending on the goals of the project. Various statistical packages (e.g., SPSS, SAS) and desktop applications (e.g., MS Excel Pivot/Powerpivot) were used for the initial analysis of the data. However, with ongoing prospective data collections, the need for analytical tools supporting big data would need to be used. With the increasing use of large data, especially in health care, the need for identification and use of data analytical tools should be an important part of the requirements. Health care data satisfies the basic core of what makes *big data*; the volume of data being generated is ever-increasing with the use of multiple systems, procedures, and documentation needs, and the frequency with which it is being generated is the fastest it has ever been. The multiple different forms and types of data that are being generated is also of note since there are structured, semistructured, and unstructured data being generated in a health care environment.

Education and multidisciplinary functioning in the advanced automation culture are the only ways to progress past these complexities. This is especially true with the evolving nature of health information tools and initiatives. With the new classification system (ICD-10-CM/PCS) to be implemented in October 2014, along with other initiatives, the information systems used by organizations would constantly need to be evaluated and maintained to keep current and provide the most accurate information for clinical decision support. This would be possible by encouraging interdisciplinary collaboration among the different entities in the organization and routinely performing educational and information sharing sessions.

CONCLUSION

Health care leadership including clinicians, researchers, health information management, finance, information technology, and administration should plan for the investments, organizational structure, and culture changes that come with migrating toward an organization that is data driven and maximizes data assets for both operations and research. Indeed, data governance with standardization of primary and derived data variables affords the opportunity to advance all aspects of health care. (An example of a primary variable might be weight, and the derived variable might be the body mass index.) For too long individual business units have been considered islands not only with their own rules and practices but also with their own terminology. Worse still, terms are often shared across business units, but underlying definitions may not be such that heart failure may be one thing in a clinical database and something else for billing purposes. In the extreme, the terms may not even be consistent across outpatient and inpatient or primary care and subspecialty records.

Researchers experienced in EHR-based investigation have long understood this lack of systems noninteroperability and have created data dictionaries and mapping algorithms specific to their projects. However, these solutions are usually not shared even across investigators—much less the system as a whole—and are typically dismantled and discarded after each specific project is completed. Transactional systems platforms must be augmented by technology investments in the form of data models that are both specific to analytics' needs and technologies but also generalizable across all business units so that they can extract and map data from legacy information systems platforms in a consistent and universally accepted way. Likewise, human resources from all aforementioned disciplines must be involved in this data transformation process as well as the ongoing governance of analytics programs.

REFERENCES

Cooper, B., H. Watson, B. Wixom, and D. Goodhue. 2000. Data Warehousing Supports Corporate Strategy at First American Corporation. *MIS Quarterly* 24(4): 547–567.

Folland, S., A. Goodman, and M. Stano. 2013. *The Economics of Health and Health Care*, 7th ed. Upper Saddle River, NJ: Pearson Education, Inc.

Kappelman, L., and J. Zachman. 2013. The Enterprise and Its Architecture: Ontology & Challenges. *Journal of Computer Information Systems* 53(4): 87–95.

Oborn, E., M. Barrett, and G. Racki. 2000. aosb. *Journal of Health Organization and Management* 27(4): 412–431.

Ogunyemi, O., D. Meeker, K. Hyeon-Eui, N. Ashish, S. Farzaneh, and A. Boxwala. 2013. Identifying Appropriate Reference Data Models for Comparative Effectiveness Research (CER) Studies Based on Data from Clinical Information Systems. *Medical Care*, Electronic Data methods (EDM) Forum Special Supplement, 51(3): s45–s52.

Wager, K.A., F.W. Lee, and J.P. Glaser. 2009. *Health Care Information Systems: A Practical Approach for Health Care Management*, 2d ed. San Francisco, CA: Jossey-Bass.

4

The Ecosystem of Federal Big Data and Its Use in Health Care

Ryan H. Sandefer and David T. Marc

CONTENTS

OBJECTIVES

After reading this chapter, the reader shall be able to:

- Describe the Open Government Initiative and the types of big data it includes
- Explain limitations of the data.gov data sets
- Articulate the metadata of the Meaningful Use attestation data
- Show the application of open-source analytic software to Meaningful Use attestation data

ABSTRACT

In this chapter we review the federal government's open data initiative that is generating large amounts of data at the community, state, and national levels. A variety of analytical tools can transform this data into information useful in health planning. Our analysis of Meaningful Use attestation illustrates this transformation of data into information using an open-source analytics platform.

INTRODUCTION

The topic of big data in health care has gained much attention in recent years in part due to increased adoption of the Electronic Health Record (EHR). An example of a big data application in health care is the Institute of Health Improvement's (IHI) development of a framework for optimizing the health system. The framework has been labeled the Triple Aim and focuses on improving patient experience, improving population health, and reducing cost (IHI 2013). The Triple Aim concept design is intricately linked to an ecosystem of data that flows from a variety of sources that allow for the measurement of quality at both the level of an individual and population. The design relies on measures of population health, patient experience, and per capita cost that are acquired from multiple sources, including patient generated data, survey data, administrative data, clinical data, and claims data. The Triple Aim is just one example of big data in health care. As Feldman, Martin, and Skotnes (2012) summarize, "The potential of Big Data allows us to hope to slow the ever-increasing costs of care, help providers practice more effective medicine, empower patients and caregivers, support fitness and preventive self-care, and to dream about more personalized medicine" (p. 5).

Big data has been defined multiple ways. It generally refers to "datasets too large for typical database software tools to capture, store, manage, and analyze" (Seffers, 2013). For the purpose of this chapter, big data can be summarized as data that have a very large quantity (volume), take many forms (variety), are generated quickly (velocity), and have varying levels of quality (veracity). These big data dimensions have been dubbed the four V's (Feldman et al., 2012). The volume of electronic health care data is quickly increasing, leaving questions as to what we should do with this this deluge of data. "Experts estimate that in 2013, 3.6 zettabytes of data will be created, and the amount doubles every two years. A zettabyte is equal to 1 billion terabytes, and a terabyte is equal to 1 trillion bytes" (Seffers, 2013). With the focus on digitizing health information, the amount of health care data is also growing exponentially. "The volume of worldwide healthcare data in 2012 is 500 petabytes (10^{15} bytes) = 10 billion four-drawer file cabinets. That is estimated to grow in 2020 to 25,000 petabytes = 500 billion four drawer file cabinets—a fiftyfold increase from 2012–2020" (Feldman et al., 2012, p. 6).

The large volume of data provides an opportunity to apply big data analytics for organizing information and ultimately improving health processes. For instance, Russell (2010) explains how large-scale analytics with health care data can benefit health care providers in clinical quality initiatives, operational efficiencies, financial performance management, and pay-for performance initiatives. Pharmaceutical and biotech companies can utilize analytics for comparative effectiveness research, adaptive trials to support personalized medicine, consumer and physician engagement, and decision support. Academic medical centers can adapt analytics for translational, clinical, and comparative effectiveness research and for collaborative and extra-enterprise research. Finally, public health initiatives can utilize analytics for disease surveillance and clinical utility studies. The opportunities offered through big data analytics is ample and will continue to grow as the big data era expands.

The U.S. government is a significant contributor to the growth of big data. According to one estimate, U.S. federal agencies currently store 1.6 petabytes of information, and the level of data storage is predicted to grow to 2.6 petabytes between 2013 and 2015 (Higgins, 2013). Because of the rising level of data housed by federal agencies and the potential information that can be gleaned from analyzing these data, the government is investing heavily in big data projects. "Federal agencies spent about US$4.9 billion on Big Data resources in fiscal 2012. The annual amount of such spending will grow to $5.7 billion in 2014 and then to $7.2 billion by 2017" (Higgins, 2013). The federal government is a major player in terms of big data in large part because of the role of the federal government in health payment—Medicare has 50 million participants. Medicare accounts for 16% of the federal budget, and Medicare accounts for 21% of total U.S. health care spending (KFF, 2012).

OPEN GOVERNMENT INITIATIVE—DATA.GOV

> My administration is committed to creating an unprecedented level of openness in Government, We will work together to ensure the public trust and establish a system of transparency, public participation, and collaboration. Openness will strengthen our democracy and promote efficiency and effectiveness in Government. (Obama, 2009)

While the federal government collects and stores massive amounts of data, it has a history of making the data inaccessible to the American people (Coglianese, 2009). In an effort to change the culture regarding governmental transparency and information sharing, then presidential candidate Barack Obama pledged to "create a transparent and connected democracy" (Obama, 2007). On January 21, 2009, the day President Obama was sworn into office, he signed the Memorandum for the Heads of Executive Departments and Agencies: Transparency and Open Government. It outlined the Obama Administration's Open Government Directive, which contained actionable steps and deadlines that federal agencies were required to take to promote the principles of transparency, participation, and collaboration. The first step outlined in the memorandum reads: "Publish Government Information Online... To increase accountability, promote informed participation by the public, and create economic opportunity, each agency shall take prompt steps to expand access to information by making it available online in open formats."

Important for the future of big data research, the memorandum includes the following statement: "Within 45 days, each agency shall identify and publish in an open format at least three high-value data sets . . . and register those data sets via Data.gov. These must be data sets not previously available online or in a downloadable format" (Figure 4.1). High-value information is defined in the document as "information that can be used to increase agency accountability and responsiveness; improve public knowledge of the agency and its operations; further the core mission of the agency; create economic opportunity; or respond to need and demand as identified through public consultation (Orszag, 2009).

In its U.S. National Action Plan, the government specifically highlighted its policy of "smart disclosure," or releasing high-quality, complex information in "standardized, machine-readable formats" that can improve decisions and aid scientific research. The action plan also notes the

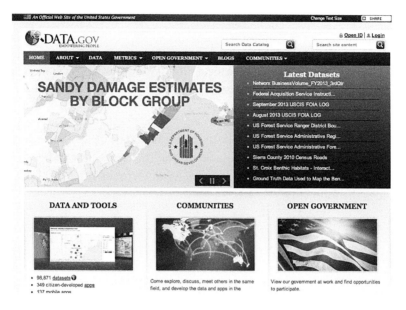

FIGURE 4.1

Homepage of Data.gov on October 21, 2013.

government's intent to develop federal guidelines on scientific data (OGP, 2011). Federal agencies were encouraged to release a variety of smart disclosure data that met the following characteristics (Sunstein, 2011):

- Accessible
- Machine readable
- Standardized
- Timely
- Adaptive and innovative to markets
- Interoperable
- Deidentifed

There are obvious reasons for why the federal government is making these high-quality data available for research and use by the public, including benefits related to the goals of collaboration, transparency, participation, and research. The overarching benefit of these data, as well as big data, is the potential to improve decisions based upon knowledge.

Smart disclosures can help consumers to find and use relevant data, including data about the effect of their own past choices and those of others, to make decisions that reflect their individualized needs, and to revise and improve those decisions over time or as new circumstances arise. . . . Smart disclosure initiatives can help promote innovation, economic growth, and job creation in the market for consumer tools. Smart disclosure of consumer data yields other benefits, including allowing consumers to monitor more easily the accuracy and use of the information that companies hold on them. (Sunstein, 2011)

The Open Government Initiative has resulted in an explosion of governmental data that are available on the Internet that can be viewed, downloaded, and analyzed by anyone. As of October 21, 2013, Data.gov includes the following:

- 98,871 data sets
- 349 citizen-developed apps that relate to these data sets
- 137 mobil eapps
- Data from 175 federal agencies and subagencies
- 87 topical compilations of related data sets
- 295 government APIs

In addition to including downloadable data sets, Data.gov includes tools and resources, communities, and education regarding how to utilize the site and its data. One of those open data communities is HealthData.gov (Figure 4.2). It includes Medicare and Medicaid cost reports, public health registries, medication treatments, and county-level determinants of health. The overall impact of the Open Government Initiative on the ability to conduct research and analysis on health care generally is remarkable and cannot be overstated. Since its creation, a total of 933 high-value data sets have been published on HealthData.gov. End users have the ability to filter these data sets by subject, agency, subagency, dates, geography, and format, among others, realizing the potential of Sunstein's (2011) explanation of how decision-making can be improved.

Despite the value of publishing these data sets to Data.gov, there are limitations to the current types of data and the structure of the data files. One major limitation is the accessibility of downloadable data files. Data. gov provides only descriptions of the data sets and information on how to access them. To download the data, users are required to travel to webpages that Data.gov provides a link for and search those pages for the data file. If the data sets were stored directly on Data.gov, data searching and extraction would be more efficient. Another major limitation of Data.gov is that the various data sets are published in a format where they cannot be

FIGURE 4.2
Homepage of HealthData.gov. on October 21, 2013.

easily related to other data sets. The system would be greatly improved if the site allowed end users to extract multiple measures linked by unique identifiers (e.g., CMS certification number [CCN], national provider identifier [NPI]). Additionally, many of the data sets that are made available lack a sufficient data dictionary to fully comprehend the meaning, relationships to other data, origin, usage, and format of the data. There are also a variety of critical health care issues related to CMS that lack published health care data sets on the current site. Health information exchange, for example, is critical to both the future of health care delivery and has been included as a primary objective of the EHR incentive program. As Data.gov matures, it will be important for CMS to expand the number of data sets published, improve the format of the data sets, and also improve the ability for end users to analyze the information on the site.

Although significant limitations to data accessibility remain, the fact that data are publicly available and the volume continually grows supports an opportunity for analytics. In the following section, we introduce an example of using publically available data to gain insights related to the adoption and use of EHRs. The following analysis is possible only because we were able to utilize data made available under the Open Government Initiative.

MEANINGFUL USE AND BIG DATA

As publicly available data become more prevalent on sites such as Data. gov and HealthData.gov, opportunities to evaluate the success of federally funded health programs have increased. One critical health information technology (IT) initiative is related to the national effort to adopt an EHR known as Meaningful Use. This section will describe the EHR incentive program and the data that are being published that related to provider and hospital participation.

The 2009 American Recovery and Reinvestment Act included the Health Information Technology for Economic and Clinical Health provision, also known as the HITECH Act (ARRA, 2009). The HITECH Act included approximately $29 billion for the Centers for Medicare and Medicaid Services to help support clinical professionals and hospitals adopt and effectively use electronic health record systems by providing financial incentives for meaningful use of certified electronic health records. The HITECH Act's most substantial program is called the CMS EHR incentive program. "To receive an EHR incentive payment, providers have to show that they are 'meaningfully using' their EHRs by meeting thresholds for a number of objectives. CMS has established the objectives for 'meaningful use' that eligible professionals, eligible hospitals, and critical access hospitals (CAHs) must report on in order to receive an incentive payment" (CMS, 2013b).

In Stage 1 Meaningful Use, there are 24 objectives with associated reportable measures for eligible professionals and 23 for eligible hospitals (see CMS.gov for more details). To successfully attest that an eligible professional or hospital has met the objectives of meaningful use, data must be collected on each provider and hospital for a specific length of time and calculated based on a specific subset of patients—there are inclusion and exclusion criteria for each objective. In other words, meaningful use is driven by electronic data capture, management, analysis, and reporting. As of August 2013, the EHR incentive program has made a total of 201,927 payments to Medicare eligible professionals, 101,544 payments to Medicaid eligible professionals, and 4,098 payments to eligible hospitals. These payments have resulted in a total of $16,239,050 in incentive payments for meaningful use of electronic health records (CMS, 2013c).

Because the EHR incentive program is based on the collection, calculation, and reporting of clinical and administrative data regarding patients and health care processes, the program has led to a massive increase in the level of data collected by U.S. health care organizations. In accordance with the Open Government Initiative, the Centers for Medicare and Medicaid Services has published multiple data sets related to the program, one of which relates to the recipients (both eligible professionals and eligible hospitals) of the Medicare EHR incentive program. The file contains the names, Medicare ID numbers, business phone numbers, business addresses, program year, and the calculated payment for all recipients of Medicare-based EHR incentive payments (Figure 4.3). As of October 2013, the data sets include information on 213,813 eligible professionals, 21,847 Medicare Advantage eligible professionals, and 3,812 eligible hospitals.

The Centers for Medicare and Medicaid Services have also published a public use file (PUF) related to all eligible hospitals and eligible professionals who have attested for Meaningful Use. While the PUF files do not allow identification of the eligible hospitals or eligible professionals who have attested, the data sets include the data that are reported for each

	A	B	C	D	E	F	G	H	I	J	K	L
	PROVIDER NPI	PROVIDER N.	PROVIDER S1	PROVIDER CI	PROVIDER A	PROVIDER ZI	PROVIDER ZI	PROVIDER PI	PROVIDER PI	PROGRAM YI	CALC PAYMENT	AMT ($)
1												
2	ELIGIBLE PROVIDERS											
3	1811044605	Abbas, Rashi	Alabama	Huntsville	930 Franklin	35801	4312	(256) 539-40		2012	$18,000.00	
4	1689659021	Abbott, Joel	Alabama	Birmingham	2145 Highlar	35205	4006	(205) 933-03	1004	2012	$18,000.00	
5	1669420394	Abele, Donal	Alabama	Pell City	2805 Dr Johr	35125	1448	(205) 814-21		2012	$18,000.00	
6	1255525945	Abrahim, Shc	Alabama	Mobile	610 Provider	36695	4622	(251) 378-39		2013	$15,000.00	
7	1770537573	Abrams, Gar	Alabama	Montgomery	2055 E Soutr	36116	2001	(334) 613-70		2013	$15,000.00	
8	1891835294	Abrams, Johr	Alabama	Auburn	1548 Profess	36830	2857	(334) 826-29		2012	$18,000.00	
9	1013010164	Abroms, Jam	Alabama	Birmingham	1817 Oxmoo	35209		(205) 870-40		2011	$18,000.00	
10	1013010164	Abroms, Jam	Alabama	Birmingham	1817 Oxmoo	35209		(205) 870-40		2012	$12,000.00	
11	1508043605	Acharya, Dee	Alabama	Birmingham	500 22nd Str	35233	3110	(205) 731-96		2012	$18,000.00	
12	1205902541	Adams, Brad	Alabama	Auburn	2408 E Unive	36830	9403	(334) 821-25		2012	$9,058.17	
13	1720039175	adams, chris	Alabama	opelika	121 north 20	36801	5457	(334) 749-83	3030	2012	$18,000.00	
14	1467463299	Adams, Davi	Alabama	Opelika	122 N 20th S	36801	5442	(334) 745-46		2011	$18,000.00	
15	1467463299	Adams, Davi	Alabama	Opelika	122 N 20th S	36801	5442	(334) 745-46		2012	$12,000.00	
16	1629023205	Adams, Geor	Alabama	Homewood	3485 Indepe	35209	5603	(205) 930-09		2012	$18,000.00	
17	1033164371	Adams, Jame	Alabama	Birmingham	2018 Brookw	35209	6898	(205) 250-81		2011	$18,000.00	
18	1033164371	Adams, Jame	Alabama	Birmingham	2018 Brookw	35209	6898	(205) 250-81		2012	$12,000.00	
19	1093991754	Adams, Mar	Alabama	Birmingham	800 Saint Vir	35205	1620	(205) 271-16		2012	$1,347.61	
20	1457589350	ADARALOYE,	Alabama	DOTHAN	1118 ROSS C	36301	3002	(989) 895-46		2011	$14,237.42	
21	1457589350	ADARALOYE,	Alabama	DOTHAN	1118 ROSS C	36301	3002	(989) 895-46		2012	$12,000.00	
22	1184688582	Adcock, Jon	Alabama	Birmingham	2006 Brookw	35209	6899	(205) 397-90		2012	$13,574.91	
23	1235178070	Adcock, Roni	Alabama	Daphne	27900 N Mai	36526		(251) 621-12		2011	$10,085.05	
24	1235178070	Adcock, Roni	Alabama	Daphne	27900 N Mai	36526		(251) 621-12		2012	$12,000.00	
25	1013951185	Adderholt, Jc	Alabama	Florence	426 East Dr.F	35630	6625	(256) 764-77	217	2012	$18,000.00	
26	1285610576	Agagan, Caes	Alabama	Mobile	100 Memori	36608	1183	(251) 343-68		2011	$18,000.00	
27	1285610576	Agagan, Caes	Alabama	Mobile	100 Memori	36608	1183	(251) 343-68		2012	$12,000.00	
28	1588725881	Aghedo, Osa	Alabama	Selma	731 Dallas Av	36701	5452	(334) 872-47		2012	$18,000.00	
29	1740397744	AGRO, ANGE	Alabama	ANDALUSIA	300 MEDICA	36420		(334) 427-24		2013	$14,700.00	
30	1003856600	Ahmed, Ali	Alabama	Birmingham	500 22nd Str	35233	3110	(205) 731-96		2012	$12,334.95	
31	1396996245	Aikens, Alan	Alabama	Birmingham	832 Princeto	35211	1320	(205) 206-84		2013	$15,000.00	
32	1841212974	Ajamoughli, i	Alabama	Fort Payne	1040 Glenn E	35967	8413	(256) 845-69		2013	$15,000.00	
33	1477695088	Akinsanya, O	Alabama	Gadsden	200 S 3rd St	35901	4210	(256) 543-30		2012	$18,000.00	
34	1649284308	Aland, Jack	Alabama	Birmingham	833 Saint Vir	35205	1606	(205) 933-92	518	2012	$18,000.00	
35	1992791297	Alapati, Anja	Alabama	Huntsville	201 Sivley Rc	35801	5134	(256) 265-26		2012	$18,000.00	
36	1225081177	Albares, Rob	Alabama	Dothan	480 Honevsu	36305	1156	(334) 836-12		2012	$18,000.00	

FIGURE 4.3
Example of data contained in CMS EP data set.

Meaningful Use objective by each entity during the attestation process. The PUFs include information regarding each measure of Meaningful Use, such as program year, eligible hospital/eligible professional type, and the percentage reported by hospitals regarding computerized provider order entry. Figure 4.3 is one example of data contained in the CMS EP data file.

The Office of the National Coordinator for Health Information Technology (ONC), the federal agency responsible for policy, coordination, and innovative programs related to the HITECH Act, has made available a data set that includes data on all providers and hospitals that have attested for both Medicare and Medicaid EHR incentive programs. The data currently include information on 307,902 reporting entities. The data

Variable	Description
EHR Certification ID	A unique ID for different combinations of EHR products
Vendor Name	Name of EHR Vendor
EHR Product Name	Name of EHR Product
EHR Product Version	Version of EHR product
Product Classification	Complete/Modular. Complete products meet all the Meaningful Use (MU) requirements. Modular products meet one or more of the MU requirements but not all.
Product Setting	Ambulatory/Inpatient. Practice setting for which the product was designed.
Attestation Month	Month in which the attestation was approved successful. May not match Program Year or Payment Year due to delays in processing.
Attestation Year	Year in which the attestation was approved as successful.
Business State/Territory	Business location of provider who successfully attested to MU.
Provider Type	EP/Hospital. Whether the provider is an eligible professional (EP) or an eligible hospital (Hospital).
Specialty	The specialty of the eligible professional who attested (derived from PECOS).
Program Year	Indicates the year of participation (2011, 2012, 2013...).
Payment Year	Indicates the year of participation (1,2,3,4,5...) that matches up the program and actual attestation.
Program Type	Whether the provider attested under the Medicare or Medicare/Medicaid EHR Incentive Program.
Attestation ID	Unique ID for each attestation
Provider ID	Unique ID for each provider

FIGURE 4.4
ONC Meaningful Use attestations by vender dataset.

set includes multiple variables, including EHR vendor, provider specialty, and hospital type. See Figure 4.4 for a complete list of the data set variables and their descriptions.

HEALTH CARE DATA RELATED TO MEANINGFUL USE ATTESTATIONS

Because the EHR incentive program is funded by CMS and the data sets related to meaningful use attestation are identified using a professional's or hospital's CCN, multiple open-source data sets can be used in combination with this data. CMS has published a tremendous amount of data related to the health care programs that fall under its banner, including Medicare and Medicaid. CMS has even created a data navigator to identify data related to specific programs, settings of care, topics, geographies, or document types. In other words, this CMS data navigator allows individuals interested in publicly available data related to the topic of national Medicare admissions to find it easily. Figure 4.2 shows the CMS data navigator website.

One particular data set CMS has published is Hospital Compare. The purpose of this data is to improve hospital performance by publishing objective data regarding a variety of measures related to hospital quality of care, such as payment, clinical quality measures, patient satisfaction, and efficiency. Hospital Compare contains data regarding all hospitals that have registered with Medicare. Medicare has similar compilations of data sets related to the following:

- Nursing homes
- Physicians
- Home health
- Dialysis facilities
- Supplier directories

Many additional federal open-source data sets can be used in concert with these data health care data sources. The Health Resources and Services Administration (HRSA) annually publishes the Area Health Resource File. This data set combines multiple data sets from across the federal government (over 50 data sources) into one file. It contains information on population-based counts of health professionals, health facilities, population, economics, health care costs, and education, among others (HRSA, 2013). The U.S. Census Bureau also publishes data sets including the Geographic Shapefiles that contain an extraordinary amount of information and are very useful for working with EHR incentive program data. For example, the TIGER/Line Shapefiles Pre-joined with Demographic Data provide information down to the county and census-tract level on attributes related to age, race, sex, housing, and household size, among others (TIGER/Line, 2010).

The Agency for Health Research and Quality (AHRQ) publishes the Healthcare Cost and Utilization Project (HCUP), which includes aggregate data on hospital length of stays, hospital readmissions, emergency department use, and AHRQ quality indicators. While the HCUP system is aggregate, it allows users to compare the cost of diagnoses and procedures by state (HCUPnet, 2013).

Medicare also publishes a data set related to specific hospital charge data that include "hospital-specific charges for the more than 3,000 U.S. hospitals that receive Medicare Inpatient Prospective Payment System (IPPS) payments for the top 100 most frequently billed discharges, paid under Medicare based on a rate per discharge using the Medicare Severity Diagnosis Related Group (MS-DRG) for Fiscal Year (FY) 2011" (CMS, 2011).

Recently, CMS has published another data set called the Medicare Claims Synthetic Public Use Files (SynPUFs; CMS, 2010). These files contain millions of records but protect individual patient identity. According to CMS, the files can be used to do the following:

1. Allow data entrepreneurs to develop and create software and applications that may eventually be applied to actual CMS claims data
2. Train researchers on the use and complexity of conducting analyses with CMS claims data prior to initiating the process to obtain access to actual CMS data
3. Support safe data mining innovations that may reveal unanticipated knowledge gains while preserving beneficiary privacy

These data sets are a few examples of federal open-source data sets that can be considered big data in health care. With the expansion of these data sets, there is a large effort to expand open-source analytic platforms. These platforms can offer analytic and storage capabilities of very large data sets that do not require costly development and maintenance operations.

OPEN-SOURCE TOOLS TO ANALYZE OPEN-SOURCE DATA

Analytic software that can be applied to the aforementioned open data sets can be expensive. Out-of-the-box solutions may not meet organizations' needs. The expansion of open-source options is beginning to provide organizations with a plethora of software options for a variety of analytics tasks. The attraction of open-source platforms is their ability to be customized based on the organization's needs at relatively reasonable cost. For example, analytics tasks can be supported with open-source options for relational database management systems and statistical computing software.

MySQL is said to be the world's most popular open-source database (Oracle, 2013). MySQL supports big data analytics through the acquisition and organization of data in a relational database. A relational database stores data into many tables rather than storing all of the data in one large spreadsheet. A relational database can facilitate rapid and specific data extraction. The database is said to be relational because the tables can be related to each other based on common data attributes (i.e., keys). The data can be extracted from a relational database using a standardized language known as structured query language (SQL). SQL allows user to insert, query, update, and delete data into a database. MySQL databases can be managed and queried using MySQL Workbench, a free integrated environment that is easy to use.

In cases where rigorous analytics are required, the R statistical computing platform is a powerful open-source option for carrying out a wide variety of analytic tasks (Ihaka and Gentleman, 1996). R provides a wide variety of statistical (e.g., linear and nonlinear modeling, classical statistical tests, time-series analysis, classification) and graphical techniques for analyzing data. Also, R is highly extensible through a multitude of packages that can be downloaded and installed. Some of these packages include the following (CRAN, 2013):

- RStudio: An alternative integrated development environment for R that offers improvements in the organization of graphs, data, and scripts than base R (Figure 4.5)
- Rattle: A graphic user interface that facilitates descriptive and predictive data-mining tasks with easy model deployment using the predictive model markup language (PMML)

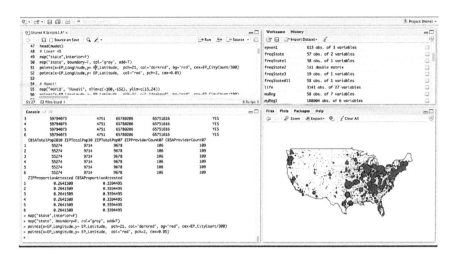

FIGURE 4.5
The RStudio package is an alternative graphical user interface to the base R program.

- ggplot2: Expands the graphics capabilities of R
- maps: Supports geospatial mapping of data based on latitude and longitude

Collectively, MySQL and R can provide organizations an opportunity to adopt large-scale analytics at no cost. The open-source market is in constant expansion; therefore, the adoption of big data analytics is not limited to any particular organizations due to economic constraints.

CASE STUDY: MAPPING MEANINGFUL USE ATTESTATION DATA FOR EP AND EH

To provide an example of an analytics application of open-source software using open-source data, the authors of the chapter provide a case study using meaningful use attestation data. As mentioned already, CMS publishes meaningful use data for all eligible providers and eligible hospitals that have attested. As of July 2013, the data set was made available on the CMS website (CMS, 2013a) and includes the data elements shown in Table 4.1.

TABLE 4.1

The Data Elements Available in the CMS Attestation Data Set

• Provider NPI	• Zip4
• Provider CCN	• Phone number
• Provider/Organization Name	• Phone extension
• State	• Program year
• Address	• Payment amount
• Zip5	

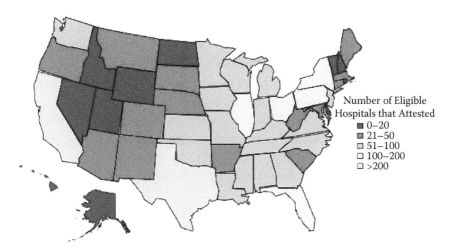

FIGURE 4.6
Count of stage 1 Meaningful Use attestations in each state.

In addition to attestation data, facility and geographic data from Hospital Compare and census public use data were used to develop a geospatial representation of the density of eligible hospitals within each state that attested to meaningful use. This was carried out using several packages in R. In the first plot, the "map" package was used to plot the density of 90-day attestations for the eligible hospitals for every state (Figure 4.6).

Figure 4.6 may appear to be informative but actually can be quite misleading. The plot is representing the number of eligible hospitals that attested in each state. A large number of attestations may not actually be a marker of Meaningful Use stage 1 success for any particular state but rather result due to a larger number of hospitals that are present in those states. To determine the relative success of each state, we generated another plot by calculating the proportion of hospitals that attested in each state using data from the Hospital Compare public use data (Medicare, 2013) as the denominator for determining the total number of hospitals in each state (Figure 4.7).

As shown in Figure 4.7, it appears as though some of the rural states are less likely to attest to meaningful use. To evaluate this observation empirically, and at a lower level of description, the proportion of attestations by eligible hospitals were calculated by core-based statistical area (CBSA). A CBSA is defined as a geographic area surrounding an urban center of at least 10,000 people. A CBSA can be further defined as either micropolitan or metropolitan. Micropolitan areas are urban clusters of at least 10,000 people but fewer than 50,000 people. Metropolitan areas are urban clusters greater than 50,000 people. A non-CBSA area is generally defined as rural. The associated CBSA for each hospital was determined by mapping their zip codes to corresponding CBSAs using data from the 2010 census derived from the "UScensus2010" package in R. The number of attestations in each CBSA was divided by the total number of hospitals in those areas as determined from the hospital compare data set (Table 4.2).

It is evident that rural areas (non-CBSA) are attesting at slightly lower rates than other areas. We also wanted to develop a more granular visualization for the location of eligible hospitals that attested. Therefore,

FIGURE 4.7
Proportion of hospitals that attested for stage 1 Meaningful Use in each state.

TABLE 4.2

Proportion of Hospitals that Attested for Stage 1 Meaningful Use Based on Their CBSA

	Proportion of Hospitals that Did Attest
Micropolitan	503/883 = 57.0%
Metropolitan	1882/3130 = 60.1%
Non-CBSA (rural)	422/877 = 48.1%

we generated another figure using the "map" and "zipcode" package in R. In this example, the "zipcode" package provided the latitude and longitude ordinances for each zip code. We appended the attestation data with the corresponding latitude and longitude ordinances for each eligible hospital. Using the "map" package, the ordinances for each of the eligible hospital's zip code was plotted as a point on a map of the United States. However, we had to account for the issue of representing more than one hospital within a particular zip code. We did so by changing the size of the points on the map. To carry this out, the graphical attribute "cex" controls the size of the points on a plot in R. We set "cex" as the count of the occurrence of each zip code. Therefore, the size of the dots is directly proportional to the number of hospitals in a particular zip code (Figure 4.8).

The results of the analysis thus far reveal that some states are attesting at lower rates than other states. In particular, attestation rates for urbanized areas appear greater than rural areas. To gain an understanding as to a possible cause for lower attestation in rural areas, we evaluated attestations by the hospital type: Critical Access Hospital (CAH) or Other. Further analysis revealed that the attestation rates for CAH may partially be the reason that disparities in attestations exist in rural areas. In non-CBSA areas, CAHs account for 74.1% of all hospitals, but they account for only 36.9% and 11.4% in micropolitan and metropolitan areas, respectively. If you take CAHs out of the calculation when evaluating attestation rates in non-CBSA areas, 71.5% of non-CAHs have attested. In addition, 70.1% of non-CAHs in micropolitan areas have attested. However, when you examine the attestation rates, CAHs are attesting at a significantly lower rate than non-CAHs (Table 4.3). In fact, only around 10% or less of the CAHs in Alaska, Hawaii, Nevada, and Utah have attested. The highest attestation rates for CAHs were at about 70% in Florida and New Hampshire. Our analysis suggests that rural areas are attesting to meaningful use at lower rates than urban areas. We discovered that this is largely due to CAH attesting at lower rates and CAHs dominating rural areas.

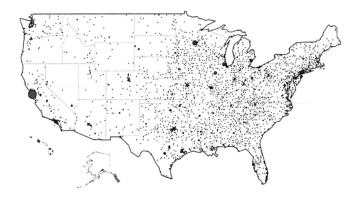

FIGURE 4.8
Location of hospitals that attested based on their zip codes.

TABLE 4.3

A Comparison of Attestation Rates for Stage 1 Meaningful Use for CAH versus Non-CAHs

	Proportion of CAHs that Attested	Proportion of Non-CAHs that Attested	Chi-Square Results
Non-CBSA (Rural)	265/650 = 40.8%	157/227 = 69.2%	< 0.001
Micropolitan	129/326 = 39.6%	374/557 = 67.2%	< 0.001
Metropolitan	141/356 = 39.6%	1741/2774 = 62.8%	< 0.001

This case study is a great example of how open-source data and open-source analytic tools can be used to generate useful insights. That is, lower attestation rates were not found to necessarily be related to hospitals in rural areas; rather, CAHs, which dominate rural areas, were attesting at lower rates regardless of their location and consequently driving down the overall attestation rates in rural areas. We were able to conclusively establish that CAH across all geographic strata (rural and urban) are attesting to meaningful use at significantly lower rates than their prospective payment system hospital counterparts. This is just one example of the insights that can be gained from publicly available big data sources. The availability of open-source data and tools is rapidly increasing, thereby providing opportunities for organizations to carry out similar large-scale analytics on data that are relevant for their own purposes.

CONCLUSION

The amount and complexity of health care data that is being made available to the public for analysis is unparalleled—open-source data have become big data. Moreover, the software tools that are being made freely available to students, faculty, researchers, policy makers, and anyone else interested in acquiring, organizing, analyzing, and using data for decision-making is unprecedented. Yet there seems to be a disconnect between the availability of data and its analysis. Thus, the question remains: How can we encourage the analysis of open-source health care data in an effort to improve care outcomes and reduce costs?

This chapter provides an overview of the Open Government Initiative and its role in promoting the expansion of publicly available data sets. As shown in the case study using Meaningful Use Stage 1 attestation data, there is an opportunity to analyze these data sets for a multitude of reasons, one being the ability to gain insights into the success of a federally funded program. Ideally, the opportunities that the open-source data and open-source analytic tools provide will be realized by academics, healthcare organizations, and other industries. The big data era is not just about collecting and storing data. Instead, the big data era is about the potential of knowledge generation through large-scale analytics. Health care is one particular industry in which big data and analytics has great implications for identifying factors that can lead to better care at lower costs. A good place to start the big data initiatives in health care is with open-source data and analytics.

REFERENCES

American Recovery and Reinvestment Act (ARRA). 2009. Health Information Technology for Economic and Clinical Health (HITECH) Act. *Title XIII of Division A and Title IV of Division B*. Available at http://www.hhs.gov/ocr/privacy/hipaa/understanding/coveredentities/hitechact.pdf

Centers for Medicaid and Medicare Services (CMS). 2010. Medicare Claims Synthetic Public Use Files (SynPUFs). Available at http://www.cms.gov/Research-Statistics-Data-and-Systems/Statistics-Trends-and-Reports/SynPUFs/index.html

Centers for Medicaid and Medicare Services (CMS). 2011. Medicare Provider Charge Data: Inpatient. Available at http://www.cms.gov/Research-Statistics-Data-and-Systems/Statistics-Trends-and-Reports/Medicare-Provider-Charge-Data/Inpatient.html

Centers for Medicaid and Medicare Services (CMS). 2013a. EHR Incentive Programs. Available at http://www.cms.gov/Regulations-and-Guidance/Legislation/EHRIncentivePrograms/Downloads/EH_ProvidersPaidByEHRProgram_Sep2013_FINAL.zip

Centers for Medicaid and Medicare Services (CMS). 2013b. Meaningful Use. Available at http://www.cms.gov/Regulations-and-Guidance/Legislation/EHRIncentivePrograms/Meaningful_Use.html

Centers for Medicaid and Medicare Services (CMS). 2013c. October 2013 Payment and Registration Summary Overview. Available at http://www.cms.gov/Regulations-and-Guidance/Legislation/EHRIncentivePrograms/Downloads/October2013_PaymentandRegistrationSummaryOverview.pdf

Coglianese, C. 2009. The Transparency President? The Obama Administration and Open Government. *Governance* 22(4): 15.

Comprehensive R Archive Network (CRAN). 2013. The Comprehensive R Archive Network. Available at http://cran.us.r-project.org

Feldman, B., E.M. Martin, and T. Skotnes. 2012. Big Data in Healthcare: Hype and Hope. *Dr. Bonnie 360: Business Development for Digital Health.* Available at http://www.scribd.com/doc/107279699/Big-Data-Healthcare-Hype-and-Hope

HCUPnet. 2013. Healthcare Cost and Utlization Project. *Agency for Healthcare Research and Quality.* Available at http://hcupnet.ahrq.gov/

Higgins, J.K. 2013. Feds to Spend Big on Big Data. *E-Commerce Times.* Available at http://www.ecommercetimes.com/story/77690.html

Health Resources and Services Administration (HRSA). 2013. Health Resources and Services Administration. *U.S. Department of Health and Human Services.* Available at http://arf.hrsa.gov/index.htm

Ihaka, R., and R. Gentleman. 1996. R: A Language for Data Analysis and Graphics. *Journal of Computational and Graphical Statistics* 5(3): 15.

Institute for Healthcare Improvement (IHI). 2013. The IHI Triple Aim. Available at http://www.ihi.org/offerings/Initiatives/TripleAim/Pages/default.aspx

Kaiser Family Foundation (KFF). 2012. Medicare Spending and Financing Fact Sheet. Available at http://kff.org/medicare/fact-sheet/medicare-spending-and-financing-fact-sheet/

Medicare. 2013. *Hospital Compare.* Available at http://www.medicare.gov/hospitalcompare/search.html

Obama, B. 2007. The Obama-Biden Plan. Available at http://change.gov/agenda/technology_agenda/

Obama, B. 2009. Transparency and Open Government. Available at http://www.whitehouse.gov/the_press_office/TransparencyandOpenGovernment

Open Government Partnership (OGP). 2011. The Open Government Partnership: National Action Plan for the United States of America. Available at http://whitehouse.gov.

Oracle. 2013. MySQL and Hadoop—Big Data Integration: Unlocking New Insight. *MySQL White Paper.* http://www.mysql.com/why-mysql/white-papers/mysql-and-hadoop-guide-to-big-data-integration/

Orszag, P.R. 2009. *Memorandum for the Heads of Executive Departments and Agencies.* Edited by Executive Office of the President: Office of Management and Budget: White House. Available at http://www.whitehouse.gov/sites/default/files/omb/memoranda/2010/m10-33.pdf

Russell, J. 2010. "The Role of Analytics in Transforming Healthcare." *Bio-IT World.* Oracle Health Sciences. Available at http://www.ehidc.org/policy/pol-resources/doc_download/225-white-paper-the-role-of-analytics-in-transforming-healthcare-data-and-analytics

Seffers, G.I. 2013. U.S. Government Bets Big on Data. Available at http://www.afcea.org/content/?q=node/10489

Sunstein, C.R. 2011. *Memorandum for the Heads of Executive Department and Agencies.* Executive Office of the President: Office of Management and Budget Available at http://www.whitehouse.gov/sites/default/files/omb/inforeg/for-agencies/informing-consumers-through-smart-disclosure.pdf

TIGER/Line. 2010. TIGER/Line Shapefiles Pre-joined with Demographic Data. Available at http://www.census.gov/geo/maps-data/data/tiger-data.html

5

Big Data from the Push of Clinical Information: Harvesting User Feedback for Continuing Education

Roland Grad, Pierre Pluye, Michael Shulha, David L. Tang, Jonathan Moscovici, Carol Repchinsky, and Jamie Meuser

CONTENTS

OBJECTIVES

After reading this chapter, the reader shall be able to:

- Explain how physician-alerting services provide big data for continuing medical education
- Describe the Acquisition–Cognition–Application–Levels of Outcome (ACA-LO) model and its application to physician alerting
- Differentiate one-way from two-way knowledge translation
- Explain how big data can aid in the construction of online questionnaires

ABSTRACT

In meeting their commitment to lifelong learning, physician participation in continuing medical education (CME) programs involving email alerts of clinical information has been strong and sustained. In CME programs involving email alerts, our research group analyzes ratings submitted by participants. Since 2006, we have collected more than 1.5 million ratings on email alerts from about 10,000 Canadian physicians and pharmacists. In this chapter, we discuss strategies to harvest "intelligence" from physician ratings of email alerts, considering two separate case studies. We also lay out a vision for the future of this work and describe challenges for analysis of this type of big data.

INTRODUCTION

Almost two decades ago, it was estimated that a generalist physician would have to read about 19 articles a day to keep pace with the medical literature reporting the results of primary research (Haines, 1996). However, patients expect health care providers to keep up with new developments in medicine while health professionals strive to be "evidence informed" in their decision-making. As such, educational strategies (e.g., alerting services) are needed to help clinicians integrate the findings of new research in practice. Alerting services are a type of push technology—in existence at least since 1996, when PointCast delivered customized news to about one million users. With regard to the continuing education of clinicians, we coined the term *clinical information channel* (CIC) to refer to a communication infrastructure (involving email systems, apps, or RSS feeds) to channel research-based information from providers to individual practitioners. CICs ask the user to subscribe to a channel (e.g., a mailing list) or a set of channels (e.g., via a multichannel app). To explain how CICs work, we proposed a push–pull framework, based on a critical literature review that covered the health sciences, communication, education, information, and knowledge translation (Pluye et al., 2010). The literature showed CIC users are more likely to use information retrieval technology, perceive CICs as useful for individual learning in the CME context, and report high levels of satisfaction with the delivered information. In an updated framework presented in Figure 5.1, we see that pushed information is typically stored in a database for later retrieval (sequence: object O1 delivery, latent period, clinical question followed by object O1 retrieval). In addition, the delivery of information objects can directly stimulate

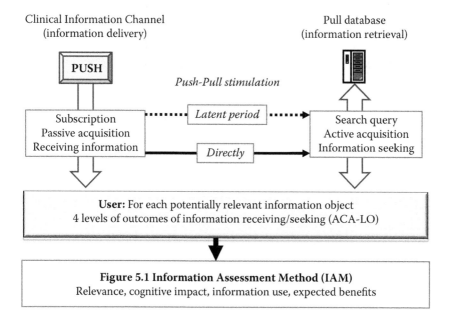

Clinical Information Channel
(information delivery)

Pull database
(information retrieval)

PUSH

Push-Pull stimulation

Subscription
Passive acquisition
Receiving information

Latent period

Search query
Active acquisition
Information seeking

Directly

User: For each potentially relevant information object
4 levels of outcomes of information receiving/seeking (ACA-LO)

Figure 5.1 Information Assessment Method (IAM)
Relevance, cognitive impact, information use, expected benefits

FIGURE 5.1
The "push-pull" conceptual framework.

a clinician to browse a database and retrieve other objects (sequence: object O1 delivery followed by object O2 retrieval) (Grad et al., 2011).

Information alerting services for clinicians help fill an essential need for lifelong learning. Alerting services have become a key strategy for clinicians to be more evidence informed—that is, to be alerted to what they do not know or to what is new in their discipline. In medicine, the general approach involves scheduled reading of information alerts such as the daily POEM (Patient-Oriented Evidence that Matters; Shaughnessy, Slawson, and Bennett, 1994). While an evaluation of 18 unique alerting services in medicine found a wide variation in their quality, the very existence of so many services (with some being over two decades old) is a testament to their popularity (Strayer et al., 2010). As we know little about the impact of alerting services on the health professions, our research group has studied how these services influence clinicians and their practices. At the very least, alerting services raise awareness of new findings by delivering abstracts or synopses of primary research studies to physicians. More importantly, patients can realize health benefits if their clinician becomes aware of a synopsis containing a diagnostic or treatment recommendation, agrees with this recommendation, and then adopts and adheres to it in practice. Interestingly, physicians do report using abstracts or synopses to guide their decision-making (Barry et al., 2001; Fontelo, Gavino, and Sarmiento, 2013).

In 1996, the CanMEDS Framework defined the elements (or roles) at the core of physician competency (Frank et al., 2005). As scholars, physicians must demonstrate a lifelong commitment to reflective learning as well as to the creation, dissemination, and application of medical knowledge. As a demonstration of their competency in meeting the scholar role, physicians must be able to maintain and enhance their professional activities through ongoing learning. In this sense, the use of email alerting services, tailored to the individuals' clinical discipline, can be considered a competency of the twenty-first-century physician. To meet this competency, the physician must be able to (1) identify and consistently make use of alerting services that are tailored to their scope of practice, and (2) acquire the evidence they need for practice, through push (alerting) services and pull databases that allow searching of knowledge resources developed specifically for answering questions that arise from practice.

For the continuing education of health professionals and in partnership with national organizations of physicians and pharmacists, our group developed the information assessment method (IAM). When linked to one object of clinical information such as that delivered by an alerting service, the IAM questionnaire provides a basis for understanding the impact of that information on patient care and systematically documents its value from the reader's perspective. The IAM questionnaire is available at http://www.mcgill.ca/iam.

The IAM questionnaire is based on a model called Acquisition–Cognition–Application–Levels of Outcome (ACA-LO). The ACA-LO model is an extension of a theory of human information interaction for research on the value of information (Saracevic and Kantor, 1997). Presented more fully elsewhere, the ACA-LO model explains the value of information, that is, how information is valuable from the user viewpoint (Pluye et al., 2013). In our model (Figure 5.2), four levels of outcomes (LO) are associated with a process that includes three iterative steps of human information interaction (the ACA cycle). To illustrate this process in the push context, health professionals subscribe to an alerting service and then acquire a passage of text (acquisition), which they read, understand, and integrate (cognition). Subsequently, they may use this newly understood and cognitively processed information for a specific patient (application). The four levels of outcomes are as follows: the situational relevance of the information (level 1), its cognitive/affective impact (level 2), the use of information (level 3), and subsequent health benefits (level 4). These are four levels because relevance is necessary for information to have a positive cognitive impact. In turn, a positive cognitive impact is necessary for using information, which could eventually result in health benefits. The outcomes are operationalized by the IAM questionnaire items.

The ACA cycle is associated with 4 Levels of Outcomes

Human information interaction process depicted by the ACA cycle

Outcomes captured in the Information Assessment Method (IAM) questionnaire

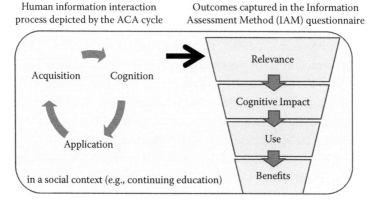

FIGURE 5.2
ACA-LO Theoretical Model.

Specifically, the ACA-LO model conceptualizes the health benefits expected by physicians as a consequence of applying clinical information to the care of their patients. Three types of health benefit are represented by three generic items:

1. This information will help to improve this patient's health status, functioning or resilience (i.e., ability to adapt to significant life stressors).
2. This information will help to prevent a disease or worsening of disease for this patient.
3. This information will help to avoid unnecessary diagnostic procedures, treatment, preventive interventions, or a referral for this patient.

With regards to item (3), later in this chapter we elaborate on the link between alerting services and their potential to help reduce the problem of overuse of health care services.

CONTENT VALIDITY OF THE IAM IN THE PUSH CONTEXT

Assessment tools (like the IAM) must be validated to know whether such tools actually evaluate what they intend to evaluate (Carmines and Zellers, 2013). Since the content validity of instruments depends on the context of their utilization and information retrieval (pull) and delivery (push) are different contexts in terms of the value of information, we have evaluated the content validity of the IAM for both contexts (Badran, Pluye, and Grad, 2013; Bindiganavile Sridhar, Pluye, and Grad, 2013; Grad et al., 2007; Pluye et al., 2010). Thus, the content validity of IAM is now well documented as is the potential for IAM to stimulate reflective learning, related to the Schön concept of reflection on action (Leung et al., 2010; Schon, 1983). Self-directed learning activities that include a reflective component are highly valued because they promote the types of learning outcomes desired by national physician organizations.

In 2013, one of our graduate students helped us revisit the content validity of the IAM for alerting services. In this work, he measured the relevance and evaluated the representativeness of all IAM items. To assess the relevance of IAM items, we analyzed more than 234,000 IAM ratings of email alerts submitted in 2012 by members of the Canadian Medical Association (CMA).

A relevance ratio, (R), was calculated for each IAM item, using (R) = the number of completed questionnaires (where the IAM item was selected) divided by the total number of completed questionnaires for the parent construct. An item was deemed relevant when R was 10% or higher. At this point, two items were recommended for removal because of a low value of relevance. To evaluate the representativeness of IAM items, 15 family physicians participated in semistructured face-to-face interviews. A thematic analysis (inductive-deductive) of interview transcripts revealed all remaining IAM items to be representative of their parent construct. From this work emerged a content validated version of IAM for alerting services.

CASE STUDIES FROM HEALTH CARE

With national organizations of physicians and pharmacists, we have taken a participatory research approach to evaluate how alerting services can influence clinical practice. We studied the delivery of two types of clinical information in two separate case studies.

Case Study 1

In 2005, the CMA began offering their physician members email delivery of one synopsis of clinical research called an InfoPOEM. One InfoPOEM was delivered daily from Monday to Friday. Written by American family physicians and a doctor of pharmacy, these are synopses of articles of primary research, selected for their relevance and potential to change the practice of primary health care.* In 2006, the InfoPOEMs CME program was accredited, meaning that in the context of this CME program Canadian physicians became eligible to earn credits for reflecting on each InfoPOEM they read. In this program, reflection on each InfoPOEM synopsis was guided and documented by the completion of one IAM questionnaire.

Case Study 2

In 2010, the Canadian Pharmacists Association (CPhA) began offering email delivery of Highlights to 17,000 physician members of the College

---

* http://essentialevidenceplus.com explains the process of producing InfoPOEMs.

of Family Physicians of Canada. Highlights are therapeutic recommendations from *e-Therapeutics+*, selected by pharmacists who produce and update a knowledge resource for primary health care.* In this CME program, Highlights were chosen by clinical editors at the CPhA and vetted by the director of continuing professional development at the College of Family Physicians. Upon clicking on the title of a weekly Highlight (delivered on Wednesday), physician participants accessed that Highlight embedded within the chapter of *e-Therapeutics+* from which it was derived. Highlights were linked to the IAM questionnaire to enable participants to document their reflective learning. As in case study 1, for each submitted IAM questionnaire, family physicians earned credits.

Case Study Comparison

As we compare the findings of these two case studies, we ask the reader to keep in mind the differences between InfoPOEMs and Highlights. The former are synopses of primary research studies, while the latter are therapeutic recommendations that summarize evidence from primary research, systematic reviews, and guidelines.

At the time, both case studies were not traditional methods of CME, in the sense that traditional CME involved large group lectures for improving disease specific knowledge. In contrast, these case studies involved self-learning through *spaced online education*—an experimentally tested method that was shown to increase knowledge retention among medical students, residents, and urologists in practice. The pedagogical benefits of spaced online education also extend to the delivery of health services. In one study of 95 clinicians in primary care, the method of spaced online education reduced inappropriate prostate cancer screenings by 26% over a 36-week period (Kerfoot et al., 2010). In another trial conducted in Canada and the United States, 78% of 720 urology trainees stated a preference for spaced online education over an online education module (Kerfoot and Baker, 2012). These studies of spaced online education took advantage of two effects described in educational psychology: (1) the spacing effect; and (2) the testing effect (Cepeda, Vul, and Rohrer, 2008; Pashler et al., 2007). While both of our case studies used the spacing effect, rather than developing test questions on hundreds of email alerts for health professionals to assess their knowledge, our team developed one questionnaire to guide

---

* http://www.etherapeutics.ca

clinicians to reflect on what they have just read, by thinking about the value of that information for at least one patient in their practice. This is a pragmatic approach to assessing the value of a large number of unique objects of clinical information delivered as email alerts through the use of a generic questionnaire.

QUANTITATIVE ANALYSIS AND FINDINGS

Case Study 1: InfoPOEMs

We analyzed all 2012 InfoPOEM ratings and tabulated frequency counts of responses of all 23 items in the IAM questionnaire. With regard to the IAM question on the clinical relevance of the information, the response choices were: (1) *totally relevant*; (2) *partially relevant*; and (3) *not relevant*. By selecting (1) or (2) the physician was obliged to answer the next question concerning the use of this information for a specific patient. To estimate the clinical relevance of each InfoPOEM, we applied a new metric called the clinical relevance of information index (CRII) (Galvao et al., 2013). This index is of interest, as synopses of low relevance (low CRII) are typically not used for patient care. Furthermore, as one increases the proportion of information in an alert that is regarded as clinically relevant, greater attention to the message should result (Kreuter and Holt, 2001). The CRII was calculated from a count of the number of totally relevant, partially relevant, and not relevant ratings received by each InfoPOEM. As participants in this CME program are not obliged to rate each InfoPOEM they read, the total number of ratings received for each InfoPOEM differed. Therefore, to make these different values comparable, the CRII computed a harmonic mean based on proportions to return a number between 0 (no clinical relevance) and 1 (maximum clinical relevance).

Following the branching logic of the IAM questionnaire, an InfoPOEM synopsis must be clinically relevant and used for a specific patient before any health benefit can be expected. With regard to the types of health benefit expected by physician participants for their patients, we calculated proportions for each of the three items of patient health benefit associated with each InfoPOEM. In particular, we identified the 2012 InfoPOEMs with the highest proportion of ratings directly linked to reducing overdiagnosis or overtreatment, captured through the item, "This information will help to avoid unnecessary diagnostic procedures, treatment, preventive interventions or a referral, for this patient."

In 2012, 20,375 CMA members received InfoPOEMs. A total of 3,056 (15%) of these members submitted at least one completed questionnaire (equivalent to one IAM rating). This group of physicians included 2,343 participants who described themselves as family physicians or general practitioners and 713 participants from 31 different specialties or subspecialties.

Ratings of all 271 InfoPOEMs delivered in 2012 were included, if they were received by the CMA from January 1 to December 31, 2012. We analyzed 226,119 ratings linked to 271 InfoPOEMs delivered in 2012, for an average of 834 ratings per InfoPOEM. Here, we descriptively summarize these InfoPOEM ratings by each of the four constructs covered by the IAM questionnaire:

1. Cognitive impact: Question—What is the impact of this information on you or your practice? Participants can report more than one type of cognitive impact for each InfoPOEM. Figure 5.3 displays the distribution of ratings for all 10 items of cognitive impact considering all 2012 InfoPOEMs. Not surprisingly for a CME program, the most frequently reported item of cognitive impact was, "I learned

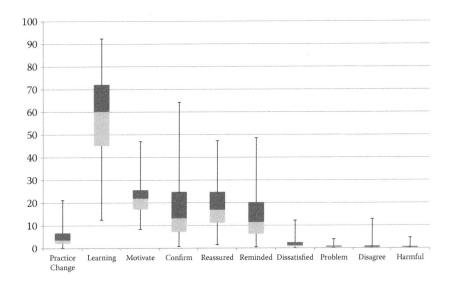

FIGURE 5.3

Q1. What is the impact of this *InfoPOEM* on you or your practice?

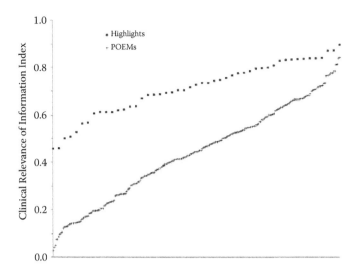

FIGURE 5.4
Email alerts: Each point represents the relevance rating of a single alert.

something new." In addition, participants frequently reported that the clinical information from InfoPOEMs "reassured" them or "confirmed they did (are doing) the right thing." Items of negative cognitive impact such as, "I disagree with this information" were reported, but rarely.

2. Clinical relevance: Question—Is this information relevant for at least one of your patients? Figure 5.4 reveals that the clinical relevance of InfoPOEMs (represented in the figure by the bottom line) varied widely in 2012. As most of their country is free of dangerous snakes, for Canadian physicians the least relevant InfoPOEM in 2012 was titled "Three-Step Identification Method for Recognizing Dangerous Snakes"* (CRII = 0.07). For this InfoPOEM, nearly all participants reported this information was "not relevant." In 2012 the most relevant InfoPOEM was titled "ASA: Not for Primary Prevention"[†] (CRII = 0.81). Most physicians rated the information in this InfoPOEM to be "totally relevant."

---

* Daily POEM delivered March 2012. Primary study by Cardwell MD. Recognizing dangerous snakes in the United States and Canada: A novel 3-step identification method. *Wilderness Environ Med* 2011;22(4):304–308.

† Daily POEM delivered March 2012. Primary study by Berger JS et al. Aspirin for the prevention of cardiovascular events in patients without clinical cardiovascular disease: A meta-analysis of randomized trials. *Am Heart J* 2011;162(1):115–124.e2.

TABLE 5.1

Q3. Will you use this *InfoPOEM* for a specific patient?

	Yes	Possibly	No
Median (%)	15.5	28.7	52.9
Range (n)	13–588	15–449	82–812

3. Use of this information: Question—Will you use this information for a specific patient? Table 5.1 presents descriptive statistics on the intention to use 2012 InfoPOEMs. Participants frequently reported the potential for InfoPOEMs information to be used for specific patients. For example, with respect to the InfoPOEM titled "Intermittent steroids effective for children with recurrent wheezing"*—the item "I will use this information for a specific patient" was endorsed in 53.4% of 1,064 ratings. As physicians do not typically rate an InfoPOEM in front of the patient (what is called the *point of care*), participants more commonly reported that InfoPOEMs information will be "possibly used" than "used."

4. Health benefits: Question—For this patient, do you expect any health benefits as a result of applying this information? The expected health benefits arising from the use of InfoPOEMs information for specific patients is presented in Table 5.2. In 13.3% of all ratings, participants reported an expectation of a health benefit for a specific patient. This ranged from a low of 1.8% of ratings for the InfoPOEM titled "Friday the 13th? Bring It On"† to a high of 47.8% of ratings for the InfoPOEM titled "Exercise Decreases Depressive Symptoms of Chronic Illness."‡

Case Study 2: Highlights

In 2010 (year one of this program), 5,346 family physicians submitted at least one Highlight rating (Grad et al., 2014). Of all participants, 91% of participants reported they were in family or general practice while 85% were in full-time or part-time practice. A total of 31,429 ratings on

---

* Daily POEM delivered March 2012. Primary study by Zeiger RS et al., for the CARE Network of the National Heart, Lung, and Blood Institute. Daily or intermittent budesonide in preschool children with recurrent wheezing. *N Engl J Med* 2011;365(21):1990–2001.

† Daily POEM delivered September 2012. Primary study by Lo BM et al. Answering the myth: use of emergency services on Friday the 13th. *Am J Emerg Med* 2012;30(6):886–889.

‡ Daily *POEM* delivered March 2012. Primary study by Herring MP et al. Effect of exercise training on depressive symptoms among patients with a chronic illness. A systematic review and meta-analysis of randomized controlled trials. *Arch Intern Med* 2012;172(2):101–111.

TABLE 5.2

Q4. For this patient, do you expect any health benefits as a result of applying this *InfoPOEM*?

	Yes	No
Median (%)	13.3	86.7
Range (n)	8–582	162–1034

49 Highlights were received in 2010, for an average of 667 ratings per Highlight (range 415–1176). The median number of Highlight ratings per participant was 2 (range 1–49). Among participants who submitted more than two Highlight ratings, the median number of ratings was 7 (mean 11.9). Participants reported the clinical information from Highlights was totally or partially relevant for at least one patient 90% of the time. To identify which Highlights were most or least relevant, we again calculated the CRII from the responses to question 2. The CRII value ranged from 0.46 to 0.90 per Highlight (mean 0.71). With regard to their practice, participants reported that Highlights will be used "for at least one patient" in 59.2% of all ratings. In 41% of all Highlight ratings, participants expected patient health benefits, such as avoiding an unnecessary treatment or preventive intervention.

There are several comparisons to make between these case studies. First, Highlights were delivered much more slowly to participants than InfoPOEMs (weekly versus daily). At this time, we do not know the optimal speed for delivery of brief educational content, and different alerting services provide their content on a daily, weekly, or monthly basis. Concurrent to the Highlights program described in case study 2, about 3,000 Canadian family physicians used IAM to rate InfoPOEM synopses in 2010. Given the groups of physicians rating InfoPOEMs and Highlights are not identical, any comparison of ratings of these two types of clinical information must be interpreted with caution. Furthermore, InfoPOEMs differ from Highlights, as the former are synopses of recently published research articles with a focus not limited to therapeutics. However, we provide Figure 5.4 to simply illustrate the results that might be obtained, for example, in randomized trials of alerting services to test the clinical relevance of delivered information as perceived by the target audience. In Figure 5.4, the clinical relevance of InfoPOEMs distributes over a wider range than Highlights (the top line). In addition, the clinical relevance of InfoPOEMs delivered in 2010 was generally lower than Highlights.

A total of 126 (0.4%) comments on 31 Highlights from 116 family physicians were confirmed as constructive feedback comments because they led to a change in *e-Therapeutics+*. On average, each of the 31 Highlights was associated with 4.1 constructive feedback comments (min 1; max 25). We categorized all 126 constructive feedback comments into four types, and Cohen's Kappa was calculated for each type (N; %; Kappa score): (1) suggestion for additional content (79; 62.7%; 0.82); (2) reservation or disagreement (26; 20.6%; 0.74); (3) suggestion to consider contradictory evidence (24; 19.0%; 1.00); and (4) need for clarification of content (9; 7.1%; 0.65). Given that 12 comments were coded to two types of constructive feedback, the cumulative percentage is greater than 100. Agreement between raters fell into the range of substantial or perfect agreement. Thus, the proposed coding scheme to categorize constructive feedback comments is reliable, and the CPhA presently uses this process to identify potentially constructive feedback.

Overall, constructive feedback is rare ($N = 126$), representing 3% of all written comments ($N = 4,166$). This low frequency confirms the quality of information in Highlights from *e-Therapeutics+*. The information provider valued the systematic collection and integration of user feedback in their editorial process.

Using Two-Way Knowledge Translation to Create Better than Best Evidence

We define two-way knowledge translation as a continuous interactional process between information providers who update and deliver best evidence and information users who assess this evidence and submit constructive feedback. In turn, information providers may integrate this feedback to optimize their evidence, which is then rereleased for retrieval by information users as needed. Stated otherwise, research-based information delivered to health professionals can be enhanced by experience-based information from health professionals. In line with Collins and Evans (2002), we submit that most physicians are not scientists. Typically they do not have graduate training in research, are not directly involved in research, and do not interact with researchers; however, they have "special technical expertise in virtue of experience" (p. 238), which legitimates their discourse about research-based information. In other words, research-based information involves people with three types of expertise: experiential, contributory, and interactive. People with practical experience in the topic area covered by the research-based information (e.g., physicians) have expertise "technically-qualified by experience" (p. 238). Core experts are research scientists with "enough expertise to contribute to the science of the field" (p. 254), which is contributory expertise. People with interactive expertise (e.g., editors) have "enough expertise to interact interestingly" (p. 254) with researchers and can carry out research synthesis. These three types of expertise are not mutually exclusive "ideal types." For specific information objects, some people may combine all three types of expertise and be concomitantly a researcher, practitioner, and clinical editor. To enable a successful two-way knowledge translation process, our case study suggests information providers must recognize information users as technically qualified experts who bring suggestions to clarify or add content as well as editorial attention to the most recent developments in the field, contradictory evidence, or regional differences in recommendations (Table 5.3).

This two-way knowledge translation process appears to be unique with regard to the information management of knowledge resources (Tang, 2012). We reviewed the literature and could not find other work that described or examined how feedback from health professionals is used to improve knowledge resources. Before the use of IAM, the CPhA only rarely received comments (perhaps two per week). IAM stimulated physician feedback in response to Highlights from *e-Therapeutics*+ and allowed for two-way knowledge translation. This process was beneficial to both the information provider and the participants. From the organizational point

TABLE 5.3

One- vs. Two-way Knowledge Translation

	One-way Knowledge Translation	**Two-way Knowledge Translation**
Key role	Information providers (contributory or interactive expertise)	Information users (experiential expertise)
Information process	Information providers summarize research in their resource and send it to users	Information users send constructive feedback to providers
	Information users receive it and then retrieve it as needed for practice	Information providers integrate this feedback into their resource
		Information users retrieve it as needed
Information use	"Best" evidence can be used for a patient	"Better than best" evidence can be used for a patient

of view, the editorial process and the content of their knowledge resource was optimized by user feedback. As for the physician participants, their voices were heard and they contributed to the creation of better than best evidence. In line with the literature on relational marketing, being open to user feedback and handling such feedback in a timely manner can improve a knowledge resource and help information providers to sustain relationships with their customers by valuing their expertise (Palmatier et al., 2006).

LIMITATIONS OF THIS WORK

In both case studies, physician participants reported that the application of clinical information delivered by an alerting service will be associated with better outcomes for patients and the health care system. A limitation of this finding arises from the self-reported nature of the data. As with any self-report measure, the IAM data is subject to bias on the part of the participant. We acknowledge that the benefits physicians expect to realize by applying InfoPOEMs to specific patients may not be achieved. Given this uncertainty, we recommend further research to objectively document the contribution made by information alerting services to the clinical outcomes of specific patients. Until this work is conducted, all we can say is that physicians do report that these services have the potential to improve their patient care. For patients, the most common type of expected health benefit is avoiding an unnecessary test or treatment, which would help to reduce overdiagnosis and overtreatment.

In our case studies, we did not measure how frequently Highlights or InfoPOEMs were read and not rated. If alerts are more likely to be rated by physicians when they are relevant to at least one of their patients, then our data overestimate the clinical relevance of these objects of information. As a general rule, CME programs do not randomly select their participants. Therefore, physicians in our case studies were more motivated to receive email alerts as well as to read and rate them. Nevertheless, knowing that any CME program can lead to health benefits for specific patients is potentially important to improving the outcomes of clinical practice. In 2012, a program for Canadian pharmacists mirroring the program for family physicians was launched by the CPhA. The continuation of this program leaves the door open to further research.

ANALYTIC CHALLENGES

With respect to the educational outcomes of physician participation and reflective learning, we would like to identify the best response format for the IAM questionnaire. Because we have an ongoing program of research, the response format of the IAM questionnaire used in case study 1 differs from what was implemented in case study 2. By this, we mean that case study 1 participants use a "check all that apply" response format whereas those in case study 2 are forced to respond to each questionnaire item with a "yes, no, or possibly," with the default response set as "no." This difference between case studies reflects our lack of knowledge with respect to the type of response format that should be deployed to optimize educational outcomes. Inherent in research involving survey methodology is the issue of participant response and response formatting. In other words, what should participation feel like for the user, and how can this experience affect the data? For example, between cases 1 and 2, which had the better response format?

Presumably, a survey that is more tedious to fill out would have a negative impact on response rates, while a more convenient format would in fact encourage participation. Methods for comparison of response formats are not well documented at the moment, but the surge of IAM data that became available allowed us to analyze response rates from a survival analysis standpoint. In other words, through counting the number of responses and nonresponses for each format as well as taking into account the time-to-rating of InfoPOEMs, inference could be made on the efficacy of each response format, using participation as a primary measure. This occurs much in the same way as the efficacy of a drug that is assessed by measuring time-to-death for each subject in the treatment or control group. Although in this case, some additional techniques were used to account for clustering in the data (i.e., different InfoPOEMs generated different response rates, and each physician has his or her own rating habits, aside from any effects of the response format itself). One of us performed a retrospective analysis of case 1 response formats, testing for differences in risk of rating between a "check all that apply" format and a forced "yes" or "no" format. We found the latter format to be significantly associated ($p < 0.001$) with a 44% lower hazard of rating (95% CI: [29.7%, 55.8%]) compared with the former (Moscovici, 2013). Ultimately, it is CME providers who will judge whether a drop in participation is compensated for by enhanced educational outcomes (i.e., better thought out responses to a questionnaire that promotes reflective learning).

In this way, not only did we capitalize on big data to collect feedback from participants, but we also used time-to-event frameworks to inform decisions on response format. This approach is not yet common practice in survey methodology but may become so in the near future. Therefore, we can now assess how different response formats impact participation as well as the nature of collected data. In the age of big data in health care, these discoveries emphasize the potential to better understand the effect of questionnaire response format in future work through the prism of careful statistical analysis.

Unlike IAM ratings, which can be efficiently analyzed using relational databases, another big data challenge resides with the free text feedback comments that require manual screening for interpretation. You may recall that some information providers want to identify constructive feedback. However, the high level of participation in our CME programs involving alerts means that feedback data sets grow rapidly. As a result, keeping up with the flow of textual feedback in the form of free text comments from thousands of physicians is a challenge. The sheer volume of IAM ratings and the low density of potentially constructive comments make it difficult to identify such feedback with existing data-processing methods. In particular, the screening task presents a big data challenge because it exceeds the capabilities of information providers for processing and analyzing domain-specific feedback data from health care practitioners.

To confront this challenge, we carried out two projects in search of an automated method to identify constructive feedback. In project 1, we collaborated with the Computer Research Institute of Montréal to explore the application of automatic text categorization (by means of supervised machine learning) to filter comments about InfoPOEMs. First, features potentially indicative of constructive comments were identified. For example, basic linguistic features included the amount of content words (e.g., nouns, adjectives), the use of domain-specific terminologies, and the appearance of negation and opinion related verbs (e.g., agree, dislike). Then, the combination and generalization of a number of features were modeled in machine learning algorithms such as Random Forest, Simple Logistic, and Naïve Bayes. The performance of these algorithms was evaluated by comparing their abilities to recognize constructive comments with human classifiers. We found that the algorithms were not sufficient to categorize constructive comments into meaningful categories such as "disagreement" or "need for clarification" and cannot replace human classifiers in that respect. However, our findings suggested a good possibility of filtering out the nonconstructive comments. For example, in a test pool of 3,470 comments, one algorithm identified 634 comments, among which 81% were truly nonconstructive. It is generally accepted that a classification performance above 80% can be practically useful for ranking or decision support.

In project 2, text-mining techniques such as clustering and descriptor extraction were applied to comments gathered in case study 2 (the Highlights CME program). In this project, every comment was considered a textual document, and each document was characterized by a document-term matrix constructed following the bag-of-related-words method (Rossi and Rezende, 2011). Documents were clustered using the fuzzy C-means clustering algorithm (Bezdek, 1981). To meaningfully identify each cluster, descriptors were extracted from documents within the cluster (Nogueira, Rezende, and Camargo, 2011). The cluster descriptors allowed us to distinguish between groups of comments and identify those that were constructive. One advantage of the fuzzy clustering approach is that it imitates reality by allowing a comment to be assigned to several clusters with different membership degrees. Therefore, varied levels of constructive feedback could be represented. The evaluation of the clustering method was conducted through comparative analysis between the automatically extracted clusters (cluster descriptors) and manually classified groups of comments (group labels). Project 2 findings again revealed that it is relatively easier to filter out nonconstructive comments than to directly identify constructive ones.

Both projects indicated that automation is helpful to some extent, and text analysis technologies can be used to filter out the nonconstructive comments. On the other hand, to target constructive comments directly is still a difficult task for machines, likely because of the domain expertise and practice-based knowledge needed to recognize any constructive value within short comments. In our studies, we noticed that even human classifiers vary in their judgment of what counts as constructive, given differences in their years of experience and field of practice. In future research, it would be interesting to test semisupervised methods where human agents concomitantly interpret a small amount of data to calibrate and correct the algorithm for uncertainties while the machine processes the bulk of data that is relatively straightforward to automatically interpret. When hard criteria for constructive comments cannot be encoded into algorithms, there remains a big data challenge.

A VISION FOR THE FUTURE

To improve decision-making by clinicians at the point of care, we see a need to help CIC users integrate the alert-based clinical information they judged as beneficial for their patients into their electronic medical record (EMR). We suggest a three-step approach to realize the integration of alerts into clinical work:

> Step 1: Physicians who use the IAM will select the alerts they believe would be beneficial for their patients, based on their answers to the final IAM question.
> Step 2: Selected alerts will be automatically linked to individual patient records in the EMR using algorithms when the information content of alerts is encoded with EMR-compatible disease or treatment codes.
> Step 3: Physicians will be reminded of their 'beneficial' alerts when they open a patient chart at the point of care.

We call this *intelligent personalized reminders* when the system reminds physicians about alert-based recommendations they themselves have chosen for application at the point of care. Intelligent personalized reminders are an evolutionary push computer system that can automatically provide information to meet the needs of the user (Pluye, Grad, Granikov, et al., 2010). These reminders will combine the intelligence of individual clinicians (using IAM-guided reflective learning) with the intelligence of EMRs. As yet, no EMR offers such a system. Our plan is to create, implement, and study this type of reminder among physicians who use an EMR and participate in alert-based CME programs.

We also see the potential to further promote reflective learning through group discussion. As we have seen in the context of the Highlights program that produced better than best evidence, constructive feedback comments from raters can be used to improve a knowledge resource and the subsequent production of new alerts. As constructive feedback comments have the potential to further stimulate learning among participants, we seek to test methods of sharing these comments (linked to InfoPOEMs or Highlights) among members of national organizations of physicians or pharmacists. While perhaps less than 5% of 1,000 ratings received on each InfoPOEM contain constructive feedback comments, in absolute numbers and for educational purposes there are a sufficient number of comments with highly relevant information. Presently, neither the CMA nor the CPhA publishes comments submitted by individual physicians participating in our case studies. Automated methods using natural language processing could help to identify comments that are potentially worth sharing. Once identified, these comments could then be posted online for program participants. In a move toward building group learning from what is presently a self-learning activity, IAM ratings are used to calculate the CRII for each InfoPOEM archived at http://cma.ca. The CRII for each InfoPOEM is then posted for all members to see and updated on a dynamic basis.

The assessment of learning needs is an essential component of curriculum development. To better guide those who provide continuing education for health professionals, traditionally the results of small surveys of physicians or planning committees are used to inform the selection of content for CME programs. Previously, we investigated whether the learning needs of Canadian family physicians could be revealed given knowledge of the clinical topics that provoke a high proportion of positive responses to one IAM item, namely, "I am motivated to learn more." In the context of the Highlights program, six CME experts believed CME planners could use IAM data as a low-cost by-product to inform decisions on the content of future CME activities, if grouped responses from family physicians were analyzed based on geographic location to obtain regional perspectives (i.e., by province or state) (Lewis et al., 2013). Further work is needed to determine if IAM data from a cohort of physicians who participate in one alerting service can reveal the learning needs of other physicians not using this service.

Finally, as a potential solution to email overload we have developed a multichannel smartphone app for Apple and Android devices. The IAM app allows clinicians to subscribe to their clinical information channels of interest and to read-rate clinical information delivered as alerts, at their own pace, away from their email inbox.

REFERENCES

Badran, H., P. Pluye, and R.M. Grad. 2013. Content Validation of the IAM for Push Technology: A Mixed Methods Study. Paper presented at 41st annual meeting of the North American Primary Care Research Group, Ottawa, ON, November 9, 2013.

Barry, H.C., M.H. Ebell, A.F. Shaughnessy, D.C. Slawson, and F. Nietzke. 2001. Family Physicians' Use of Medical Abstracts to Guide Decision Making: Style or Substance? *Journal of the American Board of Family Practice* 14(6): 437–42.

Bezdek, J.C. 1981. *Pattern Recognition with Fuzzy Objective Function Algorithms.* Norwell, MA: Kluwer Academic Publishers.

Bindiganavile Sridhar, S., P. Pluye, and R.M. Grad. 2013. In Pursuit of a Valid Information Assessment Method for Continuing Education: A Mixed Methods Study. *BMC Med Education* 13(137).

Carmines, E., and R. Zellers. 2013. *Reliability and Validity Assessment.* Newbury Park, CA: Sage.

Cepeda, N.J., E. Vul, and D. Rohrer. 2008. Spacing Effects in Learning: A Temporal Ridgeline of Optimal Retention. *Psychol Science* 19: 1095–1102.

Collins, H.M., and R. Evans. 2002. The Third Wave of Science Studies. *Social Studies Science* 32(2): 235–296.

Fontelo, P., A. Gavino, and R.F. Sarmiento. 2013. Comparing Data Accuracy between Structured Abstracts and Full-Text Journal Articles: Implications in Their Use for Informing Clinical Decisions. *Evidence Based Medicine* 18(6): 207–211.

Frank, J.R., M. Jabbour, D. Frechette, M. Marks, N. Valk, and G. Bourgeois (Eds.). 2005. Report of the CanMEDS Phase IV Working Groups. Royal College of Physicians and Surgeons of Canada.

Galvao, M.C.B., I.L.M. Ricarte, R.M. Grad, and P. Pluye. 2013. The Clinical Relevance of Information Index (CRII): Assessing the Relevance of Health Information to Clinical Practice. *Health Information and Libraries Journal* 30: 110–120.

Grad, R.M., P. Pluye, M.E. Beauchamp, J. Hanley, B. Marlow, M. Shulha, J. Johnson-Lafleur, and K. Dalkir. 2007. Validation of a Method to Assess the Impact of Electronic Knowledge Resources on Clinicians. *e Service Journal* 5(2): e113.

Grad, R.M., P. Pluye, J. Johnson-Lafleur, V. Granikov, M. Shulha, G. Bartlett, and B. Marlow. 2011. Do Family Physicians Retrieve Synopses of Clinical Research Previously Read as Email Alerts? *Journal of Medical Internet Research* 13(4): e101.

Grad, R.M., P. Pluye, C. Repchinsky, B. Jovaisas, B. Marlow, J. Moscovici, I. Ricarte, M.C. Barbosa Galvao, M. Shulha, and J. de Gaspe Bonar. 2014. *Physician Assessments of the Value of Therapeutic Information Delivered via Email. Canadian Family Physician* 2014; 60: e 258–262.

Haines, A. 1996. The Science of Perpetual Change. *British Journal of General Practice* 46(403): 115–119.

Kerfoot, B.P., E.V. Lawler, G. Sokolovskaya, D. Gagnon, and P.R. Conlin. 2010. Durable Improvements in Prostate Cancer Screening from Online Spaced Education: A Randomized Controlled Trial. *American Journal of Preventive Medicine* 39(5): 472–478.

Kerfoot, B.P., and H. Baker. 2012. An Online Spaced-Education Game to Teach and Assess Residents: A Multi-Institutional Prospective Trial. *Journal of the American College of Surgeons* 214(3): 367–373.

Kreuter, M.W., and C.L. Holt. 2001. How Do People Process Health Information? Applications in an Age of Individualized Communication. *Current Directions in Psychological Science* 10(6): 206–209.

Leung, K.H., P. Pluye, R.M. Grad, and C. Weston. 2010. A Reflective Learning Framework to Evaluate CME Effects on Practice Reflection. *Journal of Continuing Education in the Health Professions* 30(2): 78–88.

Lewis, D., P. Pluye, C. Rodriguez, R.M. Grad, C. Repchinsky, B. Marlow, and J. Bonar. 2013. Reflection on Reflective Learning for CME Planning. Paper presented at 41st annual meeting of the North American Primary Care Research Group. Ottawa, ON, November 12, 2013.

Moscovici, J. 2013. Statistical Applications in Knowledge Translation Research Implemented through the Information Assessment Method. MSc thesis, McGill University.

Moynihan, R., J. Doust, and D. Henry. 2012. Preventing Overdiagnosis: How to Stop Harming the Healthy. *BMJ* 344: e3502.

Nogueira, T., S.O. Rezende, and H. Camargo. 2011. Fuzzy Cluster Descriptor Extraction for Flexible Organization of Documents. Paper presented at 11th International Conference on Hybrid Intelligent Systems (HIS). Malacca, December 7, 2011.

Palmatier, R.W., R.P. Dant, D. Grewal, and K.R. Evans. 2006. Factors Influencing the Effectiveness of Relationship Marketing: A Meta-Analysis. *Journal of Marketing* 70(4): 136–153.

Pashler, H., D. Rohrer, N.J. Cepeda, and S.K. Carpenter. 2007. Enhancing Learning and Retarding Forgetting: Choices and Consequences. *Psychonomic Bulletin & Review* 14: 187–193.

Pluye, P., R.M. Grad, V. Granikov, J. Jagosh, and K.H. Leung. 2010. Evaluation of Email Alerts in Practice: Part 1 —Review of the Literature on Clinical Emailing Channels. *Journal of Evaluation in Clinical Practice* 16(6): 1227–1235.

Pluye, P., R.M. Grad, J. Johnson-Lafleur, T. Bambrick, B. Burnand, J. Mercer, B. Marlow, and C. Campbell. 2010. Evaluation of Email Alerts in Practice: Part 2—Validation of the Information Assessment Method (IAM). *Journal of Evaluation in Clinical Practice* 16(6): 1236–1243.

Pluye, P., R.M. Grad, C. Repchinsky, B. Jovaisas, J. Johnson-Lafleur, M.-E. Carrier, V. Granikov, B. Farrell, C. Rodriguez, G. Bartlett, C. Loiselle, and F. Legare. 2013. Four Levels of Outcomes of Information-Seeking: A Mixed Methods Study in Primary Health Care. *Journal of the American Society for Information Science and Technology* 64(1): 108–125.

Pluye, P., R.M. Grad, C. Repchinsky, B. Jovaisas, D. Lewis, D.L. Tang, V. Granikov, J. Bonar, and B. Marlow. 2014. Better than "Best" Evidence? The Information Assessment Method Can Help Information Providers to Use Feedback from Family Physicians for 2-Way Knowledge Translation. *Canadian Family Physician* 2014; 60: 415–417.

Rossi, R.G., and S.O. Rezende. 2011. Building a Topic Hierarchy Using the Bag-of-Related-Words Representation. Paper presented at DocEng' 11. Mountain View, California, September 22, 2011.

Saracevic, T., and K.B. Kantor. 1997. Studying the Value of Library and Information Services. Part I. Establishing a Theoretical Framework. *Journal of the American Society for Information Science* 48(6): 527–542.

Schon, D.A. 1983. *The Reflective Practitioner: How Professionals Think in Action.* New York: Basic.

Shaughnessy, A.F., D.C. Slawson, and J.H. Bennett. 1994. Becoming an Information Master: A Guidebook to the Medical Information Jungle. *Journal of Family Practice* 39: 489–499.

Sirovich, B.E., S. Woloshin, and L.M. Schwartz. 2011. Too Little? Too Much? Primary Care Physicians' Views on US Health Care: A Brief Report. *Archives of Internal Medicine* 171(17): 1582–1585.

Slawson, D. 2013. Re:Interesting but Potentially Misleading. Available at http://www.annfa-mmed.org/content/11/6/559/reply

Strayer, S.M., A.F. Shaughnessy, K.S. Yew, M.B. Stephens, and D.C. Slawson. 2010. Updating Clinical Knowledge: An Evaluation of Current Information Alerting Services. *International Journal of Medical Informatics* 79(12): 824–831.

Tang, D.L. 2012. Towards Optimal Management of Health Information Users' Feedback: The Case of the Canadian Pharmacists Association. PhD thesis, McGill University.

6

Addressing Social Determinants of Health Using Big Data

Gregory D. Stevens

CONTENTS

OBJECTIVES

After reading this chapter, the reader shall be able to:

- Understand how social determinants of health can be included into public health and medical practice using data

- Identify the range of social determinants that can be more consistently measured and addressed in public health and medical practices
- Understand the use of models in integrating social determinants with health conditions

ABSTRACT

This chapter explains the juxtaposition of public health and medical care in identifying individuals at risk for health conditions and improving their care. Big data enables health practitioners to identify social risk factors that are linked to specific medical conditions among the populations that they serve. Examples are then given of how data and analytics can be combined to improve medical practice.

INTRODUCTION

Avoidable health inequalities arise because of the circumstances in which people grow, live, work, and age, and the systems put in place to deal with illness. The conditions in which people live and die are, in turn, shaped by political, social, and economic forces.

World Health Organization Commission
on the Social Determinants of Health (CSDH, 2008)

The United States has experienced and, at times, has promulgated a very long history of inequality among its citizens. From civil rights violations and suffrage restrictions that only started to resolve in the past 70 years to increasing income gaps between the poor and rich that have recently dominated our national headlines, inequality pervades many aspects of modern life including income, education, employment, housing, and other life necessities. Most deeply affected have been groups delineated by race or ethnicity, socioeconomic status, immigration status, culture and language, and sexual orientation (Shi and Stevens, 2005).

Perhaps the most persistent manifestation of inequality has been an ongoing and, in many cases, increasing disparity in health and well-being across these social divisions. Today it is not considered surprising to see major health differences between whites and African Americans, the wealthy and poor, or the insured and uninsured. But perhaps it should be more surprising, considering that most health disparities are not caused by the outright lack of sanitation, famine, and absolute poverty that claimed the lives of many of this nation's underprivileged in earlier years (National Center for Health Statistics, 2006).

Things, in fact, have changed dramatically. The causes of health disparities are not always obvious and, as we now well understand, are rooted very deeply in the social context surrounding modern life (Banks et al., 2006). Public health, social sciences, and medical professions have deeply unraveled and have begun to understand the impact that personal social position and social class, racism, and discrimination, social networks, and other more relational community factors have on population health. This knowledge has been applied to better design both macro- and microinterventions to address health disparities, but most efforts are just now revealing their effects and entering an era of wider acceptance (Cooper, Hill, and Powe, 2002).

Theory regarding social determinants of health and vulnerable populations has dominated the social science and public health literature and is now common in the medical field as well (Mechanic and Tanner, 2007). The data that are gathered to inform and advance these theories are increasingly common in national and state health data. And some ambitious (if not intrepid) medical organizations and practitioners— especially those serving vulnerable populations—have ventured to make data collection on social factors a regular part of their clinical information gathering.

The measurement and collection of any data are only half of the challenge. The other is how to make these data interpretable, meaningful, and actionable for those who are familiar with the social determinants of health and compelling for professionals in public health and medicine who are new to the field. The opportunity has never been greater for data on the context of our lives to inform the way we understand and address problems, and the effective use of these data needs a framework. The purpose of this chapter is to address both challenges by making a case for big data to focus on vulnerable populations and the social determinants of health and then by introducing strategies for the collection and application of social data. Throughout, I will give specific examples of where and how big data can be used to enhance public health and medical practice.

SOCIAL DETERMINANTS OF HEALTH AND VULNERABLE POPULATIONS

Before I leap into a discussion of big data and how they can be used to inform public health and medical practice, it is worth considering why we should focus on the social determinants of health and vulnerable populations. The effort to collect and use social data is not trivial, and thus there should be a strong rationale for engaging the country in this movement. I'll begin with a brief discussion of this rationale.

Why Focus on Vulnerable Populations?

There are several overarching reasons that public health and medical professionals should focus our attention on vulnerable populations and aim to reduce disparities in health. It is worth keeping in mind that the United States was founded on the principals of both equality and freedom, and these principles have been at the core of civil rights actions. Yet health has remained conspicuously absent from the list of advocated civil rights. Evidence of this can be observed in the heated partisan debate about health care reform in the United States and the question of whether and how the citizenry should have access to health care. If equality is indeed a guiding principle for the United States, then it should be argued that disparities in health should not be allowed to persist.

Second, the health of the overall U.S. population is far behind that of many, if not most, other developed countries. For example, infant mortality, a widely accepted critical barometer of population health, remained substantially higher in the United States than in 43 other countries in 2013 (e.g., a rate of 5.9 deaths per 1,000 live births vs. 2.2 deaths per 1,000 births in Japan) (CIA, 2013). This is clearly far from what is expected of a country with the highest level of economic productivity in the world and places U.S. health on level with Croatia, Bosnia, Herzegovina and Lithuania, which face tremendous economic and political struggles. Given large socioeconomic disparities in infant mortality within the United States, achieving a level of national health that is aligned with our economic prosperity cannot be attained without attention to the most vulnerable populations.

Third, the number and proportion of vulnerable individuals is increasing in the United States. For example, the national poverty rate reached

15.0% in 2012, reflecting 46.5 million people in the United States (DeNavas-Walt, 2013). This is up from 12.3% in 2006 (or 36.5 million people), just two years before a major economic downturn (DeNavas-Walt, Proctor, and Lee, 2009). Similarly, the uninsured population has increased steadily since 1990, reaching about 15.8% of the population (or 47 million people) in 2006. It had not declined significantly through 2012, staying at 15.4% or 48 million people, just two years prior to full implementation of President Barack Obama's health care reform in 2014. Even with health care reform, millions of people in the United States will still gain affordable insurance coverage. Vulnerable groups place great demands on health care and social welfare systems and thus require substantial policy attention.

The Role of Social Determinants of Health in Vulnerability

With a rationale in hand for focusing on addressing vulnerable populations and health disparities, we now focus particularly on the role of social determinants of health. We often think about social determinants of health as the factors outside the health care system that can have an impact on personal and population health. Very generally, these include the social and economic conditions in which we live that support or detract from our ability to attain optimal health. These conditions are, of course, greatly shaped by macrolevel factors, including the political and economic systems in place.

While we might find macrolevel factors difficult to address within a health care or public health system, they are at the root of the social determinants of health and thus within the purview of our professions. Public health professionals may find this of more immediate interest than clinicians, but the social determinants of health often still arise in my discussions with physician colleagues who express frustration about patient inability to make lifestyle changes and comply with treatment recommendations. Most frequently I hear my colleagues discuss patients seem unable to adopt new health behaviors (e.g., an exercise regimen or a healthier diet) and between the lines who are often concerns about social determinants.

Let's consider the patient who has difficulty adopting a new exercise regimen. I am a moderate exerciser myself, but it does not take much to prevent me from doing so. When the weather is cold, for example, or if I'm under stress from a project deadline, I personally find it requires much greater motivation to do an evening run. For a patient with, say, diabetes, these relatively minor obstacles can be much larger. The highs and lows in blood sugar that come with uncontrolled diabetes greatly affect mood and energy, and the motivation to overcome what are relatively small obstacles can be unpredictable. With a relatively steady job, I can often find the time to exercise and can probably afford a gym membership to overcome the deterrent effects of weather. But if the patient is one of the tens of millions of people in the United States who are in much less stable part-time work (or even unemployed) in the current economy, then it is very hard to prioritize exercise over looking for more stable work, and a gym membership is a distant luxury item. The sidewalks in my rather quiet suburban neighborhood tend to be in good shape and lighted, making it a safe environment to exercise. If the patient lives, however, in one of the hundreds of thousands of lower-income neighborhoods where safety gives way to traffic-filled and poorly maintained streets and sidewalks, even the most personally motivated individual may find it an irrational choice to go for a run in that environment.

Each of these barriers that our hypothetical patient with diabetes may face can be relatively small, and the motivation of any particularly energized individual can be enough to overcome any of them. But it is clear that, in terms of social and economic conditions that favor making healthy lifestyles changes, the deck is stacked in favor of individuals of higher socioeconomic status (SES) in safer neighborhoods, those with stable and more white-collar employment, and those with lots of social support. As we begin to factor these conditions and others into our vision of health, we are acknowledging social determinants of health.

I have also heard my public health and physician colleagues adopt the opposite approach, simply writing off their target or patient populations as lazy or refusing to take responsibility, which could be true in any given instance. This approach seems to be born of frustration and particularly feeling that changing patient behaviors is beyond the scope of their professional abilities. But public health and medical professionals are finding ways to overcome these challenges—changing the way they practice, addressing more social factors in the health of their patients, partnering with agencies that can pick up where it is difficult to stretch their professional boundaries. Much of this has been fueled by the increasing demand for, and availability of, big data.

CUMULATIVE SOCIAL RISKS AND A GENERAL MODEL OF VULNERABILITY

With a rationale for focusing on vulnerable populations and a basic grasp of social determinants of health, there is now a need to understand how we can organize the social determinants into a useful structure for public health and medical professionals. Many different theories and models are useful, ranging from those that focus on specific diseases to those that address macroeconomics. A colleague and I developed a general model of vulnerability that may be more useful for big data. Rather than focus on small or rare (but high-risk) subpopulations, the general model encourages us to measure common social risk factors as they cumulatively affect a person or population (Shi and Stevens, 2005).

Figure 6.1 shows a schematic of this general model. Note that it specifically asks us to examine the combined contributions of both community and individual social risk factors to *vulnerability*. This combined effect can be handled in many ways, but the goal of the model is that it reflects some type of summation of independent risks. This level of risk, in turn, contributes to poor health outcomes at the individual and population levels. Access to medical care and the quality of care, of course, play intermediary roles in many ways, but this model importantly argues for a greater

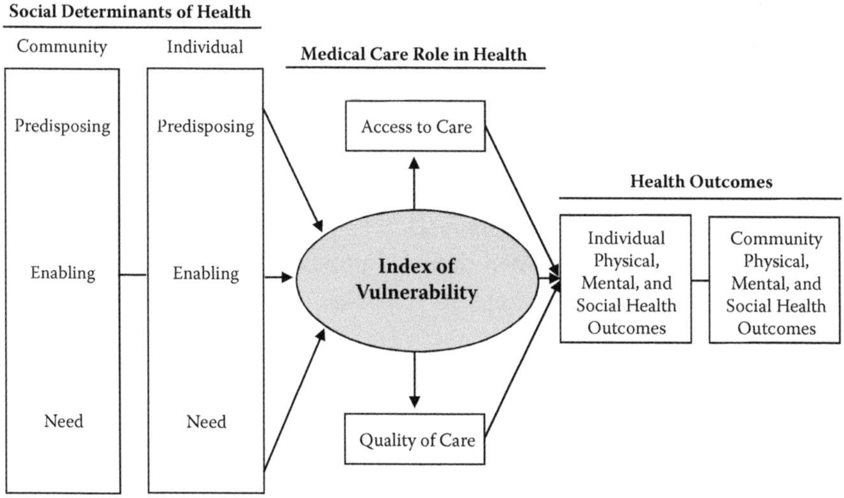

FIGURE 6.1

A general model of vulnerability applied to social determinants. *Source*: Shi and Stevens, 2005.

role of public health and medical professionals in measuring and addressing social risk factors.

The model organizes social risk factors according to *predisposing, enabling,* and *need* categories that were developed by Andersen (1995). The risk factors that fall into each category occur at both individual and community levels. *Predisposing* risk factors are those that predispose an individual to poor health including individual factors such as age, gender, race/ethnicity, and culture and community factors such as rural or urban geographic setting, the physical environment, and even the social or cultural norms of a community. *Enabling* risk factors are those that socially or even materially enhance the ability of individuals to improve their health including individual factors such as income, education, and health insurance and community factors such as the availability of well-paying jobs, excellent schools, and availability of health services. *Need* risk factors are existing health problems that may contribute to overall poor health or the ability to address other health issues including individual factors such as personal mental health issues, disabilities, and disease rates and community factors such as rates of transmissible diseases in the community, the availability of tobacco products, and even the presence of liquor stores that contribute to population rates of alcohol abuse.

The general model of vulnerability has three distinctive characteristics. First, it is a comprehensive model including both individual and community attributes of social risk. One's vulnerability is determined not only by one's individual characteristics but also by the community in which one lives. Inclusion of community factors specifically accounts for the social determinants of health, and their reduction requires societal efforts.

Second, this general model focuses on attributes of vulnerability for the general population rather than subpopulations. While the model recognizes individual variations in exposure to risks, many social risk factors are common across vulnerable groups (e.g., lack of education, low income). Their commonality lends themselves to big data, and the general model calls for an integrated approach to data collection and reporting that focuses on the most critical and common risk factors.

Third, the general model emphasizes the convergence of social risks. There is strong data showing how social risks compound and lead to poor health. Understanding gradient relationships between vulnerability status and outcomes of interest improves our understanding of how and where to intervene. For the biggest impact, the general model could be used to identify groups with the highest social risk and, at a minimum, prioritize limited resources in their direction.

Implications for Medical Professionals

For medical providers, the use of a general model of vulnerability to focus on the social determinants of health means asking about and understanding the context of their patients' lives and learning about strategies to regularly screen for and address the social risk factors as they contribute to patient well-being. For some medical providers, this is an easy extension of their regular health assessments of vulnerable patients, while for others addressing social risk factors may be an uncomfortable new facet of care.

To understand how the general model can be applied in clinical practice, it helps to walk through a specific clinical example. We can use the well-known disparity that African American adult men experience a disproportionately high rate of hypertension, a major factor in cardiovascular disease. In 2010, 42% of African American men over age 20 years reported having hypertension compared with 31% of whites and 25% of Latinos (Statistics NCHS, 2012).

Predisposing risks include a slight genetic predisposition for hypertension among African Americans (Brandon et al. 2003). Community predisposing risks include being more likely to live in inner-city areas with fewer parks and recreation areas for regular exercise and fewer and less accessible grocery stores with greater nutritional resources (Diez Roux et al., 2001; Schulz and Northridge, 2004; Schulz et al., 2002). African Americans are more likely than other groups to be employed in lower-wage and blue-collar jobs that contribute to higher stress levels (Bosma et al., 1997; Marmot et al., 1997) and perceive higher levels of discrimination, which is thought to be a form of chronic stress and has been associated with hypertension (Cozier et al., 2006; Davis et al., 2005; Din-Dziethan et al., 2004).

Enabling risk factors for hypertension include the individual lack of income that affords individuals the ability to buy hypertension-protective goods and services such as healthy foods, organized recreational activities, and leisure time away from work. Lack of health insurance limits regular access to health care services that may prevent or treat hypertension (Lurie et al., 1984, 1986). At the community level, low-income areas offer

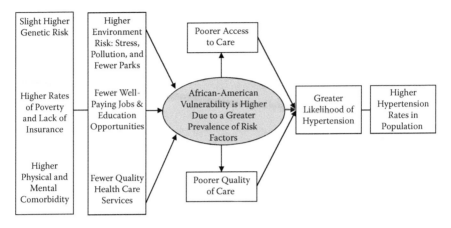

FIGURE 6.2
General model applied to hypertension among African Americans. *Source*: Shi, Stevens, Faed, and Tsai, 2008.

few well-paying jobs with health insurance, and medical providers are less likely to practice in these areas (Smedley, Stith, and Nelson, 2002). African Americans are more likely to experience these risk factors (DeNavas-Walt et al., 2005).

Taken together, these predisposing and enabling risk factors combine to affect the likelihood that African Americans will have hypertension (Figure 6.2). According to the model, hypertension rates are higher among African Americans because they (1) have a predisposition for hypertension, (2) live where stressors are higher and opportunities for health promotion are fewer, and (3) are less likely to have access to health care services to prevent and treat hypertension. The general model focuses on the complement of risk factors that, together, contribute to the presence of this problem.

Implications for Public Health and Policy

Understanding the contributors to health in this way suggests that single-pronged interventions will be less effective than those that target multiple risks. For public health professionals, this means designing new data collection strategies to monitor these critical risk factors and implementing programs that cross sectors (e.g., health promotion that focuses on educating individuals about hypertension prevention and educating private and public sector officials about urban design in low-income communities).

For policy makers who can unite public health and medical care systems, this model suggests that existing categorical approaches to funding assistance for vulnerable populations may be narrow, inefficient, and uncoordinated. Instead of funding programs for separate conditions and subpopulations, it may be more efficient to fund programs that target a range of risk factors that are common across priority health disparities.

Much of this is common sense. The general model offered here is just one tool that professionals in public health, medicine, and policy can use to better understand and address social determinants of health. Most importantly, some outstanding examples in the fields of public health and medicine provide guidance for us in how to address the social determinants of health and particularly how big data can assist.

PUBLIC HEALTH, MEDICAL PRACTICE, AND SOCIAL DETERMINANTS

There are three excellent examples of how social determinants data can be better integrated into public health practice. These examples originate both inside and outside the government infrastructure, and two were created by organizations that have a long history of serving vulnerable populations. The key element to notice about these programs is how they use social risk factors to supplement traditional health indicators and how these data were used in a way to prioritize or adapt services.

California Endowment's Building Healthy Communities Initiative

The California Endowment is the state's largest health care foundation, with nearly $4 billion in assets. Since its inception in 1996, the organization has awarded more than 9,000 grants to community-based organizations throughout the state with a goal of improving the health of minority and underserved populations. After detailed consideration and critique of its piecemeal funding strategy, the organization created a new initiative called Building Healthy Communities that was designed to better target and coordinate the scope of their funding.

The 10-year initiative invests broadly in social determinants of health to address what they refer to as their four big results: (1) providing a health home for all children; (2) reversing the childhood obesity epidemic;

(3) increasing school attendance; and (4) reducing youth violence. The focus on youth reflects the interest of the organization in promoting long-term changes. It expects each community to improve the availability of basic health care services but also the availability of healthy foods, public safety, access to parks and recreation for families, air quality, and transportation issues, among others.

Specifically, the California Endowment decided to prioritize their investments by selecting 14 of the most underserved communities in California. The communities were picked in great part by analyzing big data on the accumulation of social risk factors for poor health. These measures included poverty, unemployment and uninsured rates, measures of diversity, school absenteeism and crime rates, and other community-level risk factors. This approach of targeting specific communities using data closely reflects the general model of vulnerability by acknowledging that cross-cutting social risk factors build on one another to impact health and well-being of individuals and the community.

While the Building Healthy Communities initiative has many intermediary goals, including those around advocacy development, the initiative is highly data driven. The California Endowment has coordinated efforts with the state's largest state-representative longitudinal health survey—the California Health Interview Survey, led by the University of California, Los Angeles—to conduct an oversample of households in the 14 communities. Data on more than 7,000 randomly selected individuals from these communities are now reported in semiregular Health Profile releases and can be used to observe change over time. An excerpt from one of these profiles, specifically the South Los Angeles site, is shown in Figure 6.3.

Health Leads

Founded in Boston in 1996, Health Leads is perhaps the most profound example of how clinical practices can synthesize public health and clinical practice principles to incorporate social determinants into their routine screening and practice. Founded by a college student, the program is now a nonprofit organization that aims to break the link between poverty and poor health by recruiting college undergraduates to volunteer in community clinics to connect patients with local social resources. Their vision is that many families seek medical care while facing critical challenges in their lives, such as not having food, not having a job, and struggling to keep up with bills for gas, electricity, and rent. Clearly these challenges affect patient health, so Health Leads created a mechanism for medical professionals to address these nonclinical challenges.

Funding was originally provided by philanthropic foundations, including a $2 million grant from the Robert Wood Johnson Foundation in 2009, and from university and hospital partners. Students are asked to commit to at least six hours per week over a one-year period and help to staff family help desks

---

BUILDING HEALTHY COMMUNITIES

South Los Angeles

Health Profile

Understanding the health of your community can start with understanding the numbers. How many children have access to a safe park? How many adults have health insurance? To answer these questions, hundreds of residents in South Los Angeles participated in the California Health Interview Survey (CHIS). The survey was conducted to support *Building Healthy Communities* (*BHC*), a 10-year plan of The California Endowment (TCE) to help 14 communities develop into places where children are healthy, safe, and ready to learn.

This Health Profile describes the health of adults, teens, and children living in South Los Angeles, one of the 14 *BHC* sites. It provides a snapshot of key survey findings prior to implementing the *BHC* plan and can be used to mobilize friends and neighbors, advocate for community change, secure greater resources, and guide community planning. To learn more about *BHC*, visit: *www.calendow.org/healthycommunities/*

Selected Highlights

- 39% of adults in South Los Angeles are obese compared to 21% in both Los Angeles County and California

- Parents in South Los Angeles are less likely to report that their neighbors get along, can be trusted, are willing to help each other, or look out for their children compared to parents in Los Angeles County and California.

- Adults in South Los Angeles are less likely than adults in Los Angeles County to eat fast food 3 or more times in the last week (16% v. 26%, respectively).

- 61% of children (age 1-17) in South Los Angeles feel safe in a nearby park or playground during the day compared 87% of children in Los Angeles County and 90% in California overall.

Published November 2011

Demographics*	South Los Angeles %	Los Angeles County %
Latino	77	51
White	—	24
African American	22	8
Asian	—	15
Others**	1	2
Unemployed	29	13
Low-income households[1]	74	44
Limited English proficiency[2]	76	67

* Among adults with children under age 18 and adults age 18-40.
** Others include American Indian/Alaska Native, Native Hawaiian/Pacific Islander and two or more races.

UCLA Center for Health Policy Research | 10960 Wilshire Blvd. | Suite 1550 | Los Angeles, CA 90024 | t: 310.794.0909 | f: 310.794.2686 | healthpolicy@ucla.edu

www.healthpolicy.ucla.edu

FIGURE 6.3

California Health Interview Survey. CHIS 2009, Building Healthy Communities Health Profile: South Los Angeles. Los Angeles, CA: VCLA Center for Health Policy Research, May 2013. *(Continued)*

ADULTS *Adults with children under age 18 and adults age 18–40 unless otherwise noted*	South Los Angeles % (95% CI)	Los Angeles County %	California %
Current Insurance Coverage			
Uninsured	34 (20-48)	26	22
Insured by government program	41 (25-56)	18*	17*
Insured by private coverage/employer	26 (12-40)	56*	61*
Health Care Access and Utilization			
No doctor visit in the last year	26 (13-39)	23	24
Visited emergency department in the last year	18 (5-30)	17	18
Delayed getting prescription drugs or medical care in the last year	10 (4-16)	20*	22*
Current Health Conditions			
Obese[3]	39 (24-54)	21*	21*
Overweight[3]	28 (15-41)	30	32
Diagnosed with asthma	5 (2-7)	11*	14*
Fair/poor health	34 (19-49)	18*	16*
Serious psychological distress in the last year[4]	6 (2-11)	8	7
Binge drinking in the last year[5]	31 (17-46)	33	39
Physical Activity and Nutrition			
Regular physical activity in the last week[6]	24 (9-38)	22	24
Ate fruits and/or vegetables 3 or more times per day in the last week[7]	14 (8-20)	23*	24*
Ate fast food 3 or more times in the last week	16 (8-24)	26*	24
Drank soda 3 or more times in the last week	24 (12-37)	24	25
Neighborhood Perceptions and Civic Engagement			
Living at current residence for 5 or more years	70 (55-84)	57	50*
Neighbors get along ^	68 (51-86)	83*	85*
Neighbors can be trusted ^	43 (23-63)	80*	81*
Neighbors are willing to help each other ^	47 (27-67)	78*	80*
Neighbors look out for children ^	62 (44-81)	81*	83*
Participated in community service/volunteer work in the last year ^	26 (10-43)	39	44
Safety and Violence			
Feel safe in the neighborhood	54 (39-69)	84*	88*
Ever experienced violence from an intimate partner	4 (2-6)	11*	13*

* Denotes statistically significant difference from *BHC* site estimate. See Methods for more details.
^ Only includes parents of children under age 18.
Note: Estimates for Current Insurance Coverage may not add up to 100% due to rounding.

FIGURE 6.3 (Continued)
California Health Interview Survey. CHIS 2009, Building Healthy Communities Health Profile: South Los Angeles. Los Angeles, CA: VCLA Center for Health Policy Research, May 2013.

in pediatric and prenatal care clinics, newborn nurseries, pediatric emergency rooms, health department clinics, and local community clinics. Physicians and their staff working at these locations now regularly screen patients with regard to social determinants (e.g., Do you have heat in your home this winter?) and then prescribe food and housing assistance, public health insurance, job training, travel assistance, child care, and other social support services. Importantly, these data (often collected in previsit surveys) are recorded and become part of the medical record and can be tracked over time.

The college student volunteers (advocates) are trained to work with families to obtain these resources and services and then coordinate efforts with physicians, social workers, and even lawyers to meet the needs of patients. The advocates follow-up with patients regularly by phone and email and during clinic visits. Because the advocates are an important part of the clinical team, they provide updates on a patient's progress in securing basic resources to doctors, nurses, social workers, and other health care providers.

This approach is arguably easier to enact in larger team-based clinics that have access to a broad volunteer population because the contributions of the advocates are not as limited by time and reimbursement constraints, as are physicians. The prescription process and warm hand-off to the help desk provide a formal infrastructure for assisting families with the social determinants of health.

Health Leads now operate in six cities with 16 unique help desks staffed by 800 volunteers who serve about 9,000 families annually. During a six-month period in 2009, for example, a single help desk at Boston Medical Center assisted 205 families with securing low-income housing; 154 families with obtaining spaces in low-cost child care, after school, and Head Start programs; 135 families with accessing food stamps and other food assistance programs; and many other varied services (Garg, Jack, and Zuckerman, 2013; Garg et al., 2012). Many doctors can certainly implement a version of this in their own practices, but Health Leads should consider making templates and training materials available to facilitate adoption.

Project 50

One limitation to the Health Leads model is that there is currently no difference in the level of effort given to assisting lower-risk and higher-risk patients. If all patients can receive assistance, this is not a problem. But in situations where resources are limited it can be useful to use data to prioritize higher-risk patients in some way. Variations on the general model of vulnerability have been regularly used for triaging clinical services, but they can also be used to target additional services or support.

One widely noted example of this strategy was implemented in a handful of cities beginning in 2007 to identify the most at-risk homeless individuals living on the streets. Project 50, as it was most commonly known, used a vulnerability index to identify the 50 homeless individuals in each city at greatest risk of death based on eight indicators. The index, administered in the form of a survey, was created by Boston's Health Care for the Homeless organization, based on data showing that individuals with the following were at a 40% higher risk of premature death: (1) more than three hospitalizations or emergency department visits in the past year; (2) more than three emergency department visits in the past month; (3) age 60 or older; (4) cirrhosis of the liver; (5) end-stage renal disease; (6) a history of frostbite or hypothermia; (7) HIV or AIDS; and (8) co-occurring psychiatric, substance abuse, and chronic medical conditions. Homeless individuals were prioritized based on the number of clinical risk factors they had, in combination with how long the person had been homeless (a social risk).

This vulnerability index was used in New York, Los Angeles, and New Orleans. For three consecutive days between 3:00 am and 6:00 am, volunteers in each city walked the streets where homeless individuals were residing to gather information, taking digital photos (with permission) to be able to follow up with each person after the vulnerability profile was calculated. While the services for the prioritized individuals varied in each city, most included a multipronged intervention strategy, such as linking them with supportive housing, substance abuse treatment, extensive case management, and medical services. In Los Angeles' Skid Row, the selected individuals were given housing in the Housing Trust, which included a satellite medical clinic in the first floor of the building. The clinic housed a team of clinicians, case managers, and social workers who are part of a local community health center but dedicated to these highest-risk individuals.

The results of Project 50 have been impressive. In New York, homelessness was reduced by 87% in the 20 square blocks surrounding Times Square and by 43% in the surrounding 230 blocks. Housing costs $36 per person per night to operate compared with $54 for a city shelter bed, $74 for a state prison cell, $164 for a city jail cell, $467 for a psychiatric bed, and $1,185 for a hospital bed (Common Ground, 2010). In Los Angeles, 49 individuals moved into the Housing Trust, and by 2009 43 remained in housing. In the year prior to participation, participants had a collective 754 days in jail, 205 inpatient hospital days, and 133 emergency department visits. After intervention, these individuals had 142 days in jail, 55 inpatient hospital days, and 39 emergency department visits. Of the 36 individuals with a history of substance abuse, 22 had become sober by 2009 (Lopez, 2009).

A Strategy for Assessing Social Determinants of Health

With innovative programs demonstrating that the collection of social determinants data is feasible and helpful for public health and medical practice, one might wonder if any consensus had been reached on the most important social determinants indicators to measure and address. Particularly given the limited time and resources, a big question is where could professionals get the most value for their efforts? Since social determinants are now a core part of the activities of local, national, and international organizations, we can look to these organizations for guidance.

The World Health Organization (WHO) Commission on Social Determinants of Health has taken, perhaps, the greatest leadership role in guiding the collection and use of major data on social determinants of health. The commission released its first report in 2008 with specific instructions for member nations about data elements to collect and report, along with numerous, concrete steps to take to remedy disparities in health (CSDH, 2008). These also correspond very closely with recommended data collection and reporting from the U.S. Centers for Disease Control and Prevention, and Healthy People 2020 (Secretary's Advisory Committee on National Health Promotion and Disease Prevention Objectives for 2020, 2010).

The commission recommendations are for a strategy of monitoring inequalities in health referred to as *healthy equity surveillance.* It argues that data on important social determinants of health should be collected and analyzed together with a range of global health measures (self-assessed physical and mental health) and morbidity measures that are more disease specific. Importantly, the commission argues that surveillance should provide data on a range of social determinants of health along a causal pathway, ranging from daily living conditions to more macrolevel political and economic factors that can contribute to health inequities.

The commission recommends a specific set of social determinants measures and demographic categories that should be monitored for health inequalities. The measures come with a very strong evidence base regarding their importance to health, although the commission leaves the exact measurement techniques and methods to the WHO member nations. Figure 6.4 shows the minimum topics that are recommended for surveillance. This means that data collection should occur over time to assess changes in these factors and observe how they translate into improvements or declines in inequalities in health.

The remaining challenge is to develop opportunities for the regular measurement of social determinants and then to apply that knowledge in practice. In public health, there are many opportunities to interact and collaborate with communities, so data collection is often a regular or routine part of public health interventions and practices. Public health practitioners might look to this set of recommended topics from the WHO as a starting point for

Daily Living Conditions	Structural Drivers of Health Inequity

1. Health behaviors
  • smoking
  • alcohol
  • physical activity
  • diet and nutrition
2. Physical and Social Environment
  • water and sanitation
  • housing conditions
  • transportation and urban design
  • air quality
  • social capital
3. Working Conditions
  • material working hazards
  • stress
4. Health Care
  • coverage
  • health care system infrastructure
5. Social Protection
  • coverage
  • generosity
	1. Gender
	  • norms and values
	  • economic participation
	  • sexual and reproductive health
	2. Social Inequities
	  • social exclusion
	  • income and wealth distribution
	  • education
	3. Sociopolitical Context
	  • civil rights
	  • employment conditions
	  • governance and public spending
	  • macroeconomic conditions

FIGURE 6.4
Drivers of Risk.

ongoing data collection. With a standard set of measures, there is opportunity for comparing the relative effectiveness of varying interventions.

For medical practitioners, the challenge is a little different. Even though there is a defined patient population from which to collect patient data and engage in surveillance, it may be difficult to successfully integrate social determinants into their practices. In addition to referring to the clinical examples I described in this chapter, physicians may find it useful to look to pediatric practices where surveillance regarding social factors has been promoted for a decade or more. The Commonwealth Fund, in fact, offers an online step-by-step training for incorporating social determinants into pediatric practice, and this can certainly be relevant to other medical practices (Commonwealth Fund, 2013).

CONCLUSION

With health disparities and vulnerable populations remaining at the top of the public health and medical agendas, there is increasing attention to the social determinants of health. Especially for chronic conditions such as diabetes and hypertension, the role of behavior and influence of the physical and social environments can have a tremendous impact on the success of an individual patient and on the well-being of society at large. With the opportunities that big data presents to conduct surveillance of these social factors at the individual (or clinical) and population (or public health) level, and with knowledge and strategies for intervening, we may be ready to make substantial improvement to how we assist vulnerable populations.

REFERENCES

Andersen, R.M. 1995. Revisiting the Behavioral Model and Access to Medical Care: Does It Matter? *Journal of Health Soc Behavior* 36(1): 1–10.

Banks, J., M. Marmot, Z. Oldfield, and J.P. Smith. 2006. Disease and Disadvantage in the United States and in England. *Journal of the American Medical Association* 295(17): 2037–2045.

Bosma, H., M.G. Marmot, H. Hemingway, A.C. Nicholson, E. Brunner, and S.A. Stansfeld. 1997. Low Job Control and Risk of Coronary Heart Disease in Whitehall II (Prospective Cohort) Study. *BMJ* 314(7080): 558–565.

Brandon, D.T., K.E. Whitfield, J.J. Sollers III, S.A. Wiggins, S.G. West, G.P. Volger, G.E. McClearn, and J.F. Thayer. 2003. Genetic and Environmental Influences on Blood Pressure and Pulse Pressure among Adult African Americans. *Ethn Dis.* 13(2): 193–199.

Centers for Disease Control and Prevention (CDC). 2010. *Establishing a Holistic Framework to Reduce Inequities in HIV, Viral Hepatitis, STDs, and Tuberculosis in the United States.* Atlanta, GA: U.S. Department of Health and Human Services, Centers for Disease Control and Prevention.

Central Intelligence Agency (CIA). 2013. *The World Factbook 2013–14.* Washington, DC: CIA.

Commission on Social Determinants of Health (CSDH). 2008. *Closing the Gap in a Generation: Health Equity through Action on the Social Determinants of Health. Final Report of the Commission on Social Determinants of Health.* Geneva: World Health Organization.

Common Ground. 2010. About Us. Available at http://www.commonground.org/?page_id=24

Commonwealth Fund. 2013. A Practical Guide for Healthy Development—2005. Available at http://www.commonwealthfund.org/Resources/2006/Jan/A-Practical-Guide-for-Healthy-Development.aspx

Cooper, L., M. Hill, and N. Powe. 2002. Designing and Evaluating Interventions to Eliminate Racial and Ethnic Disparities in Health Care. *Journal of General Internal Medicine* 17: 477–486.

Cozier, Y., J.R. Palmer, N.J. Horton, L. Fredman, L.A. Wise, and L. Rosenberg. 2006. Racial Discrimination and the Incidence of Hypertension in US Black Women. *Annals of Epidemiology* 16(9): 681–687.

Davis, S.K., Y. Liu, R.C. Quarells, and R. Din-Dzietharn. 2005. Stress-Related Racial Discrimination and Hypertension Likelihood in a Population-Based Sample of African Americans: The Metro Atlanta Heart Disease Study. *Ethnic Diseases* 15(4): 585–593.

DeNavas-Walt, C., B. Proctor, and C. Lee. 2005. *Income, Poverty, and Health Insurance in the United States:* Washington, DC: U.S. Census Bureau.

DeNavas-Walt, C., B. Proctor, and C. Lee. 2009. *Income, Poverty, and Health Insurance Coverage in the United States: 2008.* Washington, DC: U.S. Census Bureau.

DeNavas-Walt, C., B. Proctor, and J. Smith. 2013. *Income, Poverty and Health Insurance in The United States: 2012.* Washington, DC: U.S. Census Bureau.

Diez Roux, A.V., S.S. Merkin, D. Arnett, L. Chambless, M. Massing, F.J. Nieto, P. Sorlie, M. Szkio, H.A. Tyroler, and R.L. Watson. 2001. Neighborhood of Residence and Incidence of Coronary Heart Disease. *New England Journal of Medicine* 345(2): 99–106.

Din-Dzietham, R., W.N. Nembhard, R. Collins, and S.K. Davis. 2004. Perceived Stress Following Race-Based Discrimination at Work Is Associated with Hypertension in African-Americans. The Metro Atlanta Heart Disease Study, 1999–2001. *Social Science & Medicine* 58(3): 449–461.

Garg, A., M. Marino, A.R. Vikani, and B.S. Solomon. 2012. Addressing Families' Unmet Social Needs within Pediatric Primary Care: The Health Leads Model. *Clinical Pediatrics (Phila).* 51(12): 1191–1193.

Garg, A., B. Jack, and B. Zuckerman. 2013. Addressing the Social Determinants of Health within the Patient-Centered Medical Home: Lessons from Pediatrics. *Journal of the American Medical Association* 309(19): 2001–2002.

Lopez, S. 2009. Smart-Spending Skid Row Program Saves Lives. *Los Angeles Times,* February 11.

Lurie, N., N.B. Ward, M.F. Shapiro, and R.H. Brook. 1984. Termination from Medi-Cal—Does It Affect Health? *New England Journal of Medicine* 311(7): 480–484.

Lurie, N., N.B. Ward, M.F. Shapiro, C. Gallego, R. Vaghaiwalla, and R.H. Brook. 1986. Termination of Medi-Cal Benefits. A Follow-Up Study One Year Later. *New England Journal of Medicine* 314(19): 1266–1268.

Marmot, M.G., H. Bosma, H. Hemingway, E. Brunner, and S. Stansfeld. 1997. Contribution of Job Control and Other Risk Factors to Social Variations in Coronary Heart Disease Incidence. *Lancet* 350(9073): 235–239.

Mechanic, D., and J. Tanner. 2007. Vulnerable People, Groups, and Populations: Societal View. *Health Affairs (Millwood).National Center for Health Statistics. 2006. Health, United States 2005.* Hyattsville, MD: Centers for Disease Control and Prevention.

National Center for Health Statistics, *Health, United States, 2012.* Hyattsville, Maryland: Centers for Disease Contorl; 2013.

Schulz, A., and M.E. Northridge. 2004. Social Determinants of Health: Implications for Environmental Health Promotion. *Health Education Behavior* 31(4): 455–471.

Schulz, A.J., D.R. Williams, B.A. Israel, and L.B. Lempert. 2002. Racial and Spatial Relations as Fundamental Determinants of Health in Detroit. *Milbank Q.* 80(4): 677–707.

Secretary's Advisory Committee on National Health Promotion and Disease Prevention Objectives for 2020. *Healthy People 2020: An Opportunity to Address Societal Determinants of Health in the U.S. 2010.* U.S. Dept. of Health and Human Services. Available at www.healthypeople.gov/2020/about/advisory/reports.aspx

Shi, L., G.D. Stevens, P. Faed, and T. Tsai. 2008. Rethinking Vulnerable Populations in the United States: An Introduction to a General Model of Vulnerability. *Harvard Health Policy Review* 9(1): 43–48.

Smedley, B., A. Stith, and A. Nelson (Eds.). 2002. *Unequal Treatment: Confronting Racial and Ethnic Disparities in Health Care.* Washington, DC: National Academy Press.

Statistics NCFH. 2013. *Health, United States, 2012.* National Center for Health Statistics (US). 26(5): 1220–1230.

UCLA Center for Health Policy Research. 2011. Building Healthy Communities Health Profile: South Los Angeles. Availble at http://healthpolicy.ucla.Edu/chis/bhc/ Documents/ BHC_Fact_Sheet_South.A.pdf Accessed Auguest 7, 2014.

7

An International Perspective: Institutionalizing Quality Improvement through Data Utilization at a Multicountry, Multiclinic Level

Martine Etienne-Mesubi, Peter Memiah, Ruth Atukunda, Constance Shumba, Francesca Odhiambo, Mercy Niyang, Barbara Bastien, Patience Komba, Eva Karorero, Mwansa Mulenga, Lanette Burrows, and Kristen Stafford

CONTENTS

OBJECTIVES

After reading this chapter, the reader shall be able to:

- Explain the use case of quality improvement for HIV care in resource-constrained countries, covering the life cycle from paper- and electronic-based data collection through the calculation of indicators to the interpretation of values at the patient and population levels
- Describe the impact of this process on the implementation of care delivery and outcomes evaluation
- Evaluate the implications for training
- Compare the results of several use cases of continuous quality improvement for HIV care

ABSTRACT

Continuous quality improvement is just as important in developing countries as in the United States. And like the United States, data systems are the foundation for understanding and providing quality services. As part of the AIDS Relief Consortium's efforts to build HIV treatment and care services, we review best practices and lessons learned from working in eight African and two Caribbean nations.

INTRODUCTION

In any setting, the effective delivery of quality Human Immunodeficiency Virus (HIV) care and treatment is a complex undertaking. Infrastructure and knowledge gaps, while major challenges in resource limited settings, do not negate the need for and achievability of quality care and treatment for people living with HIV/Acquired Immunodeficiency Syndrome (AIDS). As such, the backbone component of medical capacity building is assessing care and helping to devise and implement continuous quality improvement programs at the clinic level. Working to assure and improve the quality of medical care provided through continuous quality improvement (CQI) not only is crucial for the growth of global HIV programs but also impacts patients' health and lives. In this chapter we explain the training, technology, and clinic practices needed to institutionalize quality improvement. While HIV medical care is the focus of this chapter, the lessons learned from this effort also can apply to the treatment and prevention of other diseases.

Improving the quality of health care cannot be fully complete without accurate and reliable medical information (AbouZahr and Boerma, 2005; Aiga et al., 2008; Chan et al., 2010; Nash et al., 2009). As many countries report their progress toward achieving the United Nations (UN) Millennium Development Goals, the need for high-quality data has never been greater (Millennium Development Goals, 2011; Rugg et al., 2009). In spite of dwindling funds for public health activities, exceedingly more programs rely on the accuracy of data to determine future funding opportunities. Assuring the quality and usability of health information systems remains a challenge. It is against this backdrop that the President's Emergency Plan for AIDS Relief (PEPFAR) has had a significant impact on expanding the use of data through providing access to HIV care and treatment to millions of people in resource-limited settings. The expansion of data use through data collection and electronic medical records (EMRs) propels resource-limited countries' abilities well beyond what previously could be done.

As HIV treatment decentralizes to more rural health facilities and satellites with infrastructure limitations and as patients remain on antiretroviral (ART) treatment for longer periods of time, it becomes imperative to assess treatment outcomes to ensure that quality health outcomes are not compromised by the overwhelming demand to continue to scale. The University of Maryland's Institute of Human Virology (UMSOM/IHV) has been privileged to work as an implementing partner with PEPFAR as part of the

AIDSRelief Consortium. This consortium is composed of Catholic Relief Services (CRS), which served as the lead partner; Futures, which supported the strategic information of the programs; Catholic Medical Mission Board (CMMB), which supported the prevention of mother-to-child transmission programs and Interchurch Medical Assistance World Wide (IMA); and UMSOM/IHV, which served as the clinical mentorship arm of the consortium and provided continued medical and care delivery support to local partners and implemented continuous quality improvement interventions through the Outcomes and Evaluation (O&E) component. By the time transition of PEPFAR occurred, 276 health facilities and hospitals within eight countries in Africa (Uganda, Kenya, Tanzania, Ethiopia, Rwanda, Zambia, Nigeria, and South Africa) and two countries in the Caribbean (Haiti and Guyana) were supported. The programs were located in rural settings, semiurban settings, and urban locales with over 400,000 patients on ART and more than 800,000 patients who have received care. Our facilities were diverse in their settings, culture, and people. All programs were licensed by their respective governments and were recognized providers of care and support for people living with HIV/AIDS. In 7 of the 10 AIDSRelief countries where viral loads for program evaluation were conducted, median time on treatment was 16 months, and the average viral suppression proportion (which is the gold standard for treatment success) among a 10% random sample of all patients initiated on therapy was 88.2%, a rate comparable to or even better than those seen in industrialized countries. Our success in supporting these countries stemmed from being able to identify a benchmark and develop a general framework on which to build.

THE AIDSRELIEF HIV CARE DELIVERY MODEL

The AIDSRelief Model of Care (Figure 7.1) is built on a foundation of health systems strengthening. An effective health system will depend on the strength of each facility, its network, and its links with the public health sector and the community. With an emphasis on health systems strengthening as the foundation, our medical, strategic information, and site management program components continually worked in conjunction with each other. Additionally, the care delivery model emphasized adherence as a vital therapeutic intervention. Intensive treatment preparation, patient-specific care, and treatment plans with community-based treatment services including

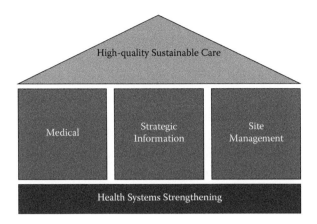

FIGURE 7.1
AIDSRelief Model of Care.

home-based follow-up during the initiation and continuation of antiretroviral treatment were key components to sustained successful outcomes. Many of these activities required specific indicators that could be measured and evaluated to improve continued care within the community. Clinical indicators such as baseline cluster of differentiation 4 (CD4) cell count, CD4 cell count overtime, identification of opportunistic infections, drug toxicities, and side effects served to provide clinicians an important background in making informed decisions for their patients. Social indicators and determinants of health included disclosure, defining catchment areas for treatment as well as training and supporting community members. All of these areas served as a part of the health system, which supported HIV care and delivery within a community and ultimately the entire country. Initially this information was captured through the use of patient management forms. However, a need was identified early on in the program for electronic capture of these large data sets to use the data effectively. The transition to electronic forms allowed for easy access to both patient and facility population data and emphasized data use for clinical management of patients and program management.

OUTCOMES AND EVALUATION

As clinical mentors, the UMSOM/IHV staff and faculty initiated components of the program that would support implementation of a care delivery model and focus on continuity of care through the collection, analysis, and use of data. The O&E component of our technical support helped to accomplish this by first identifying a set of simple indicators that would ultimately lead to the development of patient management forms. We subsequently supported the use of continuous quality improvement activities to ensure a successful continuity of care for patients within an initially burdened health system. The remainder of this chapter will describe the comprehensive work of the O&E component of our technical support and how this has led to increased use of data and ultimately improved patient level outcomes.

Data Collection

State of Data and Information Gathering Prior to PEPFAR

With its introduction, PEPFAR was able to provide access to antiretroviral treatment to health facilities in very rural areas. Although several countries had access to the Global Fund and other donors, there had never been an HIV program measured at the scale of PEPFAR. Prior to PEPFAR many rural health facilities were providing palliative care and helping people living with HIV/AIDS die with dignity. Data were collected in a register format that was more conducive to tracking acute illnesses rather than chronic disease management. Longitudinal patient medical records were nonexistent, and medical records, if they existed, contained only basic registration and demographic information rather than medical information. Continuity of patient care was a challenge for clinicians and medical professionals alike. There was a need to document patient medical information that could be useful to patient outcomes, especially in the wake of increased access to antiretroviral treatment.

Development of Indicators

We were committed to making sure that people living with HIV/AIDS enrolled in our programs have improved clinical outcomes leading to improved quality of life. To measure this we developed and integrated indicators that measured patient and family quality of life, virologic and immunologic response to treatment, adherence levels, and quality of the program into monitoring and evaluation systems. Several countries treating HIV through the Global Fund and through other funding mechanisms had already identified monitoring indicators for their programs. Yet some critical indicators were still missing that we felt should be included in the national set of indicators. A comprehensive team of clinicians, nurses, laboratory technicians, and community-based staff gathered to discuss the addition of indicators that could enable the health facility staff to make informed decisions for their patients and ultimately improve the delivery of care.

Development of Patient Management Tools

Many of the health facilities in which we worked would use thick ledgers to write down patients' names and information (Figure 7.2). The ledgers would change monthly and be stored in shelves and would no longer be useful for data or clinical purposes. The development of longitudinal patient management tools provided health facilities an easier and safer way to document their patients' information without risking a breach in confidentiality or privacy. Most important, the forms were longitudinal and could be used for the same patient every time they returned to the clinic for an appointment. Building off the clinical indicators and PEPFAR reporting requirements, a group of clinicians, monitoring and evaluation staff (Futures), and site managers (CRS) worked together to develop the AIDSRelief longitudinal medical records. These patient management tools were composed of the following forms: Enrollment, Initial Evaluation, Laboratory, Adult Pharmacy, Pediatric Pharmacy, Non-ART (antiretroviral treatment) Follow-Up, ART Follow-Up, Home Visit, Adherence Counseling Check-List, Contact

FIGURE 7.2
Picture of health ledgers.

and Care Tracking, and Patient Profile (summary sheet). A key component to the development of these forms was establishing the minimum data set. It was the critical information necessary to ensure quality patient outcomes and to adequately report to the Ministry of Health, the hospital administrators or hospital board, and the funding agencies.

There was a need for a significant culture shift at facilities to implement these patient management tools. The facilities went from acute monitoring of illnesses to monitoring of chronic disease. We were asking the facilities to collect significantly more data and to track patients throughout the facility. To facilitate this process, AIDSRelief sent multidisciplinary teams to facilitate workflow diagramming, to develop new processes, and to identify human resource gaps. AIDSRelief provided training across the facility on the patient management tools and integrated feedback from facilities to improve the tools on a routine basis. This cultural shift was facilitated by dynamic hospital administrators, clinicians, nurses, and monitoring and evaluation (M&E) staff who wanted to see an improvement in the quality of care and patient outcomes. The focus was placed squarely on reviewing clinical and program indicators, and this was enabled by the collection of quality data. IHV and Futures provided on-site technical assistance and training to collect and analyze data regularly and to improve data quality and analyses. This mechanism successfully supported the continuity of care within all participating health facilities.

Information Collected

The information collected on each patient was based on the minimal data set and contained critical variables for clinical management and program reporting. In resource-constrained settings, facilities are oftentimes understaffed and overflowing with patients waiting to be seen. This leads to challenges in collecting essential information. At AIDSRelief-supported facilities, clinicians would rush to see as many patients as possible in an effort to decrease patient wait time, yet the information needed to provide continuity of care was being jeopardized. On several visits clinicians and nurses did not have time to record every data point, which resulted in missing or incomplete data. Working day to day with the field teams provided our technical teams with valuable insight that would help to refine and adjust the patient management forms for future use.

The field experience allowed us to revise the patient management forms several times until we accurately captured the most crucial indicators on forms that could be easily filled out by the clinician and the nurse as they were observing their patients. The indicators collected were based on clinical and nonclinical criteria for initiating antiretroviral treatment. The clinical criteria included presentation with an AIDS-defining condition, a CD4 cell count below 350 cells/µL (cells per millions per microliter), pregnancy or World Health Organization (WHO) stage III or IV disease (Phair et al., 2002). The nonclinical criteria included evidence of ability to be adherent to antiretroviral treatment (ART), such as regular attendance at the health facility or adherence to cotrimoxazole prophylaxis, and demonstrated understanding of the basics of HIV infection and ART. Our patient management forms ensured a standardized approach to patient care across our partner health facilities.

The initial evaluation included a detailed medical history, physical examination, and baseline laboratory tests that included CD4 cell count, liver function tests, creatinine, and a chest x-ray. Patients were seen in the health facility weekly or fortnightly during the first month of ART and were closely monitored for early toxicities and problems with adherence. Once stable on treatment, all patients visited the health facility bimonthly to pick up their prescriptions. CD4 count testing was routinely done every six months but more frequently when clinically indicated (WHO, 2006).

e-Health Tools and Electronic Medical Records

Supporting 270 facilities and over 800,000 patients meant that the program had a significant amount of data to monitor and analyze. Moreover, within a single facility physical paper records were not conducive to analyzing patient trends and outcomes. Futures developed a series of software applications, called International Quality Solutions (IQSolutions), to address the expanding needs of facilities and the program to effectively use data for decision-making. These applications were built on the AIDSRelief quality improvement model and based on the patient management tools. We know that each country and each hospital have different clinic processes and reporting needs. IQSolutions met those needs and helped the clinics effectively provide and improve patient care through providing a platform for capturing quality data and visualization of the data. Different systems within IQSolutions meet varying capacity levels and needs of HIV care and treatment providers. In addition to the use of IQSolutions, we supported the national electronic systems when they existed. The team provided technical assistance around the implementation and maintenance of national systems at the local facility level.

One core application within IQSolutions is the EMR system, IQCare. This is a robust and comprehensive data capture and reporting system with patient management tools designed to measure patient outcomes. IQCare helps clinics collect clean and ensure accurate patient data and provides flexible reporting leading to enhanced data use and analysis. One of the cornerstones of the PEPFAR and global health initiative (GHI) focus is on mothers and exposed children. IQCare includes a form builder and separate modules for prevention of mother-to-child transmission (PMTCT), maternal and child health (MCH), TB, and so forth. The PMTCT module covers HIV-infected pregnant women prenatal, delivery, and postnatal services as well as exposed infant follow-up. In this module, countries are able to create their own forms based on MoH forms/cards. Similarly, MoH reports are integrated into the system, and countries can develop their own queries through the custom reporting feature. It is critical to ensure that facilities have access to all the data they capture. IQSolutions empowers facilities to use the data they are collecting to inform patient treatment plans and program management.

In conjunction with IQCare and other national EMRs, IQTools is an application used to assure quality data and contains a variety of data cleaning and patient and facility-level reports. IQTools works in conjunction with other systems to improve their data management and functionality. IQTools links to a variety of databases including CTC2 in Tanzania, i. Sante in Haiti, and the Management Sciences for Health (MSH) pharmacy stock-tracking tool.

AIDSRelief completed the development of the Site Capacity Assessment dashboard, a visualization tool to aid all levels of users in decision-making. Global-level users (program headquarters, country managers, health facility managers) can compare aggregated results between countries and within a country. They can identify and address overarching problems. Country managers can compare selected facility segments and regions. They can drill down to view component and facility score trends over time. Health facility managers can query site-level indicators and look at the individual pieces that are required to meet a specific score. They can create action plans for improvement where additional focus is needed. The dashboard aggregates data at the global, country, and facility levels by component and functional areas. Maps, charts, and tables are automatically generated and are color-coded to match the sustainability ranges so that it is easy to analyze the results at different levels of detail.

These e-health applications and others used within AIDSRelief provide the tools necessary to perform analytics on large data sets as well as inform individual client decisions. The tools can send patient reminders to individual patients and evaluate the percentage of those patients receiving an appointment reminder that were retained in care and treatment. It was critical to strengthen the capacity at facilities to implement these systems.

Patient-Level Outcome

At the time of program implementation, routine use of viral load testing for patient management was not recommended in resource limited settings. For many of these countries, this test was much too costly and the resources needed to maintain the viral load machine were too great and at the time seemed unsustainable. However, an integral part of our ART program was ongoing program evaluation and patient-level outcomes (PLO). The PLO involved an annual nonexperimental quality assurance survey of a randomly selected subset of patients receiving care at each site. Deidentified information was collected and analyzed centrally to evaluate program-level measures of quality of care as well as outcomes of care. The information was fed back to the facilities and guided targeted technical assistance to each site for program quality improvement. Information obtained in the survey included baseline demographic and clinical data, antiretroviral regimen information, biannual CD4 test results, opportunistic infections, drug toxicities, and side effects. In addition, the program provided viral load testing and collection of self-reported adherence information for a minimum of 10% of patients accessing ART at each site as part of the program.

The first round of the PLO survey was carried out in Kenya and Uganda between February and March 2006. Eight sites in Kenya and five sites in Uganda were included. All patients who began receiving ART at any of these sites between August 2004 and April 2005 were considered program year one patients and potentially eligible for inclusion in the survey. Of all eligible patients at each site, 10% were randomly sampled to participate in the PLO survey. Active patients were defined as those still receiving ART and in care, whereas inactive patients were defined as having stopped their ART and no longer in care. Demographic and clinical information, free of any individual identifiers, was collected for all survey participants through abstraction from both the electronic database and the patient medical charts using a standardized abstraction tool.

Active survey participants were also administered an adherence questionnaire that obtained self-reported adherence information. Preliminary analysis was done at IHV, and the information was fed back to the sites. This allowed for real-time use of the data, implementing positive changes as a result of patient outcomes for continued program quality improvement.

Sustainability of the PLO Activity

The initial PLO activity was also an opportunity to mentor the sites to be able to carry this out on their own. We worked hand in hand with the site staff from calculating the sample size to collecting patients' medical information as well as specimens for viral load analysis to reporting the findings. Our team ensured that this was an activity that could be carried out in our absence. Several years later with support from the IHV to analyze the samples and the data, the sites continued to perform their PLO activities and began to focus on targeted populations such as pediatrics and pregnant women. (PLO activities were expensive to carry out, and due to budgetary constraints we could not sample all patients on ART. The 10% sampling method helped give us a general picture of the health of our program, and additionally it gave clinicians extra information that could be used to make appropriate clinical decisions for their patients.)

TRAINING OF HEALTH CARE PROVIDERS

As the technical arm of the consortium UMSOM/IHV conducted baseline assessments of knowledge that would help enhance programmatic and clinical support. This provided for useful information that would guide our own technical support and provided a true assessment of the work we were doing. The IHV housed senior infectious disease clinicians who were responsible for individual partner countries within the consortium. The senior technical advisors worked with the Ministries of Health and partner sites within each country to ensure that the clinical needs were met for that country. The advisors led a comprehensive team of clinicians, nurses, laboratory specialists, CQI specialists, and community-based treatment supporters (CBTS) who were responsible for each aspect of the program.

Meeting the Site-Level Needs for Quality Data

A collaborative effort between UMSOM/IHV CQI specialists and Futures strategic information staff were responsible for training the health facility teams on all aspects of data, including data entry, data quality and management of information, facility assessment, and quality assurance. This included quality data collection through the patient management forms, data entry into the EMR, and data use for optimal clinical and program outcomes. A key objective of training and technical assistance was to make data relevant, valid, accessible, and useful to the facility for patient care and effective program management. Ultimately, it was the facility that had to take ownership to drive their individual quality improvement program. Additional objectives were (1) to have data that were clean, comprehensive, and valid; (2) to ensure that the data system maintained patient confidentiality; (3) to facilitate accurate and timely submission of required reports; (4) to ensure that facility M&E teams provided information to the clinical care team and key stakeholders for planning and adaptive management; (5) to provide data that can be used to enhance access to and retention in quality care; and (6) to provide data to enhance efficiency and effectiveness of the program and management at the facility. Training and targeted technical assistance were designed based on the capacity at the facility, the local context, and the priorities of the country program and MoH.

Through the use of EMRs, facilities were empowered to use their data for decision-making and ensure information was entered correctly or missing data was completed. Routine weekly and monthly data cleaning processes were put in place by facilities. In most facilities, we used a mixed model of paper-based and electronic data entry. This allowed facilities to cross-reference the records and conduct data quality audits.

Curriculum Development

The O&E component of the consortium supported the development and implementation of sustainable CQI programs from the national to the health facility level. The CQI programs in many of our partner countries were harmonized with the national program. This encouraged the continued use of data to assess, measure, plan, and improve performance for all health sectors including HIV/AIDS care and treatment at all levels of the health care system. To carry out this task effectively, we needed to develop a useful curriculum that could be sustained overtime and used in multiple settings. The curriculum had to include didactic and, most important, hands-on technical training filled with examples and field-based activities that would be useful to health care professionals. Quality improvement teams were formed in about 250 health facilities. The quality improvement teams were composed of health staff from various disciplines (e.g., medicine, nursing, social support, health records, pharmacy, laboratory). This multidisciplinary approach lends itself to enhanced staff cooperation and satisfaction as well as opportunities to solve problems jointly across disciplines. Meetings were held as needed but no less than quarterly to design quality improvement activities, establish objective criteria for use in monitoring, develop plans for improvement based on findings, assess the effectiveness of these plans after implementation, and refine the plans as needed.

Training of Trainers—Localized and Regionalized Training

All the quality improvement (QI) teams were trained and continuously mentored. The main purpose of the training was to provide a platform for the uses of data. Health care providers were exposed to the concepts of quality improvement and how this could be relevant in their daily work. At the end of the training and through continuous mentorship, the QI teams, within their own context were able to do the following:

1. Describe the overall management approach to quality and what is to be accomplished (goals) over a defined time frame.
2. Develop a plan to elicit patients' expectations and prepare a proactive quality management plan to meet those expectations.
3. Define key terms relating to quality improvement that were well-known across disciplines within the facility and could be used by all disciplines. It was also important to have consistent language throughout the health facility to avoid misconceptions and unclear messages.
4. Describe how the quality initiatives would be managed and monitored. Some health facilities adopted a formal HIV clinic QI team approach to manage and prioritize the quality activities, while others used an existing management committee structure to accomplish the coordination of quality improvement activities.

5. Describe the process for selecting quality improvement projects through understanding the project cycle and selecting team leaders.
6. Describe the quality process and quality tools and techniques to be utilized throughout the health facility. Graphs were used to present outcomes data (Figures 7.3 through 7.10). This format allowed the clinicians in often busy clinics to quickly assess information in areas for improvement.
7. Describe the importance of sustainability and progress and how planned QI activities and processes should be updated for the management and staff on a regular basis keeping them informed on progress and achievements.
8. Describe any quality roles and responsibilities that will exist in the organization (e.g., sponsor, team leader, team member, facilitator) during or after implementation.

A set of performance indicators was introduced to help assess performance and prioritize areas for improvement. QI team meetings and

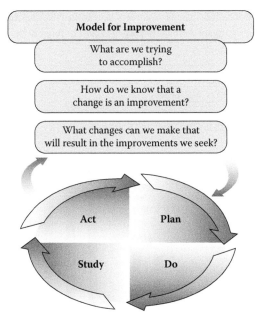

Reference Langley G. Nolan T. Norman C. Provost L (1966).
The improvement Guide: a Practical approach to enhancing
organisational performance, Jossey Bass publishers, San Fransico

FIGURE 7.3
Model for improvement.

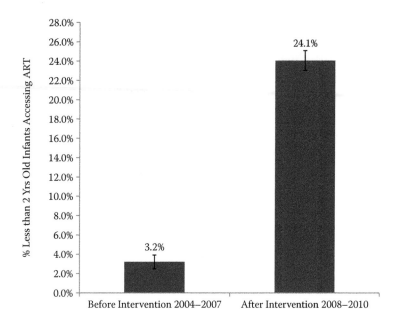

FIGURE 7.4

Proportion of HIV-infected infants < 2 years accessing ART among all HIV-infected children less than 15 years on ART between 2004–2010 in AIDSRelief sites.

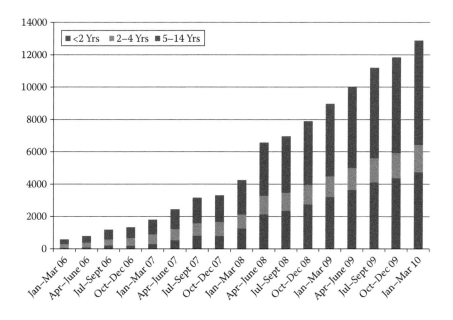

FIGURE 7.5

Total number of children enrolled into care and treatment in AIDSRelief 2006–2010.

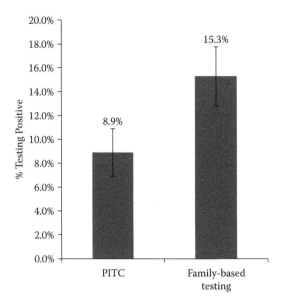

FIGURE 7.6
Use of family-based testing compared with provider initiated testing (PITC) as entry point to care and treatment of children.

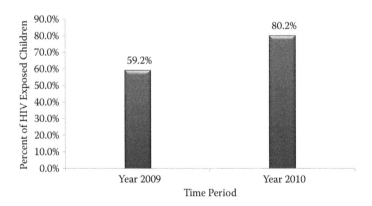

FIGURE 7.7
HIV-exposed infants enrolled for follow-up from 2009–2010 at Bunda DDh RCH.

trainings centered on setting clear targets for what the facility wanted to achieve through the use of quality improvement tools such as root cause analysis to understand system barriers, process mapping to understand patient flow and clinical pathways, and data review and patient chart analysis to identify opportunities for improvement.

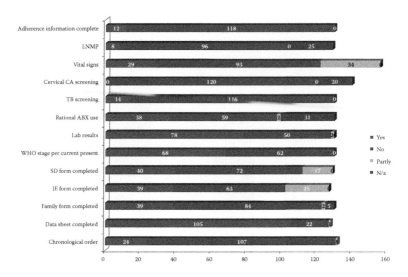

FIGURE 7.8
Medical records completeness.

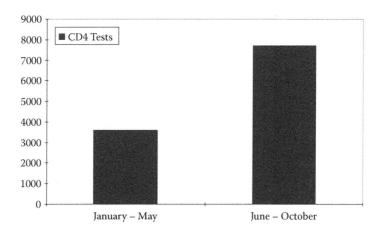

FIGURE 7.9
Increase in the number of CD4 tests.

The Culture of Routine Data Use in Rural Health Facilities

Dynamic strategic information systems were at the core of AIDSRelief's quality improvements and clinical excellence. Careful program monitoring allowed health facilities and AIDSRelief to make day-to-day and long-term decisions to ensure that activities were carried out as designed and altered when necessary. Evaluation enabled AIDSRelief and its local

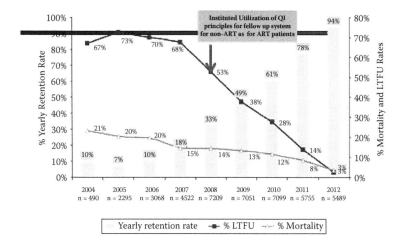

FIGURE 7.10
Care of pre-ART patients in the 29 faith-based facilities supported by AIDSRelief—Kenya
n = 42,647.

partners to understand and demonstrate the results of their work, to determine the best strategies for achieving their goals, and to document lessons learned.

The program cultivated a culture of data demand and information use (DDIU) and CQI that encourages collaboration and improvement across all technical areas with the shared goal of optimal patient outcomes. AIDSRelief supported existing and established new health management information systems as appropriate for each country's context. The IQSolutions software applications, developed by Futures, are flexible and responsive to evolving information needs and have been well received by stakeholders from the facility level to the national level. In 2010, a WHO evaluation rated IQCare (an EMR system) as one of the best health management information system in Kenya.

DATA DEMAND AND USE AND SUSTAINABILITY

Resource-limited settings experience challenges in providing chronic HIV care resulting from system failures. In these settings the critical functions of the health system often are challenged by inefficient standards, lack of evidence-based practice, inadequate data, and information use.

QI measures have been proven to be highly effective in the poorest health systems, but they are not often applied appropriately. QI offers providers a standardized approach for addressing appropriateness of care that can be applied even in the most resource-limited settings. Within the O&E component of the UMSOM/IHV, quality improvement is defined as a process that addresses identified gaps in performance and assists in improving care to produce more consistent outcomes. Improvements are achieved through repeated cycles of testing changes to the system, measuring the impact, and then adapting or expanding the changes based on the results. Ideally for most health facilities, QI efforts help to strengthen critical systems by ensuring that services are delivered according to accepted standards of care and lead to desired outcomes. As QI is data-driven, performance must be measured for quality to be improved.

Creating Data Demand

Health facilities are usually complex adaptive systems. Suggesting changes to improve quality of care can therefore become quite challenging. Fundamentally it required us to gain an understanding of the daily occurrences within the delivery of health services. It was important for our teams to assess which factors affected care delivery and how we could facilitate health care improvement. Solid evidence was needed to support decision-making rather than information based on isolated occurrences, assumptions, emotions, or politics.

The Approach

The teams adopted the plan–do–study–act (PDSA) cycles to test process changes in multiple settings. This model for improvement, developed by Associates in Process Improvement, provided a framework for developing, testing, and implementing change and is a powerful tool for accelerating improvement (Langley, 2009). The model for improvement is used to successfully improve care processes and outcomes by numerous health care organizations (Speroff et al., 2004). The model (Figure 7.3) is composed of three improvement questions:

1. What are we trying to accomplish? A QI team's response to this question helped to clarify which improvements it should target and their desired results. Since system failures varied by clinic, QI teams

generated multiple ideas for change across each step in the clinical care pathway to improve patient outcomes. QI teams adapted ideas from the clinical literature and used HIV performance standards. Findings from the PLO activity as well as the site capacity assessment (SCA) tool were used to identify opportunities for improvement. The SCA is a specialized tool developed by our consortium and is used to assess each health facility's overall capacity to deliver quality HIV care and treatment. The SCA also serves as a tool for routine program monitoring and supporting the long-term sustainability of health facilities. Measures were developed to assess the impact of individual changes and to identify changes associated over time with documented improvement in processes and system performance.

2. How will we know that a change is an improvement? Actual improvement could be proven only through measurement. We asked the health facility partners to describe what they wanted to change within their health system. A measureable outcome that clearly demonstrated movement toward the desired result was considered an improvement.

3. What changes can we make that will result in improvement? Improvement occurs only when a change is implemented, but not all changes result in improvement. One way to identify which change would result in improvement was to test the change before implementing it.

Sustainability Plan

The amount of time for improvement cycles to be completed varied across hospitals. Most facilities also struggled with resistance to change, resource limitations to maintain quality-related investments, and complacency with achieving past improvements. While virtually most of the healthcare providers agreed in theory on the need to reduce errors, there was resistance to some of the actions associated with the QI approaches. For example, nurses viewed the new reporting requirements as an additional burden rather than an integral part of their daily routine. Clinicians had to give up some autonomy and independence when asked to adopt best practices as their behaviors and practices would easily be audited. To address these challenges facilities were encouraged to use a cascade approach in educating staff. The most effective educational strategy happened through small groups. For example, CQI training involved 2–10 people at a time over two days. Also effective, were one-on-one meetings with QI core team

Health facility CQI teams used data from key indicators such as VCT, TB, and PMTCT enrollment, missed ARV pickup, missed CD4 tests, and cohort mortality. Data helped program staff monitor missed appointments, manage clinic schedules, and examine lost-to-follow-up and mortality rates. After identifying a challenge through observation or data analysis, AIDSRelief and facility staff discussed why the challenge might have come about and how it could be addressed. By making and observing incremental modifications to a process or system, teams were able to isolate simple variations to the status quo that made an impact before rolling out an expensive or complicated response that might not work. This paper-based longitudinal system linked to computerized data management system is highly effective and could be utilized in any resource-limited country to support improved patient outcomes.

REFERENCES

AbouZahr, C., and T. Boerma. 2005. Health Information Systems: The Foundations of Public Health. *Bulletin of the World Health Organization* 83: 578–83.

Aiga, H., C. Kuroiwa, I. Takizawa, and R. Yamagata. 2008. The Reality of Health Information Systems: Challenges for Standardization. *Bioscience Trends.* 2: 5–9.

Chan, M., M. Kayatchkine, J. Lob-Levyt, T. Obaid, J. Schweiyer, Sidibe, M., et al. 2010. Meeting the Demand for Results and Accountability: A Call for Action on Health Data from Eight Global Health Agencies. *PLoS Medicine.* 7: e100022.

Langley, G.J. 2009. *The Improvement Guide: A Practical Approach to Enhancing Organizational Performance.* San Francisco: Jossey-Bass.

Millennium Development Goals. 2011. How Can We Track MDG Progress? New York: United Nations Development Programme. Available at http://www.undp.org/mdg/progress.shtml

Nash, D., B. Elul, M. Rabkin, M. Tun, S. Saito, M. Becker. 2009. Strategies for More Effective Monitoring and Evaluation Systems in HIV Programmatic Scale-Up in Resource-Limited Settings: Implications for Health Systems Strengthening. *Journal of Acquired Immune Deficiency Syndrome* 52: S58–62.

Phair, J.P., J.W. Mellors. 2002. Virologic and Immunologic Values Allowing Safe Deferral of Antiretroviral Therapy. *AIDS* 16(18): 2455–2459.

Rugg, D., H. Marais, M. Carael, P. De Laz, and M. Warner-Smith. 2009. Are We on Course for Reporting on the Millennium Development Goals in 2015? *Journal of Acquired Immune Deficency Syndrome* 52: S69–76.

Speroff, T., B.C. James, E.C. Nelson. 2004. Guidelines for Appraisal and Publication of PDSA Quality Improvement. *Quality Management in Health Care* 13: 33–39.

World Health Organization (WHO). 2006. Antiretroviral Therapy for HIV Infection in Adults and Adolescents in Resource-Limited Settings: Towards Universal Access: A Public Health Approach. Available at http://www.who.int/hiv/pub/guidelines/WHO%20Adult%20ART%20Guidelines.pdf

Section II

8

Big Data: Architecture and Its Enablement

Bruce Johnson

CONTENTS

OBJECTIVES

After reading this chapter the reader should be able to:

- Articulate the need for and advantages of an enterprise-wide data architecture encompassing the data life cycle
- Describe the main database designs for big data
- Describe the relationship between data architecture and data governance

ABSTRACT

The concept of big data is just that: a concept for the value an organization can realize from in-depth analysis of all data. The concept of big data is therefore not a database or data architecture but is more the solutions that leverage any and all data, wherever they come from. In health care, the concepts of big data are enabled only in organizations that focus on data—capture, management, and usage. Health care data is extremely broad, deep, and complex, yet the needs for data access are even greater and ever evolving. To meet such needs, effective data architecture must be intertwined with a formal data governance program. This combination unlocks analytics and begins to leverage big data. It is emerging as a critical best practice to all health care analytics efforts.

INTRODUCTION

Big data takes on new meaning when applied to health care. In most industries, the collection, usage, and analysis of data are the foundation of leveraging facts to understand, grow, and improve business performance. Finding ways to thus incorporate unstructured data, images, and geographical uniqueness leads to the concept of *big data*. Health care data is almost unmatched by other industries due to its challenges in collection, breadth, width, and mass amounts of unstructured data. Most industries leverage basic reporting and analytics for operational effectiveness and focus on advanced analytics and data mining to identify future direction, process improvement, and R&D.

In contrast, health care has almost limitless basic reporting and analytics needs that are dependent upon data capture challenges. Data capture is complicated by the various areas of practice, unique data specific to those areas, and individualized characteristics that each patient possesses. While standards for data collection across practice areas abound, there are few if any standards that readily can be applied across health care organizations to serve as a solid foundation for data architecture and design.

In the past decade, significant requirements for quality reporting have led to mass efforts within health care organizations to create, adopt, and internalize tracking, monitoring, and process improvement over all areas of care. This focus has given those organizations that are able to build solid data architectures much better capability to focus on improving patient care, patient outcomes, and patient satisfaction as well as operational effectiveness. Yet many organizations are still in the early stages of mass capture of data. Growth and changes by electronic health record (EHR) software vendors have made this easier in recent years but also have added massive expense to establish this foundation of data capture. Limited funds are left for the production of reporting and analytics, let alone the advanced analytics that drive research and quality improvement (Millard, 2014).

Advanced analytics in health care require the blending of the mass amounts of structured data captured by EHRs with images, textual notes, genomics/proteomics, video/audio, and geographical data. With this wide variety of data types comes an almost limitless opportunity to leverage every advanced analytics technique and mass computer processing to correlate, identify, study, and analyze. This multiplicity becomes evident when considering the mass numbers of resources devoted to medical research and quality improvement around the world. These processes are paramount to disease research and management, drug development and monitoring, individualized medicine, medical devices, and bending the cost curve that has plagued our health care systems.

At the heart of the need to serve big data to the health care world lays data architecture. Effective data architecture must lay out the life cycle of data, from definition to capture, storage, management, integration, distribution, and analysis. The need for coherence across this life cycle requires explicit linkage among data standards, governance, architecture, and analytics. We now focus on understanding each of these concepts in relation to the others.

DATA STANDARDS

As health care practices and specialties exist across organizations, data sharing becomes critical to effective data analysis and research. To share data requires consistencies in data terminologies, ontologies, and data keys—that is, agreement as to what "words" we use, what those words mean, and how they are uniquely defined for proper definition. Think of communication among people who speak different languages: if there are 10 people in a room all speaking a different language and they know only their own language, it is nearly impossible for them to communicate effectively. While sometimes the words may sound the same, different meanings can cause misinterpretation. And when dealing with the health and well-being of our patients, it could spell disaster. While there has been significant migration to data and reporting standards, there is still little in the way of common data definition across vendor- and internally developed systems to ease sharing. Within any organization that has built an effective data architecture, a solid data model and associated standards/definitions exists to provide the foundation for data standards.

Data Governance

Data governance for the data itself establishes data standards and continues to grow them. For how it is used, data governance establishes the rules of the data-use game. Data governance becomes the function that owns the quality of data across the organization. The participating policy makers ensure that standards are in place, that data quality is monitored, and that new/emerging data and data sources are always tied into the rest of the data picture for the business. As many industries have very refined data that is easier to capture and always consistent, data governance is sometimes viewed as an information technology (IT) function. In health care, this would equate to technical people having to define the concepts of medical definitions, views, interpretations, and even disease associations. While data governance relies heavily on technical resources to provide the tools and monitoring to ensure data integrity, it is also a business function operated by those who know the business. Data governance requires balancing data security and privacy concerns against the need for knowledge from the data. As an IT graduate myself, I would not want to be responsible for establishing that mission-based balance.

Data Architecture

The concept of a data architecture in health care is interpreted many different ways across the industry. Up until the early 2000s, very few formal data architectures were in use. Health care IT systems were implemented for practice areas or for specific needs as they were identified, and thus a mass of systems with no integration or standards evolved. For example, within a large hospital system, clinics would have their own EHR that could not exchange information with billing systems, pharmaceutical systems, or other clinical systems within the facility. As health care needs for access to data grew, custom solutions were created for each need furthering the conundrum. As such, there was limited experience with multiple architectures that would identify what works best. Each organization thought up what they figured might work, with little to draw from successful examples, or simply purchased a solution from a vendor that the vendor used in a simpler industry but hadn't tried in health care. The more those solutions became a part of the culture of an organization the harder it became to change to a planned approach.

With the emergence of Meaningful Use requirements and broad adoption of EHRs has come a required focus on creating an overall data architecture that serves all the needs of a health care organization, at the same time that the Affordable Care Act (ACA) is exerting pressure for the organizations to change their business. The requirements and needs for analysis have also changed significantly with the emergence of the Triple Aim—looking for ways to drive down costs and improve population health and the patient experience. Thus, the need for integrated data that gives various views across the spectrum of data has become critical. For one organization to satisfy so many data needs requires a formal data architecture.

Many complex analytics in health care have been kept separate from more basic health care data by resources that want to control their data. However, that balkanization limits access to other data and to building consistent, standardized data. The best example here is how to incorporate research data. Researchers are very protective of their data, and rightfully so. However, their data could be insulated within a larger architectural structure at the same time that they are updated with much more accurate and timely clinical data, with greater ease and efficiency than researchers' current practices. Disease registries for research comprise a common example where basic clinical data is not kept up to date, because of the current practice of manual curation, even though the data exist within the EHR that could provide automated updates. Linking the research database structurally to the EHR would make research systems much more diverse and powerful.

There are three main data architectures, from broader to narrower reach, that can accommodate the needs we have laid out:

- Enterprise architecture: Covers integration of end-to-end data from EHRs and operational data collection systems into enterprise data warehouses (EDWs), whose data are made accessible through topical data marts
- Health care specific analytics topics: Designed to accommodate broad needs across large topics of analytics such as quality, finance, supply chain, operations, and research
- Targeted analytic solutions: Cover specific areas of analytic needs for operations, a specific practice area, quality reporting/analytics, and specific research needs (like disease registries, cohort identification, population analysis, studies, or omics analysis)

We will examine each of these data architectures to further describe the purpose, approach, and design to identify which ones are best for what needs.

Enterprise Architecture

The most significant challenges organizations face in providing appropriate access to all the right areas/individuals in a timely fashion to support organization wide analytics is the data itself. While data in other industries are much more defined and structured, as such they enable technology to tie systems together to leverage data from disparate systems. However, in health care different standards, definitions, and even capture make actually pulling different data fields from various systems virtually impossible. Unimaginable funds have been spent with vendors to try to build the ultimate technology that eliminates the need for data interation/standardization, yet all of the successful solutions have this as a foundation of their architecture. Thus, the enterprise architecture focuses first and foremost on data integration to enable analytics. Highly complex and even private data-like research data can be fully integrated as long as governance puts in proper controls on usage and viewing.

The main focus areas of an enterprise analytics solution are data standardization, data integration, data preparation, and data delivery. Figure 8.1 depicts the connectivity of a formal enterprise analytics environment.

Data standardization requires a formalization of data definitions, valid values, terminologies, and ontologies, resulting in standards for how data are captured or integrated. If data are standardized at the source, it is much easier to integrate and leverage. If not, standardization is incorporated into the data integration process. With the mass of different data from difference sources (like practice-specific systems and research study data), it is unreasonable to expect all source data to be fully standardized; thus, data integration is critical.

Data integration leverages business rules and standards (ideally from a formal data governance or standards area) to build the rules and systems that perform the integration. This information is stored in some database designed for storing or delivering data, most typically an EDW.

Data preparation then takes the integrated data and defines the data tables/structures that are designed for ease of getting data out (i.e., data marts, mining marts, and super marts). These structures are designed and built in very similar fashion to the category of healthcare specific analytics topics. While the goal of data integration

Healthcare Enterprise Data Architecture Phases

Data Capture Systems	Data Standardization	Data Integration	Data Preparation	Data Delivery
Internal • EMR • Practice Specific • Financial • Operational • HR • CTMS **External** • Public sources • Collaboration • Payers • Research • Vendor	• Manage organizational standards • Apply external standards • Apply internal standards • Associate to terminologies and ontologies	• Apply standards • Synthesize to rules • Resolve discrepancies • Create gold standard • Data quality assurance • Source system feedback	• Measure/metric definition • Measure/metric compilation • Data aggregation • Topical database population • Monitoring and performance management	• Standards portal(s) • Dashboards and scorecards • Data mining • Data feeds • Data extracts • Reporting • Research • Ad-hoc Query

FIGURE 8.1

Components of the data life cycle within an enterprise.

is to get the data in, the goal of preparation is to make it easy for application and tools to get it out.

Data delivery is thus aimed at getting data to the hands of users in an easy-to-use, timely fashion, supporting their needs. Leveraging business intelligence (BI) tools, analytics tools, and portals for information delivery is much faster and more effective with a sound enterprise architecture than with standard, siloed sources. Organizations having bad data often tend to find good tools ineffective and draw a negative response to those tools. On the other hand, organizations with sound architectures of integrated data can even make moderate to simple tools look excellent. Many BI vendors are now focusing on that target market for their tools and being very open with customers about the separation of tools and data.

Health Care Specific Analytics Topics

One common solution approach less comprehensive than the enterprise-wide strategy is to target solutions around specific practices or areas of analytics needs. Having a handful of separate data warehouses that can serve these areas enables businesses to prioritize and work on these efforts independently. When not a part of an enterprise approach, each of these solutions builds its own data extracts to integrate and populate data for the purposes desired. For small- to medium-sized organizations, this can be an effective approach and help them keep all of the associated costs under control. For large organizations or those that have many practice areas, it can quickly get out of control to the point where there are hundreds of resources pulling from the same systems but using data and metrics quite differently while incurring repeated costs for the hardware and services to manage them all.

Targeted Analytic Solutions

Targeted solutions are often vendor products for specific needs. While many vendors will say their data warehouse is enterprise in fashion, it should be quickly discernable that it indeed covers only the purpose at hand. These solutions can be quite valuable for that one need but tend to proliferate, and suddenly there are dozens or even hundreds of them. Taking a single solution approach to all analytics would be akin to not implementing an EHR but instead buying or building a data capture system for every health care need. When leveraged by an enterprise data architecture, these solutions can be very effective, but as a standard approach for an organization this approach should be taken only by small, very targeted organizations focusing on one practice area. These solutions can be very cost-effective for what they do, but when one considers the mass amount of analytics needs and the constant emergence of new needs the ability to keep up quickly inundates those that choose solely this approach.

DATABASE DESIGNS

Several aspects to database design need to be understood and compared before determining the exact analytics architecture for an organization. While each can be very effective with the right architecture, they can be equally ineffective in the wrong architecture. Each of these databases needs to be modeled, designed, and implemented somewhat differently based on their inherent uniqueness. The incorporation of complex data types, images/video, and unstructured data also needs to be carefully considered. While all of these data can be fully integrated, they may overwhelm the structure. Leveraging connections and linkages from the various databases to the complex data sources, like imaging picture archiving and communications (PAC) databases, is often best as long as it doesn't impact the source system negatively—looking up one record at a time shouldn't cause that. For targeted mining of said data, it is effective to pull subsets to data-mining solutions for in-depth analysis. For many analytics and certainly population health and research, external data are required as well. Big data is evident in combining clinical and operational data with externally available data on populations, biomarkers, and even aggregate statistics.

Before explaining the individual designs, we will address the *data modeling techniques* that are most effective. Most data warehousing professionals think of data modeling as either dimensional (typically used for data marts or EDWs that leverage common dimensions) or normalized in nature. Normalization is actually defined more as the level of relationship detail that is established in entity-to-entity relationships (historically called entity relationship modeling) and thus is very similar to what occurs in dimensional models as well. Highly normalized models are driven down to a very detailed level of relationships—such as a patient would have one-to-many addresses or even one-to-many email addresses. While this may be true, it is often counterproductive to establish so many email addresses for a patient when you really want to know where to get a hold of them (and thus focus only on their primary address).

Denormalized models tend to have very few relationships, and as such all patient data would fall into a single patient entity (Figure 8.2). The concept of abstraction is generally more associated with denormalization (although it can be seen in fully normalized solutions as well, which often presents enormous challenges and is only really suited to operational systems, not data warehouses). It takes an entity to a generic level—like patients are people and by categorizing them as such all patients would be in the Person entity. While this generic representation makes modeling easier, the characteristics of the various people you need to include in the system are quite different, and thus the meanings of the individual fields in the generic table tend to easily get misconstrued, making IT programming and end-user data analysis much more difficult.

One other key modeling consideration is the concept of views of data. One of the most common mistakes in modeling health care data is to try to model the concept of an *encounter*. It gets so large that every data item that relates to care is bulked into an encounter. It is also complicated by the concept that an inpatient encounter is different from an outpatient encounter.

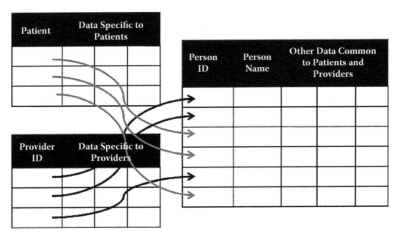

(a) Denormalized and Abstracted

FIGURE 8.2
Differences between normalized, denormalized, and abstraction in database design.

(Continued)

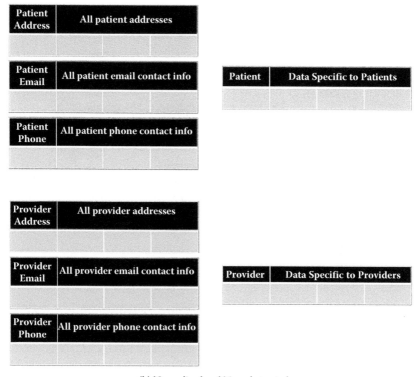

(b) Normalized and Non-abstracted

FIGURE 8.2 (Continued)
Differences between normalized, denormalized, and abstraction in database design.

When modeling, this duality of the encounter concept often leads to disagreements from the subject matter experts who provide the context required to model and ultimately only one viewpoint wins. I have seen organizations spend years trying to model encounter only to give up. However, if we separate the view from the data we can enable all views to be considered for the appropriate need. This separation is a critical component of a successful enterprise data model working effectively with effective data delivery for servicing all needs with the least effort but most accuracy and consistency.

The main database designs for a health care data architecture are EDW, operational data store (ODS), data marts, data mining, and super marts. Depending on the overall architecture, each of these can be used by itself or together (for the most effectiveness). A technical enterprise data architecture outline is included in Figure 8.3 to reference the main data movement required to support enterprise health care analytics.

We now examine the effective designs of each database.

Conceptual Data Architecture

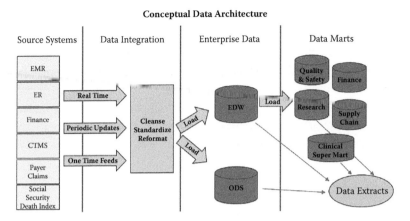

FIGURE 8.3
Main database designs for health care data architecture.

EDW

An EDW is most often thought of as the source of truth. While simply put, the word *enterprise* implies that all data from across the enterprise is contained and in a fashion that enables all enterprise analytics. However, too often databases are called EDWs but contain data for only one or a handful of purposes, discrediting the term and misleading users or executives who are dissatisfied that they cannot get what they need. An EDW is also not a simply a place to drop data—that would be a data dump—requiring IT resources to pull data for each and every need. EDWs are most often designed to be populated from source systems (including external sources) on a regular basis, with specific medical transaction data flowing through daily or weekly. Through the process of data integration with defined data standards, the source of truth aspect emerges. Considering the mass and variety of available health care data that are used for the plethora of purposes, this is where the real-world concept of big data takes its form. Data models for EDWs usually take on a mid-level of normalization, referred to as third normal form (the same for dimensional EDW models). This makes them easier to populate and deliver data for usage. While the most common effective EDW designs are not dimensional, there are some very good dimensional models as EDWs. This requires an organization to have strong data governance and controls over the definition and depth of all dimensions. While many have stated that EDWs evolve over time, data models and databases themselves in fact are not designed to evolve. They must grow in content, but any structural changes (e.g., adding tables or columns) are difficult to put into effect. For example, if you want to redefine how you identify a patient, you will have to design the tables, which would require reloading all data from the original sources (assuming you have all history) and rebuilding all of your analytics. In all likelihood, the numbers you had may change, leading to significant confusion among all users. Thus, having the right design and approach to your EDW and entire data architecture is a key aspect of success in both the long term and the short term.

One key aspect of an EDW is to get data out only through programmatic access. By connecting data marts to the EDW, data can be reloaded into data marts frequently to keep them up to date. Most analytic usage of data warehouses is focused on tabulating historical data, looking for correlations or trends over time. If users were allowed to access EDWs while they are operating (i.e., during patient care), it could result in impacting the analytics users negatively during load processes or from data changing from request to request, resulting in a query ran one minute having one result and later having a different one. This would likely result in a lack of trust in the quality and content of the data.

ODS

An ODS is very similar in context to an EDW, but slightly scaled down. It is designed to serve immediate, sometimes even real-time needs for operational access to data. In the normal operations of business, key information is required that often resides on different platforms to make quick, accurate decisions or even to monitor what is currently happening across the organization. It still has the needs to standardize and integrate data but is focused only on serving operational purposes. And oftentimes data are populated more frequently, perhaps even leveraging real-time feeds, like patient registration, admit-discharge-transmit (ADTs), or orders. Thus, it is usually much smaller than a full-fledged EDW.

The data modeling that is used for an ODS is usually third normal form or is somewhat denormalized to fit the operational analytics requirements. The biggest challenge comes when organizations try to utilize ODS structures to conduct all analytics. Combining some real-time data feeds with complex analytics will result in users looking at analytics one minute and finding one result and the next, getting a different result. Enabling direct access to an ODS is acceptable as data access for operational purposes in an ODS is targeted at watching real-time data as it changes.

Data Marts

Data mart structures are specifically designed to ease use in accessing and getting data out a data repository. Leveraging star schemas for simple data access for dashboards and scorecards, they become very effective. In other industries the concept of departmental data marts is considered a standard, but if this approach is taken in health care it could result in thousands of data marts. If not sourced from an EDW, this would mean they all have different data and results, which is terribly inconsistent for the organization. Thus, star schemas should be designed by topic, like a quality-centric data mart, which can serve needs for quality reporting and quality improvement and enable sharing for external reporting and even send data feeds. This topic-specific strategy also limits the numbers of data marts, making their production and response much more effective for serving various areas across the enterprise.

Data Mining

Snowflake designs can also serve groups of large analytics needs but are more focused on in-depth analysis needs. Having a handful of snowflakes by analysis area—like financial and research—enables in-depth analysis and incorporation of really complex data types. The primary goal of these databases is to enable the many analysis tools used across the organization to have a source to go against or extract from.

Super Marts

A super mart is a very large snowflake or star schema that is specifically designed to satisfy many needs from across the enterprise. Seldom should any organization have more than a handful of super marts, as they are quite complex. This limiting of proliferation keeps the creation and maintenance costs and time frames to a minimum while providing mass amounts of data for analysis.

Analytics

Analytics is all about getting accurate and comprehensive data into the hands of those who need them, when they need them, with security and performance that enables them to focus on the domain challenges (and not on the IT and informatics involved). The wide range of analytics available is described elsewhere in this volume. With the almost unlimited needs for data access and ways to measure and monitor health care data for various purposes, having a defined approach within a technical framework and via an approved toolset becomes a critical efficiency and cost issue. Too often health care data is thought of and delivered only via reports. Reports are focused only on operational review and are somewhat useless for most analysis and monitoring—what is mostly needed across the analytics of health care organizations. Figure 8.4 depicts a few examples of the various areas of need and the methods they might use to get access to analytics. A formal diagram of analytics across health care would be much more complex—so much so that the lines would likely blend into one another from the mass of needs. Which data warehouse tools required depends upon the chosen architecture approach and design. In an EDW design, only some data extracts and feeds would actually access the data warehouse.

Receiving the most value from analytics in a timely fashion starts and ends with access to the right data at the right time. While analysis tools can be extremely effective, they strictly are dependent upon complete and accurate data. There are many analysis and BI tools that all are very effective at delivering data. Yet most BI vendors in particular have had a hard time serving the needs of health care, and health care organizations generally are displeased with them. The real root of this issue lies in organizations hurrying to dump data into the tool and relying on the tool to

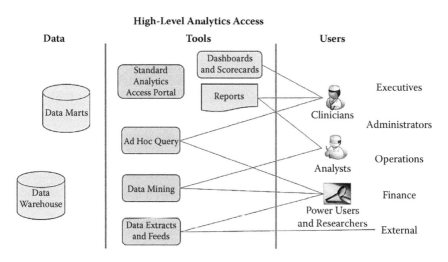

FIGURE 8.4
Relationship among data, tools, and users for analytics.

work its perceived magic while ignoring inconsistencies and inaccuracies inherent in the data. Making each one of the categories of analytics a standard is a critical part of enterprise data architecture.

In general, several categories of analysis tools need to be used across health care:

Portals: This type of access enables the easy distribution of analytics in a consistent fashion. If an organization has a good portal to deliver analytics of all kinds, all users go to one spot to see their data and each user type or usage function can still see a unique view and leverage their tools. Too often each need or area develops its own portal, and like its own data warehouse, it proliferates out of control quickly.

Analytics tools: While a goal to have one standard tool across the enterprise is noble, it is also very limiting and ineffective as different tools specialize in different analytics. With the mass of health care data analysis needs, it is inconceivable to limit all analytics to one tool. That said, it is also a logistics nightmare to try to let every user or need have its own tool, which results in the inability to build template and solutions that can be reused for similar purposes causing an organization excessive expenses for servers, storage, and IT resources.

Extracts and feeds: Health care organizations are inundated with internal and external needs for sharing data. Various frequent examples include external reporting, data sharing internally, data sharing externally (for research and collaboratives), and targeted extracts for complex analysis and research. Most health care organizations build each one of these interfaces separately and too often have to build each one from scratch, including identifying and mapping data back to original source systems. This is extremely time-consuming and costly. It also greatly limits their ability to respond to emerging analytics and reporting standards and guidelines. Having a foundational source of integrated data enables an organization to build a framework for feeds from a known source that streamlines their efforts.

Vendor solutions: There are many vendor solutions that target specific analytics or research areas. Many of these solutions have great pre-build analytics that can be easily incorporated and receive significant value from. The concept of leveraging work already done on these analytics can be a huge timesaver to any health care organization. The challenge is almost always the access to data and making sure it is consistent across the enterprise. An organization with a formal data architecture and integrated data is much more capable of achieving successful implementation and use of these tools, often rather quickly.

Analytics also requires the leveraging of internal and external metrics standards. When dealing with external organizations and governmental regulations, numerous metrics are partly or fully defined. These common needs can enable practice areas to establish standards such as the National Surgical Quality Improvement Program (NSQIP) has done to bring consistency to how data are measured within and across health care organizations (http://site.acsnsqip.org). As many standards are emerging or are yet to develop, there is also significant need for individual organizations to develop internal standards for how they view data. Key definitions are required and include what is a visit, how to report quality of care, operational effectiveness—like patient flows and volumes. Many health care organizations have multiple sites and locations that they need to look at collectively. Without those standards, they are often reporting on events slightly differently, which results in confusion of what is happening and management challenges for leadership.

TIES TO GOVERNANCE

Architecture without governance or standards is a project without a purpose. Governance or standards without an architecture is an exercise in discussion and debate—without any ability to identify if it will work but a lot of pride in thinking it is well constructed. One of the significant challenges in the world of data for health care is to bridge the expertise of medicine with technology. This requires resources on both sides to leverage their areas of expertise and to rely on the other to provide theirs. A well-aligned governance organization coordinates both areas working collaboratively under common guidance. Information technology is often thought of by users of all industries as programming. Yet aligning data, needs, and methods across those groups is what is truly required to build effective systems that impact business.

The complexities of health care make this even more relevant and pertinent. Owning data quality in health care is a business function. As the business works with IT to identify how to do that, IT resources build the systems that enable governance to own data quality. When dealing with enterprise data, this becomes even more crucial and forces a shift to an enterprise focus. Measures and metrics are yet another area that the business must define and own. When dealing with defining populations and creating metrics that can be used to measure the health of those populations, the business again must own this. IT works collaboratively with them to create views and solutions that provide that information in a timely and easy-to-use fashion to those who need it. Data governance is also the avenue for ensuring the privacy and protection of data. Data breaches are commonplace in health care today. With significant needs for data, there must be the appropriate controls to ensure the protection of patient identifiable information. Creating controls requires the definition and implementation of data privacy rules as well as the monitoring and reporting of who has access to what data for what purpose. Research has a special case in the place in the privacy discussion. They have additional rules and guidelines they have to comply with in the process of their research and as such need to make sure they are governing all research activities.

BEST PRACTICES

A nonprofit health care best practices collaborative called the Healthcare Data Warehousing Association (HDWA; http://www.HDWA.org) consists of members from several hundred health care organizations across North America. It is a volunteer organization that serves to enable sharing and thus advancement in analytics. Organizations that can leverage the work of others can respond much more rapidly to meet their needs. With the pressing need for access to data for reporting and analytics every organization faces, HDWA focuses on providing an environment for organizations to share what they are doing and what they have learned and in turn to learn from the work of others. This collaborative has helped many organizations of all sizes define, refine, and deliver solutions within their own organizations more effectively over the last decade.

While it is easy for technical resources to focus on the technical aspects of any analytics need, the business purpose and reason come back to the Triple Aim requirements. In quality improvement, for example, if we don't impact one of the three aims we should question why we are not working on things that will since there are so many areas to target. Through my work with the HDWA, I have seen many approaches, solutions, designs, and implementations intended to tackle analytics and reporting challenges in health care. Many of the bigger organizations have had the resources to learn and focus on this challenge.

I have spent time with four in particular (apologies for not including every organization that has achieved analytics successes!) that to me epitomize the success of leveraging analytics to impact their practice and research. Each of those four would tell you that it is not a destination but a journey. They all still know there is much more to be developed and incorporated into their solutions. But all are well equipped through their efforts to respond to additional and emerging needs. Each of these organizations has a somewhat different data architecture, technical tools, and even organizations of their resources. All four are also renowned for their analytics and quality improvement expertise—(in alphabetical order) Banner Healthcare, Geisinger, Intermountain Healthcare (2014), and Mayo Clinic (Chute et al., 2010). All four of these organizations have enterprise data architectures with the following features in common:

- Strong engaged leadership who understand the critical role of data to the organization and as such provide oversight, resources, and governance
- An organizational commitment to quality, not just in words but action; evident in the care they provide and also in the solutions they deploy for analytics
- A strong relationship and interaction between the technical teams, data governance, and subject matter experts from across the organization
- A formal enterprise data architecture; while the specific designs of each of these organizations may differ, each of these organizations has formal data governance, a fairly mature EDW, and solutions across analytics spectrums
- Many clinical examples of using factual data for quality improvement that is written, published, and shared via medical media or events

- Two-pronged focus on standard reporting/analytics and advanced/emerging analytics
- Effectively providing for the various reporting/analytics and external data feeds while also leveraging those data to support research and clinical operations
- Willing to share and to collaborate with other organizations on their data architecture and analytics learning, which has helped each of them in turn grow their solutions and expertise

CONCLUSION

Significant amounts of money have been spent by health care organizations, academic centers, and technology vendors to address health care's specific analytics needs, but little ground has been made to provide the foundational environment required to enable organizations to shift and adapt as the analytics requirements around them move—with confidence and accuracy and without radical financial output. Big data is no bigger and more complex in any industry than in health care (e.g., images, clinical notes, documents, research studies, genomics). Big data in health care has many variables and almost unlimited analytics needs that can overwhelm any organization.

While it is perceived that health care lags most all other industries in use of technology and data, this perception derives from the data and information being so much more complex, from data not being captured or simply being unstructured or from participants being inundated with analytics requirements, whose volume fails to promote learning. To further the cause of quality improvement and medical research, it is imperative to enable proper access to big data with sound controls. While it is easy for health care organizations to focus on the most complex data (like omics), it is equally critical to understand the complex views and correlations across all data.

As standardization of data and analytics matures across health care, the technology concepts of automated pulling of data from many sources and assembling with a tool for each need may turn into reality, but as of this writing those methods are successful only on a single-solution basis or in industries where data are much more defined, refined, and consistently applied. Database management systems (DBMS) and associated hardware are still very limited in their ability to allow access for simple or mass query while also enabling real-time entry without impacting those doing entry. (We would never allow a query on a production system if it meant providers couldn't enter data while in the room with a patient.) As the most successful organizations have made incorporation of a formal data architecture and associated business led governance the foundation of their approach, they still are constantly in learning and improvement mode. Organizations that strive for excellence will focus on factual data to drive hypothesis, quality improvement activities, research, and operational excellence.

REFERENCES

Codd, E.F. 1971. Further Normalization of the Data Base Relational Model. In Randall J. Rustin (ed.), *Data Base Systems: Courant Computer Science Symposia Series 6*. Upper Saddle River, NJ: Prentice-Hall.

Chute, C.G., S.A. Beck, T.B. Fisk, and D.N. Mohr. 2010. The Enterprise Data Trust at Mayo Clinic: A Semantically Integrated Warehouse of Biomedical Data. *Journal of the American Medical Information Association* 17(2): 131–135.

Intermountain Health Care. 2014. Data & Analytic Resources. Available at http://intermountainhealthcare.org/qualityandresearch/researchmanagement/resources/Pages/dataanalyticresources.aspx.

Millard, M. 2014. New To-Do Lists for Post EHR Era. *Healthcare IT News,* January 30. Available at http://www.healthcareitnews.com/news/new-do-lists-loom-post-ehr-era?page=1.

9

Health Data Governance: Balancing Best Practices for Data Governance and Management with User Needs

Linda Dimitropoulos and Charles (Chuck) Thompson

CONTENTS

OBJECTIVES

After reading this chapter, readers shall be able to:

- Define data governance as it relates to managing health care data in health care organizations
- Describe the types of data and information health care organizations generally require to manage their organizations
- Describe a framework for the design, implementation, and monitoring of a data management process
- Identify operational challenges and the role research plays in overcoming the challenges and expanding our knowledge of best practices
- Explore the impact of data governance on future innovations in health care management, operations, and clinical decision support
- Provide a summary of best practices and critical success factors for a sustainable data governance program

ABSTRACT

Health care data is big and growing. These massive data sets require new tools and methods for extracting the knowledge needed to improve business processes and clinical care. Data governance refers to a comprehensive, organized approach to data management that helps to ensure that high quality information is available to make decisions that affect all aspects of the organization. Many organizations struggle to understand their data, where it resides, and how it can be aggregated and used to inform decision making. Data governance programs have evolved steadily as health care organizations have come to understand the value of data to the organization and as access to advanced software and hardware needed to manage data become available. How an organization organizes and manages their data governance program depends on many factors such as the size and complexity of the organization, management structure, available resources, and culture. Creating, implementing, and managing effective data governance programs presents challenges, both for organization's implementing a new data governance program and for organizations enhancing an existing program. A health data framework is a useful tool that will help to address challenges and ensure an effective program.

INTRODUCTION

Health care organizations (HCOs), regardless of size, require a comprehensive data governance program to manage and extract knowledge from volumes of health information available to them. Data governance refers to a comprehensive, organized approach to data management that aligns an organization's strategic mission and goals, business practices, and data management policies to ensure that high-quality information is available to make decisions that affect all aspects of the organization. Data governance programs are based on proven disciplines and processes to assess, manage, use, maintain, and protect enterprise information. Many organizations struggle to understand their data, where it resides within the organization, and how it can be aggregated and used to inform decision-making. One challenge is that the data may reside in multiple repositories across the organization. A second challenge is that data collected for one purpose are being used for other purposes. The reuse of information often leads to inconsistencies in reporting resulting in a lack of confidence in overall data quality. Data governance, at the enterprise level, includes the development of data models, data quality standards, data security, and life cycle management. Using a common governance framework can address these data integration and communication needs across the health care organization. The data governance framework discussed in this chapter provides a common framework that can be used to build a new, formalized data governance program in those organizations with little to no formal data governance processes or can be tailored to optimize data governance management in organizations with existing programs.

BACKGROUND

The growing volume of digital health information is expected to transform health care; however, the information is being generated faster than people can absorb it. The current capacity to create digital health information exceeds our ability to extract the value from it. According to a report by the Institute for Health Technology Transformation (Cottle et al., 2013), U.S. health care data were estimated to exceed 150 exabytes of storage space in 2011 and are expected to soon reach zettabyte (1,024 exabytes) scale. These massive volumes of big data will require new tools and methods to extract the knowledge necessary to improve business processes and clinical care including diagnosis and treatment, patient safety, and reducing or eliminating unnecessary or ineffective interventions. A recent McKinsey Global Institute (2011) report estimated there are four major information sectors in health care: pharmaceutical research and development, clinical data, payer activity and cost data, and patient behavior and survey data. There is marked variability in the amount of information in each sector that is held in digital form. For example, payment and billing information is generally held in electronic format; however, clinical data lags behind due to the slow uptake of electronic health records (EHRs) prior to the implementation of widespread incentive programs in 2011. Approximately 30% of clinical data, including laboratory and medical surgery reports, are not currently in digital format (McKinsey Global Institute, 2011). However, advances in imaging, video technology, and data streams from connected devices are adding greatly to the size of health data files.

One example is Kaiser Permanente, which is estimated to have between 26.5 petabytes and 44 petabytes of patient data collected using an EHR, including images (Cottle et al., 2013). Health information can be defined as the information created or used by a health care organization such as a provider practice or ambulatory care center, a hospital, or a long-term care facility (Wager, Lee, and Glaser, 2009). Health information includes clinical, administrative, operational, financial and other types of information. Information may be generated within the organization through day-to-day business processes or through the patient encounter. HCOs may also use external data for decision-making. Externally generated information may include data sets used for comparative purposes or benchmarking and as a source of knowledge-based information such as is found in the published literature.

STATUS OF HEALTH DATA GOVERNANCE TODAY

Data governance programs have evolved steadily as health care organizations have come to understand the value of data to the organization and as access to advanced software and hardware needed to manage data become available. This evolution in organizational thinking has moved beyond a focus on data management systems that are transactional (e.g., administrative and billing systems and EHRs) to knowledge management systems that integrate data from multiple disparate systems so that it can be used to conduct analytics. Transactional systems are largely process management systems and are not capable of using the data beyond the transaction. Early efforts to use aggregated data from multiple disparate systems to inform enterprise-level of decision-making often resulted in reports and analyses that conflicted with one another. This is largely because the data were not collected in a standardized way that would enable their reuse for other purposes. The development of data warehouses that serve as a central data management platform to meet the needs of decision-makers across the organization has helped to resolve many of the data quality issues that result in inconsistent reporting. Data warehousing has been commonly used in commercial businesses for decades, but its use is more recent in health care. HCOs may use data warehouses to collect, store, and analyze data from both internal and external sources. Data types vary and include structured and unstructured data. Relevant regulations follow.

A major challenge that HCOs face in the design and management of their data warehouses is the implementation of measures to protect the privacy and security of protected health information and compliance with federal and state regulations and policies (Elliott et al., 2013). Numerous federal and state regulations impact organizational policy with respect to data governance of operational and clinical information. For example, the Gramm-Leach Bliley Act, which protects financial information of consumers, and the Health Insurance Portability and Accountability Act (HIPAA) of 1996 privacy rule, which regulates how protected health information may be used and disclosed. Additional regulations that may need to be considered in a comprehensive governance program (DGI, 2008; Hughes, 2002) are as follows:

Gramm-Leach Bliley Act
Medicare and Medicaid EHR incentive programs (Meaningful Use)
Patient Protection and Affordable Care Act (ACA)
HIPAA privacy and security rules
Confidentiality of Alcohol and Drug Abuse Patient Records (42 CFR, part 2)

Genetic Information Non-discrimination Act (GINA)
Medicare Conditions of Participation
Accreditation standards
Standards of practice

Designing and implementing a data governance program that is practical, meets these regulations, and is useful for all types of health care organizations can be challenging. Regardless of the size and complexity of the organization, the organization must be prepared to manage the large quantity of health care data coming into their organization from multiple sources. One of the most important aspects of managing data is the design and implementation of a data governance program that ensures control and oversight while providing high-quality data to all users whenever and wherever they need it. A comprehensive data governance framework requires balancing the business needs of the organization with the needs of the data users both internal and external to the organization. The following section provides a scalable data governance framework that provides the rigor required to develop a comprehensive data governance program for a health care organization.

A DATA GOVERNANCE FRAMEWORK: THE FOUNDATION FOR MANAGING DATA, PEOPLE, AND CHANGE

A data governance program provides the structure necessary to manage all data related to a health care provider, patients, a practice, or an entire health care organization. How an organization organizes and manages its data governance program depends on many factors such as the following:

1. The size and complexity of the organization
2. The existing management hierarchy
3. The resources (people and budget) available to support and sustain the program
4. The management tools, methods, and processes currently being used to monitor attainment of the organization's performance metrics
5. How compliant staff are with following current policies and procedures for managing data
6. The organization's culture and how people view data stewardship as a part of their everyday jobs

Many other factors may drive the design and implementation of an organization's data governance program. Conducting a comprehensive needs assessment will help to identify existing data sources and data needs that can be used to tailor the program to meet the needs of the organization. Including staff in the design and implementation of a data governance program will provide greater probability of acceptance of the governance policies and procedures established to ensure compliance. Thus a well-designed data governance framework can provide a roadmap for designing and managing the program in a health care organization.

A health data governance framework should have the following characteristics to make it useful for providing the roadmap for governing the design, implementation, and management of health data in an HCO:

- It must be comprehensive to support the organization's mission.
- It must include policies, procedures and methods designed to be consistent with the culture of the organization.
- It must be easily integrated into the existing management and oversight structure.
- It must be scalable from a small provider practice to a large healthcare organization or enterprise.
- It must be rigorous enough to ensure compliance with regulations and to achieve the desired outcomes of the program.
- It must have the support of the organization's management team—managers at all levels must fully understand all facets of the program and be prepared to teach, provide guidance, monitor, and enforce all policies and procedures.
- It must support a dynamic program, including a continuous improvement management approach that evolves and seeks better ways to adapt and manage the governance process changing the policies, procedures, and processes to accommodate best practices, staff recommendations for improvement, and changing requirements.

Figure 9.1 provides a suggested framework for health care organizations to consider when designing, implementing, and managing a data governance program. This framework was adapted from a general data governance framework proposed by the Data Governance Institute (DGI; http://www.datagovernance.com/). The structure of this health data framework uses many of the DGI concepts while integrating the desired characteristics, concepts, and components unique to the data governance requirements in a typical health care organization environment.

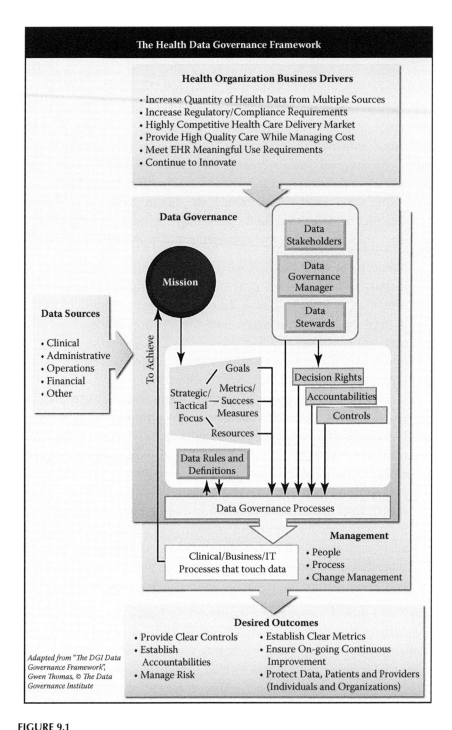

FIGURE 9.1

The Health Data Governance Framework.

HEALTH ORGANIZATION BUSINESS DRIVERS

The business drivers illustrated in the health data governance framework are business drivers commonly seen in today's health care delivery market. As noted, the drivers focus on both external and internal factors that impact health care organizations and their data. External factors include the ever-expanding federal, state, and organizational regulatory and compliance requirements related to quality of care, new federal health care reimbursement policies and regulations, and the implementation of new models of care, such as accountable care organizations (ACOs) and patient-centered medical homes (PCMHs) (Meyers et al., 2010). All of these initiatives rely heavily on high-quality data from multiple sources for analysis, operations, and reporting. As the regulatory and reporting requirements expand, the quantity of data expands, resulting in the need for a more robust data management and governance program.

Internal factors also drive the design and implementation of a data governance framework. The internal mechanisms for ensuring high-quality care impact patients, providers, and the organization as a whole. For example, the ability to have data readily available for clinical or business decision-making is dependent on the formalized data management and governance processes in place to ensure meeting the goals and objectives to meet the organization's mission. Managing and safeguarding the organization's health data effectively can also provide a competitive edge and can be a significant marketing tool for an organization to attract highly qualified health care providers and new patients.

DATA SOURCES

Health care delivery organizations rely on multiple sources of data to efficiently and effectively meet their mission requirements. In most healthcare organizations, clinical data are the predominant data. *Clinical data* include all electronic data associated with the delivery of clinical care, public health and surveillance data, and health care consumer-driven data and information. As noted in the model, all clinical processes supported by health information technology (IT) result in the creation of data that must be managed and governed. *Administrative data* include all of those data associated with an individual practice, provider, or patient. For example, it can include the basic administrative data such as location of the practice, status of accreditation, and number of employees. *Operations data* include all data related to the support of the organization's ability to run the organization on a day-to-day basis. Examples include data from logistics systems used for medical supplies, data from IT performance monitoring, staffing schedules, and medical transcription services. *Financial data* include all data related to the organization and practice management financial systems. Examples include data required for billing and reimbursement systems (e.g., UB-04 and CMS 1500 standard billing forms), systems that collect ICD-9 and 10-CM and CPT codes. and systems such as the patient appointment and scheduling systems and the system that documents encounters (aggregating the number of visits). *Other data* are data generated from sources such as remote and continuous monitoring systems, other medical equipment such as intravenous (IV) pumps, and self-generated health information collected by individuals through personal devices and applications. As technological innovations increase, the quantity of data from these other sources will continue to increase. A data governance process must take all of these alternate data sources into consideration in the creation of their data governance program.

As depicted in Figure 9.1, the data governance process centers on all clinical, business, and IT processes that touch data. Thus, the planning for a data governance program starts at support for the mission of the organization and culminates with the achievement of the desired outcomes for the data governance program. As illustrated, managing the organization, people, and all of the processes that touch data must be integrated into the planning and operations of the organization's data governance program.

MISSION

In the context of a data governance program, the mission includes a focus on both the mission of the organization and the mission of a health governance program. In most health care delivery organizations, the mission is to provide high-quality, safe, and cost-effective health care. High-quality, accurate, and timely data are required for health care providers to achieve their missions. A clear, easily understood organization mission statement can be used as the foundational element for designing the mission statement for a data governance program. The purpose or mission of a data governance program is to support the organizational mission but also to protect all data related to patients, providers, and the organization.

As seen in the framework, the strategic and tactical management focus areas help the organization focus on meeting the mission today while planning and building for the mission of the future. Strategic goals focus on longer-term, futuristic thinking and planning. Tactical goals, on the other hand, focus on shorter-term, day-to-day operations or activities. When establishing both strategic and tactical goals, the organization must consider what metrics will be used to measure success and what data will be required to provide rigor to the measurement process and ensure accurate attainment of the tactical and strategic objectives. For data governance to be practical and useful, the organization has to consider the processes that will be used to govern the quality and security of the data. The organization must measure the effect the management and monitoring mechanisms are having on achieving the goals of the program and the effect of the program on the people and their ability to access the data needed to do their jobs. Monitoring both the effectiveness of the controls needed to govern data use and the impact the controls have on health care providers and patients is important to ensure the data governance program provides the rigor to ensure protection of the data while balancing the needs of all data users. The DGI summarizes the importance of monitoring versus supporting users by stating, "Each time you consider a new set of activities, you'll want to anticipate stakeholders' expectations for monitoring efforts, measuring success, and reporting status. Your ability to deliver industry-standard metrics that satisfy stakeholders can be the difference between program activities that are chronically painful and those that become routine" (Thomas, n.d., p. 12). Balancing the needs of stakeholders requires managing people, processes, and the change management process.

PEOPLE

The DGI's framework identifies three people components that can easily be adapted to the typical health care setting. *Data stakeholders* include all internal and external people who touch data. Regardless of how they fit in the process flow of health care delivery, each stakeholder will have needs and expectations that a data governance program must meet. As the proliferation of EHRs continues to grow under the Health Information Technology for Economic and Clinical Health (HITECH) Act and healthcare organizations start to actualize the benefits of the health information exchange (HIE) in a connected health care system, meeting all of the stakeholder expectations may become more complex. This complexity will require managers to have a clear understanding of the components and processes of the data governance program so they can clearly communicate the goals of the program to internal and external stakeholders. As leaders design their data governance program, they must work in collaboration with all stakeholder groups to ensure that the program is usable, that it balances program controls with user needs and expectations, and that it is sustainable, becoming a routine part of each stakeholder's everyday job.

The *data governance manager* role can be designed to be scalable to meet the varying size and complexity needs of typical health care delivery organizations. In smaller physician practices, the data governance role may be assumed by the office administrator or the person responsible for monitoring the quality assurance and improvement activities of the practice. In larger physician practices, the role may be assumed by a physician champion or totally integrated into the office quality assurance and reporting process. For large complex organizations with multiple internal and external stakeholders and in a highly connected data-sharing environment, a data governance manager will be required. Regardless of the choice of who will manage the governance program, the responsibilities will be the same: (1) design data governance policy, processes, and methods that allow the achievement of the desired outcomes of the program while being compatible with the organization culture and needs of the stakeholders; (2) provide clearly understood metrics and measurement methods for monitoring compliance; (3) monitor and report compliance with the program goals; (4) educate all stakeholders on their role for data governance and be prepared to intervene when user practice is not consistent with the control mechanisms designed to protect data and all users.

Because all levels of staff in a health care organization touch patient data, the role of data steward can be broadened from those in jobs designated as data stewards to include all staff. Health care data consist of highly sensitive data that are protected by federal laws such HIPAA, state privacy and security requirements, and regulatory and accreditation requirements from organizations such as the Joint Commission, formerly the Joint Commission on Accreditation of Healthcare Organizations (JCAHO). The Joint Commission accredits a full continuum of health care settings from ambulatory health care to large critical access hospitals. While all staff are considered data stewards, health organization leaders are ultimately responsible for managing the health data within the scope of their organizational management and oversight. It is the responsibility of the organization's data stewardship requirement to ensure the data governance program meets all federal, state, and accreditation requirements. Data steward responsibilities in this wide continuum of care include ensuring data are managed at all times consistent with existing organizational policies and procedures that reflect compliance with all laws, regulations, and accreditation standards.

Decision rights, accountabilities, controls, and data rules and definitions are inherent in the data governance process and provide the structure, rules, and compliance mechanisms to manage the program. For healthcare data governance and management, the decision rights of who or when decisions are made regarding health data may be directed by laws or statutes, regulations, standards of practice, or scope of practice based on licensure for health care professionals. The decision rights may also be dependent on the technology, the technical requirements for using the technology, the data rules and definitions defined by stakeholders, and the HIE requirements needed to support multiple, disparate stakeholders. All stakeholders should have input to the decision rights rules, policies, and procedures created to govern the use of health care data.

The key is for all stakeholders to have consistent policies and procedures so they understand the controls and all requirements for them to be good data stewards in their day-to-day management of health data. A part of this understanding is for staff to know they will be held accountable for managing health data within the scope of their practice and by following the guidelines, policies, and directives the organization has created to govern the data and their use of the data. Stringent management accountability requirements must be visible and in place among all entities that touch data to ensure that all data stewards understand the data governance program and the implications for them personally if they fail to follow the organization's policies, procedures, and the data governance processes that have been created to protect the data.

MANAGING RISK, CONTINUOUS IMPROVEMENT, AND CHANGE

Managing Risk

Weil (2004) defines risk as the "likelihood that a specific threat will exploit a certain vulnerability, and the resulting impact of that event" (Wager et al., 2009, p. 260). As the quantity of health data and the numbers of stakeholders interacting with those data increase, the vulnerabilities and likelihood of an event occurring also increase. The essence of risk management, as a part of a health data governance program, is to recognize the trade-offs between risk and security, design controls to minimize the likelihood of a data breach, and continual monitoring of the efficacy of the data governance processes and methods to quickly act to prevent a risk event from happening—or if it does happen, to quickly contain the event. Risk management mechanisms have been integrated into the proposed health data framework and include the following:

- Integrating risk surveillance metrics into the organization goal setting
- Identifying risk management roles and responsibilities of all data users
- Ensuring risk management is an integral part of decision rights, accountabilities, and controls
- Establishing appropriate management and control mechanisms to constantly assess the organization for vulnerabilities, rapidly redesigning the data management and the governance program when vulnerabilities are identified
- Educating all data stewards on the risk management policies and procedures and ensuring all staff understand the sanctions or consequences that can result if they fail to follow the established data governance policies, procedures, and processes

Managing Continuous Improvement

An organization's health data governance program must be constantly evaluated to ensure it is accomplishing the goals established for the program and protecting all data and data stakeholders. This constant evaluation requires organization leaders to have a dynamic view of the program and be willing to improve or optimize the tools, methods, and processes to achieve the desired outcomes for the program. Health care organizations are familiar with the quality management and improvement requirements for managing their patients and their care; thus, continuous improvement (CI) for the data governance program should be acceptable to health care providers and data users and stewards as long as the CI process meets the following criteria:

- The data governance program must be practical and easily integrated into the culture of the organization, to include the existing risk/quality management and control mechanisms. Onerous control mechanisms that impede meeting the mission of providing health care delivery or are not consistent with other quality management processes will not be adopted.
- The metrics for measuring success of the program must be agreed upon by all data stewards, and they must have an opportunity to recommend improvements in the metrics and the data collection tools, methods, and processes.
- Leaders must ensure all staff understand the performance metrics and their role in achieving the desired outcomes.
- Leaders must be agile and responsive to risk events and recommendations for improvement and rapidly integrate the recommendations into the data governance processes when recommendations for change are found to be valid and useful.
- Leaders must create a CI culture that continually encourages staff to ask, "How are we doing?" and "Can we do it better?" (Edwards et al., 2008).
- Leaders must constantly listen to all data stewards and respond to staff needs, evaluate progress, and rapidly intervene to fix the program if things aren't going as planned.

Managing Change: An Integral Component of the Data Governance Process

Today's health care delivery environment is clearly stressful for many providers and their staff, and adapting to change has become a way of life in many health care organizations. Depending on the size and complexity of the health care organization and the maturity of the organization in collecting, using, and storing electronic health care data, the concept of a formalized, structured data governance program may be new to the usual management control mechanisms to which the staff currently adhere. Regardless of the complexity or maturity of an organization and the current management mechanisms currently in use, the organization leaders should plan the implementation of their data governance program using sound change management principles.

Change management is a well-developed field with evidence-based strategies and lessons learned that can be readily adapted to planning and implementing a data governance program (Campbell, 2008; Kotter, 1996). The Change Management Learning Center defines change management as "the application of the set of tools, process, skills and principles for managing the people side of change to achieve the required outcomes of a change management project or initiative" (http://www.change-management.com). There are significant similarities when the key concepts in the change management definition are compared with concepts in the health data governance definition. Key operational components such as people management; use of structured tools, processes, and methods; management intervention to achieve the desired outcomes; and the monitoring and control mechanisms to determine attainment of goals are included in both. While a full discussion of the change management theories and strategies are beyond the scope of this chapter, some change management principles are pertinent to the design and implementation of a data governance program. When these principles are applied to implementing the program, there will be a greater probability of acceptance and success of the program.* These principles include the following:

- Having leaders clearly establish the vision for and goals and objectives of the governance program.
- Establishing a data governance design team that includes representatives of all data stewards and stakeholder groups.
- Creating and disseminating an action plan (the product of the design team) to all stakeholders—the plan must be practical, feasible, have realistic time frames, and have clearly communicated, observable, and understandable performance metrics to continuously

---

* For an example of governance and change management in practice please see 2013 Davies Award application for Unity Health Care titled "Menu Case Study: Governance and Change Management" (http://apps.himss.org/davies/pastRecipients_org.asp).

monitor for compliance and to provide opportunities for continuous improvement of the program.

- Defining clear communication strategies. The leaders can work with the design team to establish both what is to be communicated and the communication mechanisms that work best in that organization. Communication strategies should be tailored to both the organization culture (methods and processes) and optimizing the use of lessons learned and feedback from all stakeholders.
- Including all stakeholders and data stewards in the design of the data governance program. It's especially important that they help create the metrics for success and understand their roles and responsibilities in achieving them.
- Continually communicating the data governance control and monitoring processes and enforcing the importance of following established policies and procedures (and the ramifications if they aren't followed).
- Being prepared to train, retrain, and provide technical assistance based on analysis of the performance compared with the metrics for success or issues related to a risk event.

OVERCOMING CHALLENGES AND ACHIEVING DATA GOVERNANCE PROGRAM DESIRED OUTCOMES

Creating, implementing, and managing a robust data governance program can present significant challenges, both in organization's attempting to implement a new data governance program and those organizations wanting to enhance or optimize an existing program. As discussed throughout this chapter, most of the challenges will ultimately be related to the culture of the organization, dealing with people issues such as change, the implementation of practical policies and processes, and the technology for collecting and storing health care data. The ultimate success of a data governance program is the achievement of the desired outcomes for the program and, more important, protecting all data users and stakeholders by preventing inappropriate use of data and containing a data risk event if it does occur. Table 9.1 summarizes the desired outcomes, the challenges for achieving those outcomes, and management interventions that can be used to overcome those challenges.

TABLE 9.1

Data Governance Program Outcomes, Challenges, and Interventions

Data Governance Desired Outcomes	Challenges to Achieving Outcomes	Management Intervention

Provide Clear Controls	• Multiple health care organizations with different data governance business rules
	• Multiple data sources with varying quality of data
	
	• Organizational history of staff not complying with policies and procedures
	
	• Staff lack a clear understanding of the vision for the program and how they fit into the program
		• Include stakeholders from all organizational entities in the design of the control mechanisms
		• Create a data governance work group to:
		  • standardize business and data rules
		  • establish common data definitions
		  • establish the data governance processes, policies, and procedures for decision rights and other controls such as risk management
		• Establish clear, written policies and procedures
		• Train all staff on all data governance processes
		• Make ramifications for noncompliance clear
		• Be prepared to monitor the program and enforce compliance
		• Leaders must have a clear definition of the governance program and clearly explain what it will look like in the organization
		• Leaders must communicate their vision for the program and the roles and responsibilities for all data stewards
		• Be prepared to train and retrain if the vision is not being actualized in practice

Establish Accountabilities	• Difficult to establish accountability among multiple stakeholders in a "connected" health environment	• Integrate DG processes within existing management processes • Establish clear guidance for data decision rights and how compliance will be monitored and reported across multiple organizations • Establish cross-functional teams to create, help train, and monitor DG protocols and procedures

	Individual managers may not be prepared to design and oversee a DG program	• Leaders shouldn't assume a "good" manager can design and oversee a complex governance program without appropriate training and coaching • Include managers, at all levels, in the design of the program • Ensure managers have a full understanding of the DG tools, methods, and processes so they have credibility with all staff and organizations external to their organization • Train and retrain as needed
Manage Risk	• Getting all staff to understand the purpose of the risk management program and how it fits into their day-to-day job • Ensuring staff understand the implications for noncompliance • Providing managers with training in managing a risk event and noncompliant staff	• Integrate risk surveillance goals, objectives, and metrics into the individual's annual performance rating • Identify the DG roles and responsibilities for all staff • Promote the concept that all staff are data stewards • Provide training on the role of risk management in a comprehensive DG program • Ensure managers understand their role in assessing vulnerabilities and reacting quickly to a risk event • Train to audit for compliance and the reporting processes and procedures • Ensure managers understand the sanctions or consequences for noncompliance and the processes for documenting
Establish Clear Metrics	• Providing metrics that the staff will understand what success looks like and what the metrics mean for their day-to-day work requirements • Providing metrics that are practical, visible, and can be easily measured	• Bring clarity to the DG program by translating goals to formal value statements • Have representatives from all stakeholders reach consensus on the metrics for the program • Ensure managers have a clear understanding of the metric and how it will be measured • Ensure staff at the operational level participate in identifying the metrics (they already know what works and what doesn't work when it comes to operational compliance), and let them apply those lessons learned and expertise to defining what success looks like from their perspective

Continued

TABLE 9.1 (Continued)

Data Governance Program Outcomes, Challenges, and Interventions

Data Governance Desired Outcomes	Challenges to Achieving Outcomes	Management Intervention
Ensure Ongoing Continuous Quality Improvement (CQI)	• Integrating the DG program into existing quality management and other oversight programs • Leaders viewing the DG program as a static program, versus a dynamic program that needs to be constantly assessed to ensure it meets the needs of the organization and all data stakeholders	• Assess current quality management programs to determine how DG can be easily integrated into existing processes the staff currently use • Design the DG program to be practical and easily integrated into the organization's current compliance culture • Identify onerous DG compliance mechanisms and streamline to meet user needs while maintaining the rigor of the program • Leaders design a program that includes constant monitoring, feedback, and reporting to fix what's not working and redesign the program as needed for both fixes and regulatory or reporting requirements that necessitate changing the processes for governing the data • Leaders create an organizational environment that encourages problem identification, rewards practical solutions, and quickly identifies staff who do not follow DG policies and procedures • Leaders need to be prepared to train and educate and respond quickly to chronic staff who fail to comply with established policies

Protect Data, Patients, And Providers (Individual and Organizations)	• To design a comprehensive DG program that balances the data needs of providers while providing the DG mechanisms to protect all data, patients, and the health care providers using those data	• Leaders must:
		  • Create the vision for a robust DG program
		  • Include representatives from all stakeholder groups to ensure their data needs are met while ensuring the DG tools, methods, and processes don't impede the availability of those data for real-time decision-making
		  • Create a CI culture that seeks to constantly improve the DG program
		  • Agile and responsive to risk events and recommendations from staff
		  • Constantly listen to all data stewards, respond to staff needs, evaluate progress, and fix the program isn't achieving the desired outcomes.

DATA GOVERNANCE IN THE FUTURE

The purpose of this chapter has been to present a data governance framework that health care organizations can use to design and implement a data governance program that maintains the balance between providing high-quality data available for real-time clinical and business decision-making while protecting the health care data, the organization, and all data users and stakeholders. For health care data, this wide scope of data includes data from individual patients to large health care organizations and health care delivery enterprises. A rigorous, user-focused data governance framework can help today's health care organizations design, implement, and govern data use in their organization. Any governance program must also be designed to be dynamic and flexible to meet the ever-changing needs for the future. Although it's difficult to know what health care delivery will look like in the future, based on current trends we do know that HIT advances will continue to be integrated into practice and the results will be a significant growth in health care data. Kohane et al. (2012) provide a glimpse of medicine in the next 100 years. The quantity and value of data for clinical decision-making, population health, and more efficient and effective health care delivery will continue to grow rapidly:

> In the decades ahead, the pace of biomedical discovery will accelerate. The state of an individual person will be characterized with increasing precision from the molecular level to the genomic level to the organ level and by interactions with medications, nutrients, the microbiome, therapeutic devices and the environment.... Precision medicine will become possible because of huge data sets on large populations, with millions of characterizations of each person.... Discovery of useful, reproducible patterns of relationships from these data will be possible because virtually all data will be in an advanced infrastructure of electronic health records (EHRs) that includes input from physiological monitoring, which is already starting to become part of the management of chronic diseases of guidelines for prevention and fitness. (p. 2538)

As data complexity and volume continue to grow, HCOs will need to become more sophisticated in their use of data. There will be a growing need for data scientists who specialize in the complexities of health care data to design and manage the software and systems needed to manage big data in small and large HCOs. A data governance approach that is policy driven will be needed. Processes for defining, implementing, and enforcing policies for data use and reuse will make it possible for standardized data to be stored in multiple places, both internal and external to the organization and be governed by the same set of policies.

Reliance on evidence derived from advanced analytics will become increasingly important as health care delivery models shift toward patient-centered, coordinated-care models. HCOs are under increasing pressure to be more cost-effective, deliver higher-quality care and meet the requirements of federal programs such as the Medicare and Medicaid EHR incentive programs and the ACA. The Medicare and Medicaid EHR incentive programs established under Title IV, Division B, of HITECH pay incentives to eligible hospitals and providers to adopt and use certified EHR technology. Together, these federal initiatives create greater need for HCOs to manage and report data in an effort to meet the requirements. Privacy, security, intellectual property, and liability policies will all need to be continually refined as more data are generated and shared across organizational and jurisdictional boundaries.

Successful data governance programs will result in clearly defined policies and accountability that covers all types of health care information, the HCOs business processes, and the IT systems used to store and analyze the data. In addition, HCOs with successful data governance programs will develop a strong organizational culture that values data-driven decision-making and is confident in the quality of the underlying data. Finally, a successful data governance program will become institutionalized and widely recognized as critical to the business of health care as other permanent business functions such as personnel management and operational planning.

The need for robust, policy-driven data governance programs will grow as well as health care organizations become more reliant on the rapidly increasing volumes of health information to manage the business of health care. Health care leaders will need scalable data governance frameworks, tools, and methods to compete in the increasingly data-driven health care marketplace and achieve the goals of safe, high-quality, affordable health care.

REFERENCES

Campbell, R.J. 2008. Change Management in Health Care. *Health Care Manager* 27(1): 23–39.
Cottle, M., S. Kanwal, M. Kohn, T. Strome, and N.W. Treister. 2013. Transforming Health Care through Big Data. Available at http://ihealthtran.com/iHT2_BigData_2013.pdf

Data Governance Institute (DGI). 2008. Current US Federal Data Laws Addressing Data Privacy, Security, and Governance. Available at http://www.datagovernance.com/adl_data_laws_existing_federal_laws.html

Edwards, P.J., D.T. Huang, L.N. Metcalfe, and F. Sainfort. 2008. Maximizing Your Investment in EHR: Using EHRs to Inform Continuous Quality Improvement. *Journal of Healthcare Information Management* 22(1): 32–37.

Elliott, T.E., J.H. Holmes, A.J. Davidson, P. La Chance, A.F. Nelson, and J.F. Steiner. 2013. Data Warehouse Governance Programs in Healthcare Settings: A Literature Review and a Call to Action. *eGEMs* 1(1): Article 15. Available at http://repository.academyhealth.org/egems/vol1/iss1/15

Franks, B. 2012. *Taming the Big Data Tidal Wave: Finding Opportunities in Huge Data Streams with Advanced Analytics.* New York: John Wiley & Sons.

Hughes, G. 2002. Laws and Regulations Governing the Disclosure of Health Information. AHIMA Practice Brief. Available at http://library.ahima.org/xpedio/groups/public/documents/ahima/bok1_016464.hcsp?dDocName=bok1_016464

Kayyali, B., D. Knott, and S. Van Kuiken. 2013. The Big Data Revolution in US Health Care: Accelerating Value and Innovation. Available at http://www.mckinsey.com/insights/health_systems_and_services/the_big-data_revolution_in_us_health_care

Kotter, J.P. 1996. *Leading Change.* Boston, MA: Harvard Business School.

McKinsey Global Institute. 2011. Big Data: The Next Frontier for Innovation, Competition, and Productivity. McKinsey & Company. Available at http://www.mckinsey.com/insights/business_technology/big_data_the_next_frontier_for_innovation

Meyers, D., D. Peikes, J. Genevro, G. Peterson, E.F. Taylor, T. Lake, K. Smith, and K. Grumbach. 2010. The Roles of Patient-Centered Medical Homes and Accountable Care Organizations in Coordinating Patient Care. AHRQ Publication No. 11-M005-EF, December. Rockville, MD: Agency for Healthcare Research and Quality. Available at http://pcmh.ahrq.gov/sites/default/files/attachments/Roles%20of%20PCMHs%20And%20ACOs%20in%20Coordinating%20Patient%20Care.pdf

Parmelli, E., G. Flodgren, F. Beyer, N. Baillie, M. Schaafsma, and M. Eccles. 2011. The Effectiveness of Strategies to Change Organizational Culture to Improve Healthcare Performance: A Systematic Review. *Implementation Science* 6(1): 33.

Thomas, G. (n.d.). The DGI Data Governance Framework. Data Governance Institute. Available at http://www.datagovernance.com/dgi_framework.pdf

Wager, K., K. Lee, and J. Glaser. 2009. *Health Care Information Systems: A Practical Approach for Health Care Management,* 2d ed. San Francisco, CA: Jossey-Bass.

10

Roadblocks, Regulation, and Red Tape: How American Health Policy and Industry Norms Threaten the Big Data Revolution

Matthew Dobra, Dorothy Weinstein, and Christopher Broyles

CONTENTS

OBJECTIVES

After reading this chapter, the reader shall be able to:

- Describe ways current U.S. health practices and policy may prevent the health care industry from realizing the opportunities and benefits that big data has to offer
- Evaluate differences and similarities between small data and big data regarding inference
- Explain the relationship between policy and the success of the big data agenda
- Explain how imperfect diagnosis by clinicians or from research leads to a bias of overreliance on comparative effectiveness research
- Analyze the implications of policy uncertainty on innovation in health care

ABSTRACT

Modern society is marked by the democratization of computing power and the ubiquity of the data it generates. Rapid innovation and the growth of technology have fostered exponential leaps in the improvement of our ability to collect, capture, and manipulate data. Among the most important applications, big data promises considerable excitement to the world of health care. As discussed extensively throughout this volume, exploiting big data in health care is expected to yield cost savings, treatment breakthroughs, and improved health. If this promise can be realized, the greatest beneficiary is likely to be each individual consumer whose health care could be customized down to the smallest genetic units. But how does the United States optimally mobilize big data to maximize benefits? This question remains an enormous challenge, not only in its technological applications and costs, but also very importantly, in how policy is crafted and implemented. It is all too easy to lose sight of the fact that there are still significant hurdles to overcome before the health fields can truly harness the power of big data. In this chapter, we focus on the many ways current U.S. health policy might hinder the creation, preservation, and exploitation of big data.

INTRODUCTION

Big data is constantly collected and mobilized in-house at large institutions like hospitals, pharmaceutical companies, and research institutions. A prominent example of the in-house application of big data is at Intermountain Healthcare. A 2013 *Wall Street Journal* article reported that Intermountain Healthcare is building an ambitious new data system to track the cost of every procedure, piece of equipment, and supply in its 22 hospitals and 185 clinics (Beck, 2013). The idea is to have data available so physicians and patients can discuss costs and outcomes before making treatment decisions.

The in-house application of big data is very important, in and of itself, but increasing the scope of big data across institutions in local, regional, national, and global applications is equally important and should correspondingly increase the benefits of big data. Our focus is specifically on this more universal aggregation of big data: Can we get "bigger" data?

Throughout American history, the public sector has played a significant role in shaping health care policy, particularly debates addressing entitlement and rights. Given the entrenched nature of government programs such as Medicare, Medicaid, and the state children's health insurance program (SCHIP); the uncertainty of the Patient Protection and Affordable Care Act of 2010 (ACA); the large-scale support in federal funding of biomedical research; and the extensive network of federal health regulations, it is likely that government will be increasingly involved in the U.S. health system. This fact places the creation of big data, as well as the definition of the parameters of its use, squarely at the feet of the U.S. government. Assuming the government possesses the willingness to address the issue of big data, our operative question centers on the capacity of the government to do so adequately.

The focus of our contribution to this volume is to explore the many ways current U.S. health practices and policy may prevent its own health care industry from unleashing the opportunities and benefits that big data has to offer. Currently, most applications of big data are executed in-house; large providers and insurance companies are already using their massive volumes of data in an attempt to improve treatment, speed up diagnoses, and cut costs. In addition, we are beginning to see efforts that cross business borders, such as General Electric's collection of multiple electronic health record (EHR) sources into a large epidemiology database. However, the ability to move beyond these individual silos of information is severely limited by current policy. Extant privacy laws impede the creation of big data, and therefore any big data created will likely be compromised and contain significant biases. Moreover, utilization of big data may generate unforeseen and countereffective issues in the area of personalized medicine, individualized care, and innovation. Finally, given the current state of uncertainty surrounding U.S. health policy and the unlikelihood of a major policy overhaul (or abandonment), those in the health care sector may remain reluctant to make extensive use of this data.

CREATING BIG DATA

Let us start by considering the ideal big data set. Imagine a world where every patient's information, as a matter of practice, is automatically uploaded to a database. This data would include socioeconomic and demographic information, health conditions, tests results, courses of treatments, outcomes, lifestyle preferences and choices, environmental influences, and DNA information. The technical feasibility of such a database is probably closer to reality than many realize—the primary impediment is the present-day high cost of DNA sequencing, though improved technology is rapidly yielding lower costs. These technical obstacles, however, are not nearly as insurmountable as those generated by the American policy landscape.

It is clear from a data-mining standpoint why we gather these independent variables about the patient. Much of the promise of big data lies in two possibilities: first in the serendipity of research, where relationships or breakthroughs are discovered (and for which there was no a priori reason to expect such a relationship); and second in the subtleties or nuances of research discovery where relationships or breakthroughs are discovered that normally are too small to find in traditional data. In other words, big data excels in helping to find statistical needles in data haystacks; in fact, and rather counterintuitively, the bigger the haystack, the easier it is to find those needles. But it is far less clear, especially to those not trained in statistical methods, that for big data to be revealing, data uploads to any database need to be comprehensive and compulsory. Without every combination of adenine, cytosine, guanine, and thymine for every human being, both alive and dead, and without matching this genomic data with measures of all the attributes that DNA is expected to influence, big data will be full of small data problems.

In pursuit of the promise, scientists, policy makers, and even the general public seem to have fetishized big data to the point of overlooking the critical fact that only some of the limitations of small data can be addressed by increasing the amount of data available (Gayo-Avello, 2012). Big data allows researchers to overcome sampling error. However, no data, big or otherwise, should be mistaken for being objectively true in any sense. Data are necessarily of human construction and design, and whether big or small the processes of collecting and defining data always have the potential to be fraught with bias. Moreover, interpreting the results of data analysis inevitably brings the preconceptions and cognitive biases of the analyst into the equation. While big data is often lauded as a way to eliminate the impact of researcher bias (a process in which the researcher influences results in order to achieve an outcome normatively viewed as being particularly desirable), this claim is dubious; after all, the researcher still chooses where to look and still must interpret results. Put more bluntly, the big data fetish seems to have given rise to two great fictions: first that it is possible for $n = N$ and $N =$ everything; and second that if the former is true, then ascertaining Truth has been reduced to a mere exercise in computation.

Let us briefly reconsider our aforementioned hypothetical ideal data set, this time looking more closely at the two assumptions made. First, we started by assuming every patient's information would be automatically uploaded to our database. This is essential if we are to avoid small data problems like selection bias, yet privacy and proprietary policy and economic obstacles are not likely to be overcome. Moreover, such a shift could have a multitude of effects on the health care industry, on both the provider level and for the R&D industry. Second, we assumed that this data set would include socioeconomic and demographic information, health conditions, test results, courses of treatments, outcomes, lifestyle preferences and choices, environmental influences, and DNA information—all data that would necessarily come from a variety of sources. We assumed not only that the sources of these data are capable of speaking with each other but also that they would have incentives to do so.*

---

* Please note that a coordinated effort to collect comprehensive data has not been realized. Policies covering the administration of Health Insurance Portability and Accountability Act of 1996, electronic health records, health information exchanges, and accountable care organizations, for example, are not currently designed or able to collect this data.

Although we have the scientific skills to collect data, we do not have the power to enforce complete, comprehensive, honest, clean, nonduplicative population participation. Given the current policy regime, we are left to question the future viability of either assumption. The remainder of this section will develop these ideas further.

Mandatory Collection

To understand the first assumption regarding automatic and compulsorily patient data, first consider the logic of, and motivation for, the randomized controlled trial (RCT), the gold standard of quality research premised on statistically robust data sets. Assume that a drug company has developed a product they hypothesize might be used to cure some disease. How might they go about determining whether or not their drug will, in fact, have the effect they expect? Suppose that they simply post ads at a local free clinic trying to find people with the disease; such a study is called a cohort study, where an established group of patients is followed forward in time. Suppose, after taking the drug, that the patients in the sample have a cure rate of 78%. Is this enough evidence to draw a conclusion? Perhaps the drug did nothing and the subjects would have improved anyway. Maybe the drug actually harmed them and had they not taken the drug 95% would have gotten better on their own. Because all the subjects came from a free clinic, they may be atypical of most sufferers of the disease—these subjects are likely to have low incomes, for example. Women may be more likely than men to accompany their children to the clinic, so it is likely that the trial group will have more females than men. Women may respond better than men to the drug. Maybe there was a placebo effect. The list goes on and on (Delgado-Rodriguez and Llorca, 2004).

What all these problems have in common is that we cannot easily isolate the effect of the drug from a wide variety of other influences that might also have had an effect, and this is where the RCT comes in: to prove the efficacy of a drug, it is necessary to design the study as well as possible so that the only difference between the treatment group and the control group (the group to which the treatment group is compared) is the treatment itself. Any differences observed between the groups can then be ascribed to the treatment and not to any confounding effect.

The same considerations for experimental design in an RCT must also be considered in the creation of big data. If the people whose records are captured in the giant health database are systematically different from those whose records are not, then it is plausible, if not likely, that any results drawn from big data are artifacts of the data collection process. For example, there are asymmetries in what data are collected or recorded, which can skew results. Moreover, physicians and patients opt for specific treatments for a wide variety of reasons, not all of which are captured in the records. Such reasons could be technical, such as limitations due to formulary choices or familiarity with certain treatments. They could be socioeconomic, such as racial bias, or selecting less expensive treatments due to affordability or insurance coverage. Or they might simply be intuitive, such as doctors using a sixth sense. These observations become particularly true if the criteria for inclusion are systematically related to factors that might influence health or presence in one health system over another.

So to clarify, if the reporting of health records to a central source is voluntary, there will certainly be systematic differences between those who report and those who do not. For example, if reporting is costly, then one should expect to see lower reporting rates among small providers than among large providers, lower reporting rates among rural providers than among urban providers, lower reporting rates among providers to the poor than among providers to the rich, and so forth. Such issues have already affected big data in health care (Hersh et al., 2013a,b). For example, Google Flu Trends dramatically overestimated U.S. flu levels in 2013 by nearly 100%, likely because the data used to generate their estimates, as big as it was, was influenced by nonrandom factors that determined what data were collected (Butler, 2013).

Collection Costs

On the other hand, implementing a compulsory system of data uploading would have widespread ramifications on the health sector. First, there would have to be a clear, quick, and large benefit to justify a compulsory system. Ignoring for a moment the issues of privacy (which we will turn to shortly), consider the simple dimension of cost. We anticipate that moving to a compulsory system would impose two types of costs on health care providers: variable and fixed costs. Variable costs can be thought of as the cost of uploading each individual piece of data. This might include the cost of coding data for each patient and transmission costs. These costs are likely to be small and constant; the cost of delivering information for 200 patients should be roughly double the cost of delivering information for 100 patients, and neither should be terribly expensive. Fixed costs might be thought of as the cost of uploading the *first* piece of data or the cost of being able to upload any data at all. This would include costs of purchasing the required software and hardware and training staff on the process and new coding requirements. Unlike the variable costs, fixed costs should be roughly the same for all providers and are likely to be high. This high fixed cost has the potential to dramatically change the health landscape because the cost of compliance per patient to small providers is likely to be much higher than the cost of compliance per patient to large providers. For example, small providers may not be able to compete in urban markets with large providers, squeezing them out of the market, and in rural areas with less competition, these costs would likely be pushed onto health consumers or government.*

Data Diversity

Returning to our discussion of our hypothetical data set, and assuming some method of compulsory participation has been agreed upon, we discuss our second assumption: that our data set would include a broad set of information including socioeconomic and demographic, health conditions, test results, treatments, outcomes, lifestyle preferences and choices, environmental influences, and DNA information. For any given patient, some of this data would come from health care providers or information aggregators (like health information exchanges), but it would be uncommon for all the health data for a patient to come from the same source. Moreover, some data would have to come from alternative sources. Information on education, socioeconomic status, income, and the like might come from a variety of sources, such as the Internal Revenue Service or the U.S. Census Bureau. Some data, such as lifestyle choices, might be available only from patients themselves (Kozak et al., 2012). For such a data set to be useful, it is essential that there is some coordinated system to mine and share these data sources and that each independent variable is translated and categorized consistently across data sets. Finally, not only

---

* We note that we have made two (perhaps heroic) assumptions here: first, that all members of the medical community will perceive this to be beneficial to them; and relatedly, that compliance will actually happen. A large portion of the medical community is still chafing at EHRs.

must these data sources be capable of speaking with each other, but also the owners of the data must also find it in their incentives to do so.*

Privacy Protection

So now we come full circle to our discussion of privacy policy and its potential to stifle both innovation and patient care. Information sharing of this sort is by definition bidirectional; therefore, privacy becomes the lightning rod for discussion of feasibility. After all, each of these billions points of data is a medical record, the privacy of which is heavily regulated, most notably through the Health Insurance Portability and Accountability Act (HIPAA) and the Health Information Technology for Economic and Clinical Health Act of 2009 (HITECH). Currently, these policies hinder the ability to share data, combine data, and create big data sets. While there is a recent trend toward open data, it historically has been the case that patients and other research subjects can give their consent for only a single research endeavor. The National Institutes of Health (NIH) has had a data-sharing policy since 2003, but academic institutions have only recently seriously considered designing their own policy on data sharing. Consortium and meetings are popping up on university campuses everywhere to discuss data-sharing policy (NIH, 2003).† More flexible forms of consent are evolving with the end goal of having sharable data; however, this evolution will not change the rights that pertain to existing data (Obeid et al., 2013). For most already-existing data, consent attaches not to the personal data but instead to the research project or site. Therefore, after a study is completed further research using patient data is off limits (Litan, 2012). As a result of these research silos, adequate study populations are incredibly expensive to assemble, if not impossible, and do not allow for data to be aggregated into larger sample sizes. This eliminates the reuse and repurposing of

---

* As a relevant historical aside, the Health Insurance Portability and Accountability Act of 1996 required all Americans to be issued a unique patient identifier (UPI), in other words, a national ID card. However, Congress blocked funding for the ID card in 1998 because of vocal public concern about the potential for breach of privacy. Patient identification cannot be overstated in its central importance to aggregating data sources into robust reliable big data sets. Yet this policy ambiguity remains without resolution, even as the health information exchanges (HIE) under the Affordable Care Act (ACA) require a centralized data collection.

† The NIH Data Sharing Policy "expects investigators seeking more than $500K in direct support in any given year to submit a data sharing plan with their application or to indicate why data sharing is not possible." Please note that most of the Institutes that comprise the NIH have their own data-sharing policies, as well" (http://grants.nih.gov/grants/guide/notice-files/NOT-OD-03-032.html).

information, a commonplace practice in other parts of the economy, such as in financial venues or in marketing and advertising practices.

Examining Policy

A quick summary of policy reveals a broad sweep of restrictions in data sharing across the health care spectrum. The impediments are both legal and incentive driven. For patients, there are airtight legal privacy rules, such as HIPAA. In R&D, particularly that of the pharmaceutical industry, data are limited by patent rules that protect proprietary information or hide failed research. In academia, there is no incentive to share data before publication since the goal is to reward original research and discovery and to be the first to publish results. The end result is that, across the health care sector, researchers guard their procured data in an environment where sharing is actively discouraged in the race to get research completed first. The Kaufman Foundation reinforces the default assumption "that information collected here stays here, unless there is a particular reason to move it somewhere else. This cultural predilection often exacerbates the already-restrictive effects of privacy constraints—and privacy constraints, in turn, often excuse the hoarding of information" (Kaufman Task Force on Cost Effective Health Care Innovation, 2012).

Federal policy is phasing in mandates for health care providers and institutions to secure patient information and data through electronic medical records. Health information exchanges (through the ACA on both the state and federal levels) could potentially allow for the electronic mobilization of health care information across organizations. Engineering the sharing of health care information throughout these exchanges would provide a vast quantity of data, but historically regular aggregation has not been important in the health care community. Even if we assume that the legal/privacy side of this problem can be solved, we are then left with the existing incentive structures in academic and R&D sectors that drive much of society's health research and are not consistent with quiet and seamless acceptance of mandated data sharing.

Among the most vexing issues confronting privacy is the question of who owns data. Increasingly, technology has allowed patients and consumers to have more information about their health. However, in a strange twist, current laws set medical records and biological samples under the ownership of the health care provider or institution, not the patient or consumer. This perplexing contradiction puts further challenges on privacy when ownership of one's own data is put into question.

The issue of privacy also presents one of the many technical limitations that health policy has created. After all, it is difficult to control for methodological issues like self-selection and other independent variables when there is complete anonymity. Moreover, without some form of universal identifier, researchers cannot cull duplicate records or multiple identifiers for the same person. It is hard to imagine a fully functioning mechanism to generate big data without the creation of a new, national health ID program to allow records from multiple sources to be linked together in a common translated language. And while appropriate technology policy can go a long way toward protecting anonymity, nothing is foolproof. No technology or policy will be sufficiently robust to prevent a determined hacker from identifying individuals (El Emam and Moher, 2013; Litan, 2012). Therefore, since policy cannot completely prevent misuse, society is faced with the need to assess the relative trade-off between the benefits of data and the risk of abuse. The Kaufman Task Force on Cost-Effective Health Care Innovation (2012) puts this challenging situation in perspective: "Instead of balancing privacy against discovery, the current system puts policy's thumb so much on the side of privacy that it has the practical effect of locking in information, restricting it to the smallest possible 'need-to-know' circle."

Privacy is paramount, of course, and leaks in confidentiality are real. John Wilbanks, one of the nation's leading data-mining scholars and entrepreneurs in this field, cautions us about the wide availability of "gifted hackers" who can easily identify people based on limited public information. Security of individual rights becomes even more daunting when data are shared and combined to create larger data sets. The ability to reidentify a formerly anonymous person (or data point) creates an imbalance in the policy process undermining confidence in protecting anonymity (Polonetsky and Tene, 2013).

While privacy concerns may be the most obvious technical limitation to linking data from multiple sources, perhaps more daunting is the fact that language must be standardized across the industry, a point we have mentioned a number of times in this chapter. Inputting, uploading, or downloading information with diverse formats is completely useless to research unless there is a way for formats to "talk" to each other and translate into one common language (Litan, 2012).

USING BIG DATA

The preceding section highlighted a variety of ways we anticipate public policy to limit the accumulation and aggregation of big data. The resolution of these issues is necessary, but not sufficient, to the policy goal of unlocking the potential of big data. After all, the creation of big data sets does not ensure their proper utilization, and again, we foresee policy roadblocks that need to be cleared before this can even occur. Much of our concern focuses on how both social and policy-driven forces might result in overemphasis of the information and scientific knowledge emanating from the analysis of big data. In addition, we anticipate that U.S. health policy's current state of constant and extreme flux will hamper these efforts as well.

Individualizing Care

Nobel laureate economist F. A. Hayek observed in 1945 that "today it is almost heresy to suggest that scientific knowledge is not the sum of all knowledge." This sentiment is echoed in the more familiar line from William Cameron (often misattributed to Albert Einstein): "Not everything that can be counted counts, and not everything that counts can be counted." Analysis of big data has the promise of generating additional information that might improve health care outcomes; we fear that this additional information will be given too much weight relative to local knowledge, effectively tying the hands of practitioners and ultimately harming—or at least reducing the benefits of big data to—patients. This potential can best be seen against the backdrop of personalized medicine.

Personalized medicine, initially a natural outgrowth of the successful sequencing of the human genome, promises the delivery of precise, individually tailored care and greater treatment effectiveness than traditional medicine. The actual practice takes an integrated, evidence-based approach to individualized treatment looking at each respective patient's unique clinical, social, genetic, environmental, and lifestyle information across the continuum from health to disease (Weinstein, 2014).

While traditional medicine has always aimed to be personal, personalized medicine refers specifically to the practice of using some form of technology, discovery, or data enabling a level of personalization not previously feasible or practical. Present-day practice has evolved from a straightforward genomic treatment approach to one that incorporates a diverse set of tools to uniquely customize a treatment plan (Weinstein, 2014). Most notable among the tools used are evidence-based practice (EBP, sometimes referred to as evidence-based medicine) and comparative effectiveness research (CER). EBP is the combination of the best available research and the provider's best clinical expertise integrated with patient values and preferences. CER augments EBP by critically synthesizing systematic research and comparing different interventions and strategies to prevent, diagnose, treat, and monitor health conditions. Evidence for the practice of CER comes from research studies such as RCTs and meta-analyses of RCTs that compare drugs, medical devices, tests, surgeries, or other ways to deliver health care.

By adding to our stock of scientific knowledge, analysis of big data has the potential to provide large gains to CER and, by extension, EBP. Ideally, CER aids consumers, patients, providers, and policy makers by supplying accurate and timely information about the most effective and least harmful treatments, both on the individual level and within specific populations (Nix, 2012). There is, however, potential cause for concern if the value of CER is exalted above that which it is scientifically due. The Institute of Medicine (2009) of the National Academy of Sciences provides a cautionary perspective along these lines about the effect of overreliance on CER: "Intended to compare available treatment options, CER can benefit patients if used for informational purposes only, but it could also be harmful in practice if used as the only variable in creating a treatment plan." A report by the Pacific Research Institute makes a similar observation regarding how CER is utilized and argues that at the federal level, a top-down approach may be misguided in crafting sound policy: "A renewed emphasis upon a 'bottom up' approach of experimentation by many millions of practitioners and patients would be a more fruitful vehicle for the acquisition of information about the comparative effectiveness of alternative clinical approaches" (Zycher, 2011, p. 8).

Both of these reports echo the same sentiment: Big data is not supposed to tie the hands of consumers, patients, providers, and policy makers in making decisions. However, while caution against the misuse of CER data are frequently overlooked, we argue that such misuse is in fact quite likely, in part due to reasons implied by Hayek (e.g., our previous suggestion that perhaps we have fetishized big data and attached undue importance to data). Data should enhance decision-making and inform policy-making. The practice of good health care needs to combine the nuance of nonquantifiable variables and the science of big data. It is our opinion that such misuse is, however, in the incentives of medical practitioners. To illustrate this concern, consider this simple game theoretic-probabilistic model of diagnosis.

Assessing Risk and Treatment Options

Assume that a physician wishes to practice EBP with her patients. When a patient walks in, the physician has a $0 < p < 1$ chance of independently and correctly diagnosing her patient's condition and a $(1 - p)$ probability of incorrectly diagnosing her patient's condition. She also uses the best available CER data in an attempt to independently diagnose the patient's condition, which similarly has a $0 < q < 1$ probability of correct diagnosis and a $(1 - q)$ probability of incorrect diagnosis. For simplicity, assume that p and q are uncorrelated and that if both the physician's differential diagnosis and CER-based diagnosis indicate the incorrect diagnosis, the same incorrect diagnosis is indicated. It is not necessary for p or q to be known ex ante, though we assume them to be known as a simplifying assumption. Finally, assume that the appropriate treatments for both the correct and incorrect diagnoses are known by the physician and that these two treatments are mutually exclusive—she must choose one or the other and cannot choose both.

The probability of both the physician's differential diagnosis and the CER-based diagnosis can be calculated as pq. For very high values of p and q (i.e., both the physician and CER have a high probability of being correct), there is a high probability of concordance between the physician and the CER. For example, if $p = .95$ and $q = .98$, then the probability of both reaching the same, correct diagnosis is just over 93%. The (hopefully rare) probability of both the physician and CER-based diagnosis is similarly $(1 - p)(1 - q)$. It is also possible that the physician and CER-based diagnoses reach differing conclusions—the probability of these outcomes is $p(1 - q)$ in the case of the physician being correct and $q(1 - p)$ in the case of the CER being correct. This basic setup is summarized in Table 10.1.

Socially, or from the perspective of the patient, correct concordance (cell a) is an unambiguously good outcome, and incorrect concordance (cell d) is an unambiguously bad outcome. In the case of disagreement between the two diagnoses, the patient would prefer that the doctor go with her gut if the physician is correct (cell b) and that the doctor stick with the CER if the physician is incorrect (cell c). In other words, from a social or patient-based perspective, there is symmetry between cells

TABLE 10.1

Probability of Physician's Differential Diagnosis and CER-Based Diagnosis

			CER	
			q	$(1-q)$
			Correct Diagnosis	**Incorrect Diagnosis**
Physician	p	Correct Diagnosis	(a)	(b)
			pq	$p(1-q)$
	$(1-p)$	Incorrect Diagnosis	(c)	(d)
			$q(1-p)$	$(1-p)(1-q)$

b and c—the patient unambiguously wishes for the physician to pursue treatment based on the objectively correct diagnosis, regardless of the basis for that diagnosis. Moreover, the patient is equally bad off if the incorrect diagnosis is chosen in cells b or c. Due to this symmetry, the patient would ideally like for the physician to act on her personal diagnosis with probability $\dfrac{p(1-q)}{p(1-q)+q(1-p)}$, and the patient would like the physician to act on the diagnosis suggested by CER with probability $\dfrac{q(1-p)}{p(1-q)+q(1-p)}$. For example, if $p = .95$ and $q = .98$, then the physician should assign a 28% chance to her diagnosis being correct and a 72% chance of the CER diagnosis being correct.

Consider next the incentives of the physician. We assume her foremost goal is the betterment of her patient, so like the patient, she views cell a as the best, along with pursuing the objectively correct course of treatment in cells b and c. Unlike the patient, however, the physician is unlikely to view each of the bad outcomes as equally bad. A quick discussion with any given group of physicians will likely reveal that their care giving is more routinized and less personalized because of the great uncertainty of health care policy and the push of time and cost pressures. First, providers are aware of lowered reimbursements and feel bound to stick to best practices to ensure any reimbursement. Second, providers may believe that strict adherence to practice guidelines is necessary to protect themselves against liability. Within the context of the model, the cost to the physician of pursuing the incorrect course of treatment is much higher in cell c than in cell b. This, in turn, is expected to bias her decision in favor of simply following the CER. This bias is more deleterious either the higher is p or the lower is q.

If it were anticipated that q would always be significantly higher than p then this may not be so problematic. But remember our discussion in the earlier section about the RCT and the importance of statistically sound research. When data are not clean or comprehensive and when studies are conducted or interpreted incorrectly, CER results will likely be inaccurate or, worse, misleading. A Lewin Group study explains this point: "The absence of [personalized medicine] considerations in CER could be suboptimal for patient interests, particularly to the extent that CER findings are used to support gatekeeping or other authoritative functions, such as product labeling, clinical practice guidelines, coverage policies, and quality measures and criteria" (Goodman, 2009, p. 22).

The model as presented has been simplified for the sake of general accessibility; hiding behind the simple probabilities is an implicit set of costs and payoffs and utility functions, and the result is driven by the assumption that the patient and the doctor have different payoffs and costs. If one presumes that the best outcome of this game is one in which the net benefit to the patient is maximized, then intuitively the solution to this dilemma lies in finding a way to alter the physician's payoffs or costs to encourage her to make decisions that are more closely aligned with the desires of the patient. At a practical level, this could be accomplished through a variety of means; examples include changes in malpractice laws or insurance reimbursement practices.

Our simple model has been framed within the context of a physician using EBP to diagnose and treat a patient. The principle, however, that a physician is likely to find it in her incentives to be biased in favor of overreliance on CER data is generalizable to nearly all areas of patient care where there might be some discord between the physician's recommendation and what is said by CER, leading to the potential for this sort of bias to have far-reaching consequences. For example, this bias may cause CER to serve as a strong deterrent to the creation and introduction of new treatments. When CER focuses too heavily on existing treatments for which data are already available, then the situation immediately stacks the deck against new treatments where little or no data are available.

Creating Uncertainty

At the core of our model is the notion of uncertainty; we contend that when faced with the uncertainty of correct diagnosis and effective treatment the incentive structure pushes physicians to make biased choices. The health profession is currently dealing with another form of uncertainty: policy uncertainty. There is economic evidence that policy uncertainty is a hindrance to the economy. For example, Bloom (2009) argues that policy uncertainty causes firms to slow their hiring and investment, and Bloom (2007) finds that uncertainty causes firms to be more cautious with respect to R&D.

Policy uncertainty has long been endemic to the area of health care, but our view (at the time of the publication of this chapter) is that American health policy uncertainty may well be at an all-time high with no end in sight. While trying to avoid a statement about the merits or demerits of the ACA, it is difficult to escape the conclusion that the reaction to the law has created an extraordinarily tumultuous health care policy climate. Highlights of this list include lawsuits over the constitutionality of the ACA, a threat of repeal following the 2012 election (if the Republicans had been more successful), and a rollout that might best be described as a debacle prompting multiple last-minute implementation changes. And these are just a select three. In short, at no point over the course of the Barack Obama presidency can health policy be said to have been stable or projectable. It is likely that this uncertainty had a wide-ranging effect on the health care industry, most notably the stifling of R&D and innovation.

While the effects of policy uncertainty are expected to span many areas of health care, we would like to highlight two that may be particularly salient to the discussion of big data. First, to the extent that one of big data's great promises is in its applicability to R&D and innovation, any factor that stifles R&D and innovation will by proxy reduce the utility of big data. Second, it is notable and certainly ironic that the application of data, big and small, could have helped the Obama administration craft sound health care policy. The healthcare.gov rollout under the ACA, however, introduced a nonviable system with fragile infrastructure. As such, the rollout in particular can plausibly be viewed as a failure to correctly use big data.

CONCLUSION

As we sit back and review the impediments to the use of big data discussed throughout this chapter, we, as authors, are faced with the challenge: What recommendations can be made to unleash big data from large enterprise silos to a global community of accessible networks? Is it possible to scale in-house application of big data research to an even larger worldwide level? Data are housed within the federal government, pharmaceutical and device industries, health care institutions, academic settings, and more. These data, when well used, are not fully leveraged, and further innovation is stymied while data sit untapped. Data are everywhere and ready and waiting for exploitation.

The following broad recommendations are offered as practical and illustrative, hoping to spur decision makers to think about other policy options.

First, tort reform in the health care arena could be redesigned to model the U.S. patent system where judges and administrators are trained in the scientific area under consideration. Such reform could play a role in curbing malpractice suits since liability concerns might be abated. Health care providers often feel bound to follow practice guidelines to safeguard against liability when other avenues of care are equally important to consider as part of larger treatment goals. A judge educated not only in the law but also in the specialty of health care may be able to examine the situation in a more nuanced light with the end result of a more balanced opinion.

Second, clarification on ownership of data is needed. Traditionally, consent to use data is given and secured to only one research project and then left to be shelved for no other use. There are vast sources of data available for further exploitation and sharing. An international consent system whereby data are released permanently with regulated patient protections would likely foster more research. Of course, this area of policy needs considerable clarification on protecting patients and their personal information. But rather than shying away from this challenging issue, policy makers need to design a mindful system with safeguards in place that protect the patient and encourage innovation and entrepreneurship.

Third, policy must address when and how to access and share data balancing the many interests of all parties involved. For instance, academic institutions need to protect data before publication, and pharmaceutical companies need to protect data prior to launching a new product. Timing of data access is complicated by current patent and intellectual property law (and subsequent agency regulations) that place vast barriers on the release of data. Examples of such policies are found in the Freedom of Information Act (FOIA), Bayh-Dole Act, and federal agency conforming regulations. Additionally, Supreme Court decisions have decided favorably on maintaining strict privacy laws (Center for Regulatory Effectiveness, 1999).

Fourth, extreme care must be given in delineating the precise role of the government in the process. It is clear that the government must do something—at the very least, health policy needs to be modified to create the capacity and incentives for big data to be created and shared more broadly than it is today. However, even in what seems to be a clear-cut case for action—the creation of a national health identifier—the federal government has at best sent mixed signals by encouraging such a program in HIPAA in 1996 but explicitly barring it from being the target of federal money beginning with the 1999 omnibus appropriations bill. Moreover, once the government does act, how large a role should the government have? It is common to presuppose that the government has both the ability and incentives to create beneficial public projects, but this is not necessarily the case. The fall 2013 rollout of healthcare.gov makes one wonder about the capacity of the government to meaningfully and successfully undertake large health programs, and the spring/summer 2013 revelations of the National Security Agency makes one wonder about the desirability of the government having access to that much data.

This chapter focuses on elucidating and deconstructing the impediments to the use of big data in an attempt to see where health care policy can be redesigned or newly crafted. We leave the question of whether big data will be seriously considered to the predictions of the political pundits. It is important to note that the relevance of the structure (e.g., single payer, ACA model, employer based, individual mandate) is unimportant in this context because policy on big data can always be incorporated in any health care system. Certainly, Americans are keenly aware of the precarious and indeterminate situation in health policy. And as this uncomfortable uncertainty becomes more embedded in our American ethos and as it streams down into our own health care, policy needs to be reexamined and reworked to regain clarity. We fully acknowledge the supreme difficulties faced in crafting health policy and the time and resources it will take our nation to undertake. However, much can be learned and improved by taking a granular look at the serious impediments to the use of big data and to potential policies that may work to improve health care delivery.

REFERENCES

Beck, Melinda. 2013. Here's What Your Operation Will Really Cost. *Wall Street Journal*, November 17.

Bloom, Nicholas. 2007. Uncertainty and the Dynamics of R&D. *American Economic Review* 97(2): 250–255.

Bloom, Nicholas. 2009. The Impact of Uncertainty Shocks. *Econometrica* 77(3): 623–685.

Butler, Declan. 2013. When Google Got Flu Wrong. *Nature* 494: 7436, February 13. Available at http://www.nature.com/news/when-google-got-flu-wrong-1.12413

Center for Regulatory Effectiveness. 1999. *Three Key Protections for Intellectual Property Under the New Federal Data Access Law: FOIA, The Bayh-Dole Act, and Agencies' Conforming Regulations*, June.

Delgado-Rodriguez, M., and J. Llorca. 2004. Bias. *Journal of Epidemiology and Community Health* 58(8): 635–641.

El Emam, K., and E. Moher. 2013. Privacy and Anonymity Challenges When Collecting Data for Public Health Purposes. *Journal of Law, Medicine & Ethics* 31(s1): 37–41. Available at http://www.ncbi.nlm.nih.gov/pubmed/23590738

Gayo-Avello, Daniel. 2012. No, You Cannot Predict Elections with Twitter. *Internet Computing IEEE* 16:6. Available at http://dx.doi.org/10.1109/MIC.2012.137

Goodman, Clifford. 2009. *Comparative Effectiveness Research and Personalized Medicine: From Contradiction to Synergy*. Lewin Group Center for Comparative Effectiveness Research, Falls Church, VA.

Hayek, F.A. 1945. The Use of Knowledge in Society. *American Economic Review* 35(4): 519–530.

Hersh, William R., J. Cimino, P.R.O. Payne, P. Embi, J. Logan, M. Weiner, E.V. Bernstam, H. Lehmann, G. Hripcsak, T. Hartzog, and J. Saltz. 2013a. Recommendations for the Use of Operational Electronic Health Record Data in Comparative Effectiveness Research. *eGEMs* 1(1): Article 14. Available at http://repository.academyhealth.org/egems/vol1/iss1/14

Hersh, W.R., M.G. Weiner, P.J. Embi, J.R. Logan, P.R. Payne, E.V. Bernstam, H.P. Lehmann, G. Hripsack, T.H. Hartzog, J.J. Cimino, and J. Saltz. 2013b. Caveats for the Use of Operational Electronic Health Record Data in Comparative Effectiveness Research. *Medical Care* 51(Suppl 3): S30–S37. Available at http://www.ncbi.nlm.nih.gov/pubmed/23774517

Institute of Medicine. 2009. *Initial Priorities for Comparative Effectiveness Research. Committee on Comparative Effectiveness Research Prioritization. Institute of Medicine.* Washington, DC: National Academies Press. Available at http://www.iom.edu/~/media/Files/Report%20Files/2009/ComparativeEffectivenessResearchPriorities/CER%20report%20brief%2008-13-09.ashx

Kaufman Task Force on Cost-Effective Health Care Innovation. 2012. *Valuing Health Care: Improving Productivity and Quality.* Foundation of Entrepreneurship. Available at http://scholarship.law.duke.edu/cgi/viewcontent.cgi?article = 5220&context = faculty_scholarship

Kozak, M.S., M.J. Mugavero, J. Ye, I. Aban, S.T. Lawrence, C.R. Nevin, J.L. Raper, C. McCullumsmith, J.E. Schumacher, H.M. Crane, M.M. Kitahata, M.S. Saag, and J.H. Willig. 2012. Patient Reported Outcomes in Routine Care: Advancing Data Capture for HIV Cohort Research. *Clinical Infectious Diseases* 54(1): 141–147. Available at http://www.ncbi.nlm.nih.gov/pubmed/22042879

Litan, R. 2012. Big Data Can Save Health Care—But at What Cost to Privacy? *Atlantic Magazine*, May 25.

National Institutes of Health (NIH). 2003. *Final NIH Statement of Sharing Research Data*, February 26. Available at http://grants.nih.gov/grants/guide/notice-files/NOT-OD-03-032.html

Nix, K. 2012. *Comparative Effectiveness Research Under Obamacare: A Slippery Slope to Health Care Rationing*. (Abstract). Heritage Foundation, Washington, DC.

Obeid, J.S., K. Gerken, K.C. Madathil, D. Rugg, C.E. Alstad, K. Fryar, et al. 2013. *Development of an Electronic Research Permissions Management System to Enhance Informed Consents and Capture Research Authorizations Data*. AMIA Summits on Translational Science proceedings AMIA Summit on Translational Science. May 18. Available at http://www.ncbi.nlm.nih.gov/pubmed/24303263

Polonetsky, J., and O. Tene. 2013. Symposium Issue: Privacy in the Age of Big Data: A Time for Big Decisions. *Stanford Law Review Online* 25: 63–69. Available at http://www.stanfordlawreview.org/online/privacy-and-big-data/privacy-and-big-data

Weinstein, D. 2014. Personalized Medicine: A Cautionary Tale or Instructional Epic. In R.K. Bali, L. Bos, M.C. Gibbons, and Ibell (eds.), *Rare Diseases in the Age of Health 2.0*, p. 196. New York: Springer Publishing.

Zycher, Benjamin. 2011. Comparative Effectiveness Reviews: Quantitative Analysis of Research and Development Investment Effects. *Pacific Research Institute*, July, p. 6.

11

Education and Training of Health Informaticists*

Lynda R. Hardy

CONTENTS

OBJECTIVES

After reading this chapter, the reader should be able to:

- Understand the types of health informatics
- Describe the growth of the field

---

* This chapter was prepared by Dr. Hardy in her UMUC capacity. The opinions expressed in this chapter are the author's own and do not reflect the view of the National Institutes of Health, the Department of Health and Human Services, or the U.S. government.

- Explain training requirements
- Summarize the professional organizations involved in health informatics

ABSTRACT

Making use of the explosive growth in information, especially health information, requires educating the current and next generation of health informaticists. Just as data analytics including health informatics and its various components (e.g., bioinformatics, clinical informatics, public health informatics) are in flux, so is the type and content of health informatics education that students can take advantage of.

INTRODUCTION

The big data explosion has caused a tsunami of information issues that are flooding academic institutions and government agencies at increasing speeds. The need to look at big data from an academic perspective is relatively new, while consumer research has been harnessing the power of data for longer periods of time. Google, Amazon, Twitter, and other consumer and social media networks have been collecting individual data to target population and individual purchasing methods as a means of expanding their market share. Trillions of data are being captured using technology-driven devices such as smartphones and tablets according to the McKinsey Global Institute (2011). These technologies continue to fuel the big data fire daily, and their technologies are now being applied to health care. The Institute estimates that Facebook generates 30 billion pieces of data monthly; each of us adds to this pool, including our health information (2011). We are heading into a new world of information and the skills, and training required for it are rapidly evolving. This chapter will focus on the impact of accumulated and stored data on the requirements to educate and train the new generation of health informaticists adept at understanding how to access, manage, and analyze extremely large and diverse sets of data.

OVERVIEW

Health informatics can be collectively defined as an interdisciplinary study of the design, development, adoption, and application of IT-based innovations that focuses on the generation, processing, use, and storage of health-related data. Health informaticists are individuals with the knowledge and skills required to manage health care information and data analytics. Bioinformatics, as defined by the National Institutes of Health (NIH) Big Data to Knowledge (BD2K) Initiative (http://bd2k.nih.gov/pdf/bd2k_training_workshop_report.pdf), encompasses biological, biomedical, biobehavioral, social, environmental, and clinical studies related to the understanding of health and disease. The terms *bioinformaticist* and *health informaticists* are occasionally used interchangeably; however, bioinformaticists have a greater focus on computational methods. They are closer in practice to data scientists, who have complex statistical skills usually applied to several fields. A related field is health information management, which includes both medical record administrators and health information technologists. In recent years, health information management has also expanded into the practice of health informatics.

Big data, defined by McKinsey as "datasets whose size is beyond the ability of typical database software tools to capture, store, manage, and analyze" (McKinsey Global Institute, 2011, p. 1), creates value on numerous fronts. Your website shopping habits allow merchants to discern previous preferences, thus giving them the ability to provide you with product information consistent with your purchasing habits. Even grocery stores, with their store-specific applications for smart devices, know your purchasing habits and will distribute advertisements when previously purchased items are on sale. The value of big data continues in the healthcare environment as the transparency of health care increases, providing near instantaneous and seamless access by all providers of your medical information.

Consider the implications of data stored in electronic medical records. These data provide information regarding health care practice and costs having the ability to modify practice, based on data collected, and to offer alternatives with better patient outcomes at lower costs. They also have the ability to provide institutions with information supporting their request for accreditation, licensing, and certification as well as reimbursement data to manage the health care corporation.

Big data also has the ability to reshape tomorrow's workforce—beginning today—based on the magnitude of daily generated data. It is estimated that industry will require additional new informatics positions in manufacturing (8,698 positions), Internet information systems (6,874 positions), National Security and International Affairs (6,602 positions), retail (4,873 positions), and health care (3,248 positions) (Education Advisory Board, 2013). Further estimates suggest that, by 2018, there will be a shortfall of 1.5 million data management positions (data interpretation, visualization, decision-making) and 190,000 data analytic positions (statistics, programming, modeling) (McKinsey Global Institute, 2011).

There is an urgent need to develop the current and next generation of health informaticists. The data explosion has increased the need for training programs and opportunities in the area of data science, specifically translational bioinformatics, clinical informatics, consumer health informatics, and public health informatics as defined by the American Medical Informatics Association (AMIA). This new informatics domain encourages increased understanding of health improvement through individual or collaborative, transdisciplinary teamwork to advance practice and improve patient outcomes. Doctoral-level programs, specifically doctor of philosophy (PhD), have been developed for more research-oriented individuals in the area of bioinformatics and data science. Many programs focus on computational biology, networks, advanced statistics, and modeling with a data-intense practicum to interact with large data sets.

One example of the urgent need for education and development of health informaticists is the need for standardized and consistent methods of data capture. It is essential to determine how data capture and analysis should be accomplished. The data point <age> can be captured in various formats—self-reported, birth date, month/year, month/day/year. To analyze multiple large data sets, it is important to either collect variables in a consistent manner or create compatible tags for different data sets to allow for meta-analyses. One method of standardization is the use of common data elements (CDE). A CDE is "a data element that is common to multiple data sets across different studies" (U.S. National Library of Medicine, 2013). Maximization of current and future data sets will be incumbent upon the use of CDEs as a means of verification of commonality among data points and data sets. The NIH Biomedical Informatics Committee Common Data Elements Working Group is developing methods of linking investigators to groups with existing validated CDEs (http://www.nlm.nih.gov/cde/). Such strategies are crucial for health informaticists to know, especially as the volume of data is only increasing.

Moore's Law states that over the course of computing history the processing power (transistor count) of computers and therefore that data have doubled—and may be expected to double—every two years. Figure 11.1 displays Moore's Law trajectory of development. If the y-axis was extended through 2013, the transistor count would expand to 5,200,000,000. If future development is even close to this target, there is an urgent need to develop health care informaticists to meet the needs of data utilization and management.

The need for health informaticists continues to grow. The McKinsey Global Institute Report on big data (2011) suggested that not only would we need additional 1.5 million data managers but also we would need trained individuals knowing what questions to ask of what data and who could manipulate multiple data sets to answer important health

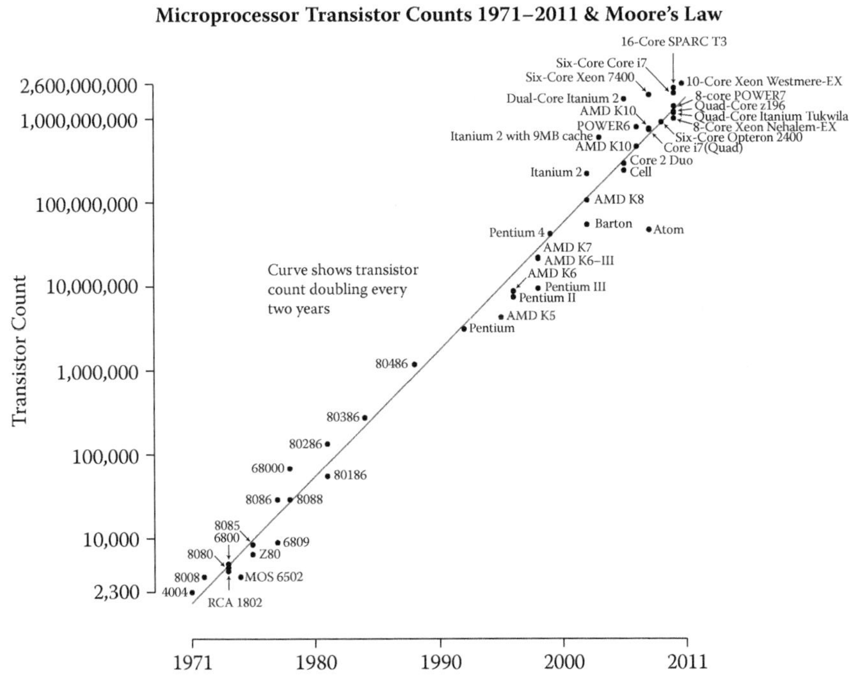

FIGURE 11.1
Moore's Law and the microprocessor, 1971–2011. Wikipedia.

care questions. These deep analytic individuals, with the expertise to mine multiple large data sets, would have the ability to develop policies that would address concerns related to data security and privacy. Jobs for the Future, in conjunction with Burning Glass Technologies, conducted a study indicating the grown of health informatics positions from 2007 to 2011 (Figure 11.2). The Education Advisory Board noted that the fastest growing positions in the United States are related to the ability to work with big data sets. Figure 11.3 provides an overview of these positions and associated experience levels. It should be noted that the degree of analytic training needed for these positions in X-2 varies from the very basic, such as medical records clerks to more sophisticated training such as clinical documentation and improvement analysts.

The following sections focus on who, how, when, and what will be required to train the next generation of health care informaticists and what standards and measures currently exist.

WHO SHOULD BE TRAINED?

Health informatics, one of the fastest growing fields within health technology, has become more than the total of all its parts. Where once it was thought that all persons interested in data collection, mining, and mathematical computation were limited to those who reviewed hospital data, today large medical reimbursement data such as found in the Centers for Medicaid and Medicare Services Virtual Research Data Center (http://www.resdac.org) or mobile and other sources are important. Currently, health informatics has expanded to include all levels of health care providers and researchers, persons with public health backgrounds, and those specifically interested in improving patient outcomes. Some refer to these two disparate areas as *quants* (those focused on quantitative research such as mathematical computation) and *quals* (those focused on qualitative research such as health care providers). One reason the quals became interested in biomedical informatics was the surge of data accumulation. Another important reason is that modifying health care practices and treatments using the gold standard of randomized controlled trials requires a lengthy time frame to get treatments from bench to bedside. The U.S. Food and Drug Administration suggests that the time required for all

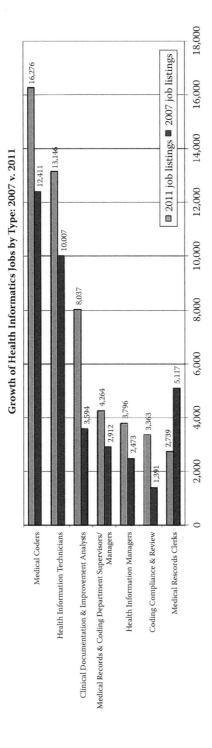

FIGURE 11.2

Growth of health informatics jobs (2007–2011). (From Jobs for the Future and Burning Glass Technologies. 2012. *A Growing Jobs Sector: Health Informatics*. Available at http://www.jff.org/sites/default/files/CTW_burning_glass_publication_052912.pdf)

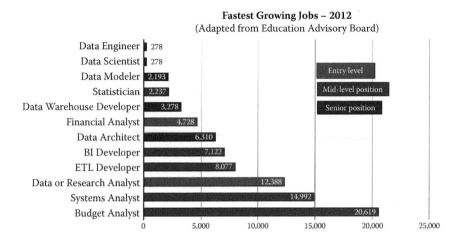

FIGURE 11.3

Fastest growing analytics jobs. (Adapted from *How Will Big Data Reshape the Workforce*, Education Advisory Board, 2013.) Fastest Growing Jobs indicates the fasted growing jobs in 2012 and the level of expertise required for each. Red indicates an entry level position; green indicates a mid-level position and blue is a senior position.

phases of drug study can be at least 12 years. Modification of indications for drug use (using an existing drug for another use) can take an additional three to five years. Researchers are showing that a more practical method of data analysis, using health care informatics and electronic medical records, can reduce the development and use time and protect patient anonymity. This was magnified as research funding levels diminished, causing researchers and health care providers to consider how they could develop alternative methods of modifying health care practices while increasing positive patient outcomes and reducing the total cost of health care.

Health informatics training is not solely for computationalists or computer experts; it is an essential part of training that should be inserted into all health care programs. Mathematical computation programs prepare individuals for careers in computer science with an emphasis on the use of the computer to mathematically solve physical problems (quants). Biobehavioral science programs prepare individuals for careers in medicine and public health with an emphasis of looking at individual behaviors and the built environment as a means of reducing physical problems (quals). The NIH BD2K Committee held workshops with expert members from government, academic, and private sectors. Members of the NIH BD2K

Workshop on Enhancing Training for Biomedical Big Data (http://bd2k.
nih.gov/pdf/bd2k_training_workshop_report.pdf) suggested that health
and biomedical informatics training should include both quantitative and
qualitative (domain specific) trainees as a means of leveraging each discipline's knowledge, thus providing a more rounded understanding of health
informatics (2013). This concept becomes more evident as health informatics course content contain computer, computational, and physiologic
coursework.

WHEN SHOULD TRAINING BEGIN?

The revised Bloom's taxonomy of learning, used by educators from pre-K
through professional, incorporates six levels of the cognitive domain:
remember (most basic; remembering taught material); *understand* (grasp-
ing meaning); *apply* (using learned material); *analyze* (break down learned
material into its basic structure); *evaluate* (understanding the value of the
learned material); and *create* (putting the learned material back together)
(Wilson, 2013). This theory presents a widely used program to classify educational competencies and curricula across the learning continuum. It provides an understanding of the steps in the learning process (Figure 11.4).

Early training of the elemental underpinnings of data and informatics
allows for the developing brain to maximize concept familiarity and
understanding. In adolescents, the brain experiences stages of *prun-
ing* and *strengthening*: neural connections that are not frequently used
are pruned, whereas those that are frequently used are strengthened.
Introducing basic human anatomy and physiology, informatics, and the
study of data during adolescence allows for neural connections associated
with thought processes required to understand and manage data to be
strengthened. Providing a basic foundation for further development of
processes required for informatics will allow for an easier transition to
future, more advanced processes.

Education at the baccalaureate level assists in solidifying and expanding processes learned earlier. The baccalaureate level provides additional
training in health data management, information systems, health care
information regulations and standards, data security, statistics, biomedical
research, software, and database construction and use. It also provides concepts of health services organization, ethics, confidentiality, and privacy.

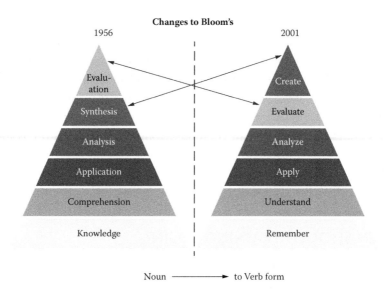

FIGURE 11.4
Revision of Bloom's taxonomy (Wilson, 2013).

This level of education would encourage individuals seeking to work in health care information systems management and maintenance, health care finance, and health practice areas.

The master's level of education continues to build on Bloom's taxonomy by reinforcing and expanding previously learned information. It builds upon baccalaureate education by expanding knowledge of information systems, analysis, design, and implementation. Increased emphasis is placed on informatics structure, function, and sociotechnical aspects of health computing and workflow processes. In addition, higher levels of computer networks, database development and systems administration and programming are added. Master's-prepared individuals may be in positions such as chief information officer, consultant, analyst, and program manager.

EDUCATION AND TRAINING METHODS

The type or level of education and training is predicated by student needs, previous education, learning style, and resources. Current and future personnel requirements for health care informaticists spurred the need to increase training and education methods. The type and level of training has been evolving and reflects levels of responsibilities. Experts, one of whom—Karen Bandeen-Roche—wrote the preface for the current book, at the NIH BD2K Workshop on Enhancing Training for Biomedical Big Data had lengthy discussions surrounding the type of educational scope of various informaticists. They agreed that there is no single best method of conducting education and training in this area but provided suggestions to educators. Suggestions included using an interdisciplinary team approach, providing practical training in addition to didactics enhancing the student's introduction to large data sets, knowledge of research design and methods to understand how to query large data sets for responses to specific questions, and have realistic goals and expectations of the data and individuals used in accessing it.

The interconnectivity of the Internet has increased the ability to meet the training demands of a greater number of students. Education and training programs are provided in multiple formats such as classroom, online, and hybrid combinations, which allow for increased access to education.

Nondegree Training

Certificate programs in health informatics are available for both postbaccalaureate and post–master's-level students. These programs generally require that a prospective student has successfully graduated their program with at least a 3.0 grade point average (GPA). Postbaccalaureate informatics certificates are designed for individuals with a computer science undergraduate degree. They require at least 36 credit hours that include courses in advanced mathematics, computer science, database structure, and systems. Students must maintain an acceptable GPA during the program with course completion within two years. Certificate programs also can focus on a specific area of health informatics.

Post–master's informatics certificates have greater rigor but also vary more than postbaccalaureate programs. The post–master's programs are designed for individuals wishing to work in public health, health policy, or quality of health care services. Each program describes their basic entry criteria. Some programs allow for either postbaccalaureate or master's degree, while others mandate conference of a master's degree but not all schools require that degree to be in computer science. Course credit hours vary as well, ranging from 15 to 40 credit hours half in core curriculum courses and half in computer science electives. Core courses, similar to the postbaccalaureate programs, include foundational courses in health informatics, information systems, and in some cases a technical practicum. Electives are varied based on student needs.

Massive open online courses (MOOCs) have been utilized as a means of reaching large numbers of students in both certificate and degree programs. They have been used by universities to reach large numbers of students who otherwise would not have the ability to attend college programs. However, they have also come under scrutiny since they present challenges in terms of monitoring and evaluating a student's success and completion. *Scilogs*, a scientific and medical library run by *Nature*, wrote an in-depth review of MOOCs providing pro and con reviews of this form of education noting that it opens education to the world—but does the world want to sit in a 160,000 student classroom (Bohle, 2013)?

Degree Programs

Education in health informatics is offered at the associate, baccalaureate, master's, and doctoral level. Degree courses may vary based on their focus (e.g., health informatics, health information management, health information technologies). Most programs require basic health care or public health courses in addition to informatics courses. Associate degrees generally offered by community colleges are two-year programs involving 60 credit hours. Baccalaureate programs require 120 credit hours over an average of four years. Master's-level programs range from 30 to 40 credit hours over a one- to three-year period. These programs allow for tailored structuring for individual student needs. Courses focus on more advanced level of informatics and statistics. Doctoral-level degree programs are tailored to the student and include areas such as bioinformatics, data science, and health informatics. These programs are research focused generally aimed at population or patient-based technologies and personalized medicine. Requirements and focus vary based on the academic institution.

Training Requirements

Colleges and universities are required to have credentialing to assure they meet nationally accepted standards, have the ability for program evaluation, and assure the reputability of the institution. Understanding the level and type of accreditation is important to program evaluation.

ACCREDITATION

Accreditation, or the assurance of meeting suitable standards, is applied to institutions of higher learning and individuals. The goal of institutional accreditation is the assurance the programmatic education meets quality standards. The U.S. Department of Education (2013), while not accrediting institutions, is required to provide a list of all colleges, universities, and institutions of higher learning.

Specialty and professional associations also provide accreditation within their respective areas. Examples of these specialty/professional associations are Colleges, the American Medical Informatics Association (AMIA) (http://www.amia.org/), the American Health Information Management Association (AHIMA) (http://www.ahima.org), the Health Information and Management Systems Society (HIMSS) (http://www.himss.org/), the American Society of Health Information Management (ASHIM) (http://www.ashim.org/), the American Nurses Association (ANA) (http://www.nursingworld.org/), and the American Medical Association (AMA) (http://www.ama-assn.org/ama).

CAHIIM

CAHIIM provides guidance and accreditation for associate, baccalaureate, and master's-level academic programs in health information management and graduate health care informatics. Students should understand the association of responsibilities to degree level when considering career choices. This guidance provides the requirements for program accreditation. Table 11.1 provides information related to curricula domains required for each level of education. These domains define the content of the degree programs previously discussed. They provide an ideal curriculum that focuses on data manipulation, medical terminology, clinical processes, and statistics. Each level indicates the increasing complexity as individuals' progress from the associate to the master's degree. The domain is further divided into curricula components the specify domain objectives. AMIA is currently in discussion for extending their accreditation to the types of informatics programs that are more technical and are of the types described earlier.

Many universities are now including doctor of philosophy (PhD) programs in biomedical informatics. Most programs require 64 academic credits that include some core courses but are individually developed to incorporate the student's areas of expertise and research course.

TABLE 11.1

Academic Education Programs for Healthcare Informatics adapted from Commission for Accreditation of Health Information and Information Management Programs www.cahiim.org/policiescurriculum.html

Associate's Level

  I. Health Data Management
  II. Health Statistics, Biomedical Research, and Quality Management
  III. Health Services Organization and Delivery
  IV. Information Technology & Systems
  V. Organizational Resources
Other: Anatomy, Physiology, Medical Terminology, Pathophysiology, Pharmacotherapy

Baccalaureate Level

  I. Health Data Management
  II. Health Statistics, Biomedical Research, and Quality Management
  III. Health Services Organization and Delivery
  IV. Information Technology and Systems
  V. Organization and Management
Other: Anatomy, Physiology, Medical Terminology, Pathophysiology, Pharmacotherapy

Master's Level—Health Informatics

Facet I. Information Systems—concerned with issues such as information systems analysis, design, implementation, and management
Facet II: Informatics—concerned with structure, function, transfer, sociotechnical aspects of health computing, and human-computer interaction
Facet III: Information technology—concerned with computer networks, database and systems administration, security and programming
Other: Biomedical sciences, Quantitative, Qualitative and Mixed methods, Epidemiology

Master's Level - Health Information Management
Domain I. Health Data Management
Domain II. Information Technology and Systems
Domain III. Organization and Management

Individual Certification

AHIMA provides for competency certification for professionals wishing to practice health information management (not necessarily health informatics) through the Commission on Certification for Health Informatics and Information Management (CCHIIM). The CCHIIM is composed of a 15-member board that establishes, implements, and enforces standard certification and recertification procedures. Eight certifications are conferred based on academic and experience eligibility and successfully passing the certification examination. The certifications are identified in Table 11.2. One of these certifications is health data analyst. It requires basic

TABLE 11.2

Commission on Certification for Health Informatics and Information Management (CCHIIM) Certifications. From: http://www.ahima.org/certification/cchiim

Title	Certification
RHIA	Registered Health Information Administrator
RHIT	Registered Health Information Technician
CHDA	Certified Health Data Analyst
CHPS	Certified in Healthcare Privacy and Security
CHTS	Certified Healthcare Technology Specialist
CCA	Certified Coding Associate
CCS	Certified Coding Specialist
CCS-P	Certified Coding Specialist–Physician-Based

statistical and health information expertise and experience. Certification provides assurance to colleagues and employers that the individual health information professional possesses the appropriate skills to perform at a functional level indicated by the type of certification. AHMA is also considering a health informatics certification.

HIMSS provides two levels of certification. Certified professional in health information systems (CPHIS) stresses the technology aspects of health data rather than analysis. This certification would be applicable for individuals with five or more years of health information experience. HIMSS developed the certified associate in health information systems, a new certification for less experienced individuals. This certification would be for entry-level persons and would serve as a pathway for CPHIS certification.

ANA provides certification for registered nurses interested in informatics specialization. Certification requirements include licensure as a registered nurse with a baccalaureate degree or higher, two years of nursing experience, 30 hours of continuing education in informatics in nursing within three years, and one of the following: (1) 2,000 hours of nursing informatics practice within three years; (2) 1,000 hours of nursing informatics practice *and* at least 12 credit hours in a graduate nursing informatics program; or (3) completion of a graduate program for nursing informatics containing 200 hours of faculty-supervised informatics practicum. Nurse informaticists are supported by the American Nursing Informaticists Association (ANIA) (https://www.ania.org/).

The American Board of Medical Specialties in 2011 approved a board subspecialty certification in clinical informatics, applicable only to MDs with a prior or concurrent primary board certification (e.g., internal medicine, radiology). The first annual certification exam was held in October 2013. By 2018, to sit for the exam candidates will have to have been trained for at least two years in an accredited program. The Accreditation Council for Graduate Medical Education published in 2013 (with modifications in 2014) the conditions for accreditation of subspecialty training programs.

Health Informatics Core Competencies

Core competencies are the combination of pooled knowledge and technical expertise that are fundamental to the performance of duty in a specified area. They articulate an individual's proficiency in the knowledge and conduct of specific tasks associated with a distinct area. AMIA developed criteria/competencies for graduate education in medical informatics (Kulikowski et al., 2012). These competencies focus on fundamental scientific skills, scope and breadth of discipline, theory and methodology, technological approach, and human and social context. Each competency further articulates subsections required by individuals embarking on a health care informatics career (Kulikowski et al., 2012). Further competencies, unique to the position of nursing leaders, have been developed to assure that roles and functions of nursing leaders included specific computer skills, knowledge, and expertise (Westra et al., 2008).

CONCLUSION

The digitization of health care data has been ongoing for more than a decade. Pharmaceutical and other organizations are aggregating databases to facilitate the flow of information. Federal and state governments continue to work to provide greater access to databases and data sets. The mushrooming of health-related data continues to grow at an unbelievable rate. While digitization efforts assist in collecting health care data continued modification, curation, and access to these data are imperative to predict health care trends, modify health care practices, and reduce health care costs. Health care informaticists play an important part of this process. Education and training of this group should begin early, should be inclusive of quants and quals, and should include interdisciplinary participants to assist in making knowledge and evidence-based decisions for individuals and health care corporations. The field of health informatics is changing and training will evolve to meet its needs.

REFERENCES

Bohle, S. 2013. Librarians and the era of the MOOC. *Scilogs.* Available at http://www.scilogs.com/scientific_and_medical_libraries/librarians-and-the-era-of-the-mooc/

Data to Knowledge to Action: Fact Sheet. 2013. Available at http://www.whitehouse.gov/sites/default/files/microsites/ostp/Data2Action%20Agency%20Progress.pdf

Jobs for the Future and Burning Glass Technologies. 2012. *A Growing Jobs Sector: Health Informatics.* Available at http://www.jff.org/sites/default/files/CTW_burning_glass_publication_052912.pdf

Krathwohl, D. R. 2002. A Revison of Bloom's Taxonomy: An Overview. *Theory into Practice* 41(4): 212–218.

Malin, B., K. Benitez, and D. Masys. 2011. Never Too Old for Anonymity: A Statistical Standard for Demographic Data Sharing via the HIPAA Privacy Rule. *Journal of the American Medical Information Association* 18(1): 3–10.

McCarty, C.A., R.L. Chisholm, C.G. Chute, I.J. Kullo, G.P. Jarvik, E.B. Larson, R. Li, D.R. Masys, D.M. Roden, J.P. Struewing, W.A. Wolf, and the eMERGE Team. 2011. A Consortium of Biorepositories Linked to Electronic Medical Records Data for Conducting Genomic Studies. *BMC Med Genomics* 4: 1–13.

McKinsey Global Institute. 2011. *Big Data: The Next Frontier for Innovation, Competition, and Productivity.* Available at http://www.mckinsey.com/mgi

National Institutes of Health (NIH). 2013. *Workshop on Enhancing Training for Biomedical Big Data.*

Spragg, R.G., D.R. Masys, D. Sergeant, T. Lawrie, and F.J. Taut. 2010. An Informatics Strategy to Assure Enrollment Criteria Compliance in Studies of the Critically Ill. *Contemporary Clinical Trials* 31: 530–535.

U.S. Department of Education. 2013. The Database of Accredited Postsecondary Institutions and Programs. Available at http://ope.ed.gov/accreditation/

U.S. National Library of Medicine. 2013. NIH. Available at http://www.nlm.nih.gov/cde/glossary.html

Wilson, L.O. 2013. The Second Principle. Available at http://thesecondprinciple.com/teaching-essentials/beyond-bloom-cognitive-taxonomy-revised/

Section III

12

Interactive Visualization

Catherine Plaisant, Megan Monroc,
Tamra Meyer, and Ben Shneiderman

CONTENTS

OBJECTIVES

After reading this chapter, the reader shall be able to:

- Describe uses of information visualization in health and health care
- Evaluate components of successful information visualization interfaces
- Explain how information visualization can be used to detect patterns of health care
- Articulate the balance between displaying as much information as possible while maintaining simplicity

---

ABSTRACT

This chapter focuses on the central role of information visualization in health analytics. From the early x-rays to 3D volume visualizations, rapid progress has been made. However, the most exciting growth is now in the area of information visualization, which offers interactive environments and analytic processes that help support exploration of electronic health record (EHR) data, monitoring, or insight discovery. For example, a health organization might want to investigate patterns of drug prescriptions in patients with asthma and compare prescribing practices with current guidelines. Temporal patterns are critical to this analysis, and interactive visualizations are beginning to support powerful temporal queries, present rich result summaries, and offer fluid interactions to identify the clinically relevant patterns hidden in the data. Visualization should soon help clinicians identify cohorts of patients who match selection criteria for clinical trials or need to be brought back to the office. Visualization can also reveal data quality problems, which are common when repurposing clinical data for secondary analysis. After a quick summary of the state-of-the-art of information visualization systems for exploring and querying EHR data, we describe in detail one recent system (EventFlow) developed by the Human-Computer Interaction Lab at the University of Maryland and illustrate its use with an asthma prescription study example.

INTRODUCTION

Visual analytics is the science of analytical reasoning facilitated by interactive visual interfaces (Kielman and Thomas, 2009; Ward, Grinstein, and Keim, 2010). Visual analytics tools often combine multiple components such as analytical reasoning, data representations, human–computer interactions, and tools for collaboration and for communicating the results of the analysis. Information visualization can be defined as the use of computer-supported interactive visual representation of abstract data to amplify cognition (Card et al., 1999). It aims to visualize and manipulate large numbers of items (10_5–10_{10}), possibly extracted or aggregated from far larger data sets or brought to the attention of users by analytics algorithms. It uses the enormous visual bandwidth and the remarkable human visual system to enable clinical researchers, epidemiologists, policy makers, and even clinicians and patients to make discoveries, make decisions, or propose explanations. While visualization tools are becoming available, the field is still in its infancy. In particular, the U.S. Institute for Medicine's 2011 Report (IOM, 2011) noted that "information visualization is not as advanced in parts of clinical medicine as compared with other scientific disciplines."

After a quick overview of the range of opportunities for the use of information visualization in health informatics, we describe in detail one example of a state-of-the-art visualization system—EventFlow—and illustrate its use with a case study of patterns of asthma drug prescriptions. EventFlow is a project of the Human-Computer Interaction Lab at the University of Maryland, College Park. The lab has a long history of transforming the experience people have with new technologies. From understanding user needs to developing and evaluating those technologies, the lab's faculty, staff, and students have been leaders in developing innovative technology, in particular in the area of information visualization.

MANY OPPORTUNITIES

While medical imagery based on x-rays, computed tomography (CT) scans, and magnetic resonance imaging (MRI) transformed medical care early on by providing 3D volume visualizations, commercial visualization tools such as Spotfire (http://www.spotfire.com) are now routinely used for pharmaceutical drug discovery, genomic expression analyses, and other applications (Figure 12.1). Researchers are actively developing novel techniques and strategies using information visualization to harness the benefits of health informatics databases and networks (e.g., Faisal, Blandford, and Potts, 2013; Rind et al., 2013). Many technologies need substantial advances to produce reliable, effective, safe, and validated systems, but the potential societal benefits are enormous. Shneiderman et al. (2013) describe the state-of-the-art of interactive visualization within three domains of health informatics (clinical, personal, and public health) and then give seven challenges to researchers. Examples of promising applications of visualization abound. Figure 12.1 provides one example.

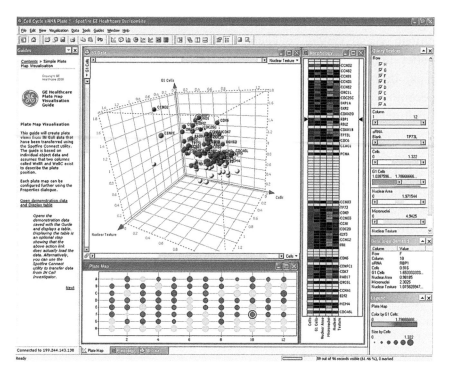

FIGURE 12.1

Using Spotfire, analysts revealed the previously unknown involvement of the retinol binding protein RBP1 in cell cycle control. (From: S. Stubbs and N. Thomas, *Methods in Enzymology*, 414:1–21, 2006.)

In the area of personal health information, personal sensors are becoming popular. Products such as Fitbit (http://fitbit.com) collect movement data, and the associated website shows retrospective temporal patterns of activity, sleep, or diet with timelines that help users reflect on their behaviors. The PatientsLikeMe website has an openness philosophy and encourages members to report in great detail on their status, treatments, and side effects for more than a thousand conditions. It then presents visual summaries of the aggregated data to the public (Figure 12.2).

In the area of public health information, visualization provides novel opportunities to present the huge volume of information collected by government organizations in compelling ways. Interactive tools can help analysts spot patterns and issues, while visual presentation of the results can guide policy makers. For example, the University of Washington's Institute for Health Metrics and Evaluation has developed a revealing

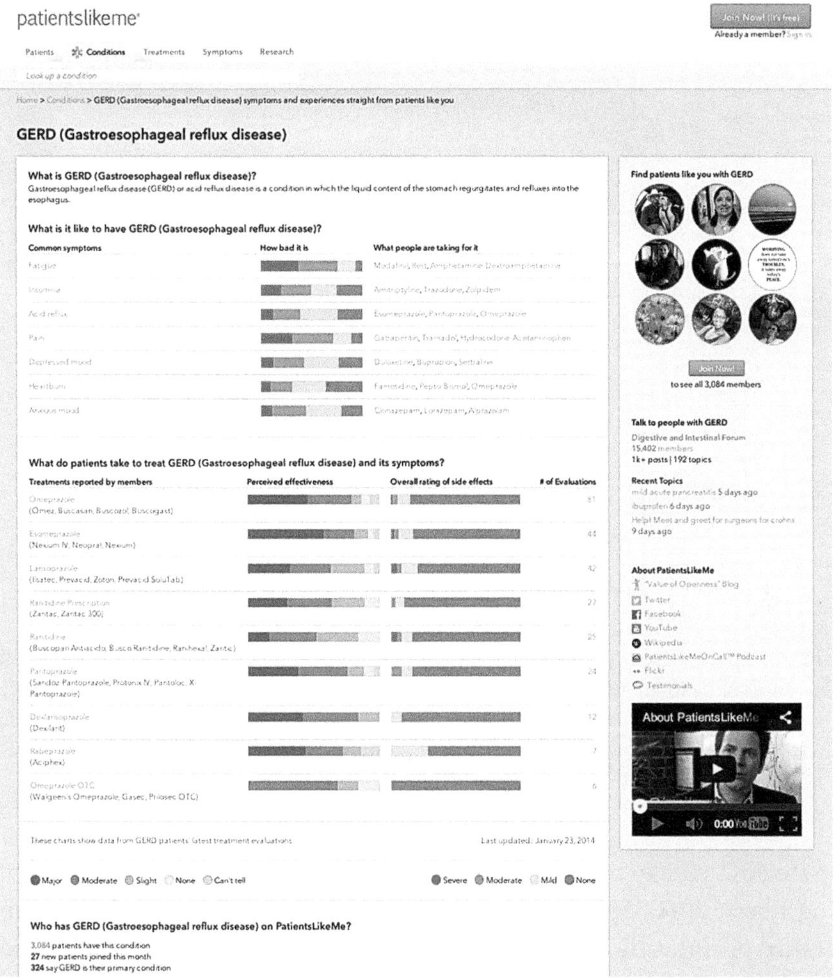

FIGURE 12.2

A PatientsLikeMe summary on gastroesophageal reflux disease (GERD) based on reports from more than 3,000 participants. (From: http://www.patientslikeme.com/conditions/78.)

visualization tool, GBD Compare, based on the global burden of disease (GBD). GBD Compare makes good use of treemaps to enable users to explore causes of death and their impact worldwide (Figure 12.3). Controlling the spread of new infectious diseases or responding to biological attacks is also an opportunity for visual analytics solutions.

Coupled with models of disease spread, visualizations are starting to help decision-makers predict the future course of the outbreak and to evaluate

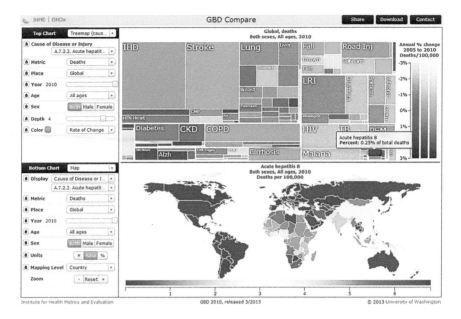

FIGURE 12.3

GBD Compare, based on the global burden of disease. At the top, a tree map shows all the causes of deaths. The size of the box is proportional to the number of deaths, and the shading indicates the changes over time (light for improving, dark for worsening). The acute hepatitis is selected, and the bottom map shows where the problem is most prevalent. (From: http://viz.healthmetricsandevaluation.org/gbd-compare/)

strategies that can be applied to control an epidemic (Afzal, Macicjewski, and Ebert, 2011). Syndromic surveillance is an important new function desired of clinically sourced systems. The Centers for Disease Control and Prevention (CDC) defines this function as "an investigational approach where health department staff, assisted by automated data acquisition and generation of statistical alerts, monitor disease indicators in real-time or near real-time to detect outbreaks of disease earlier than would otherwise be possible with traditional public health methods" (2004). Improved syndromic surveillance includes the analysis of over the counter drug sales. Data from social media is especially interesting for public health analysts (Christakis and Fowler, 2011). Clustering algorithms can sort out the active communities of discussions, and network analysis metrics help to detect key influencers (Hansen, Shneiderman, and Smith, 2010; Hesse et al., 2010) (Figure 12.4).

Finally, in the area of clinical health information Rind et al. (2013) make a survey of interactive visualization to explore and query electronic

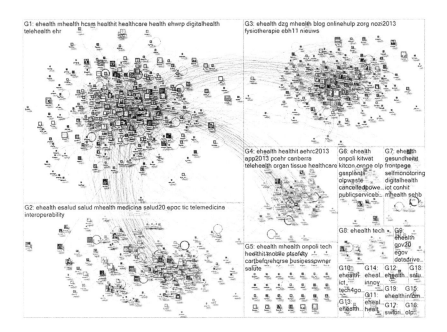

FIGURE 12.4

NodeXL (http://www.codeplex.com/nodexl) graph of 695 Twitter users whose recent tweets contained "#ehealth." Each of the 6,177 edges corresponds to a "follows," "replies-to," or "mention" relationship between those users. Users can scan representative keywords for each cluster, the most active tweeters, the URLs mentioned the most often, etc. The largest cluster is placed at the top left. It is in English—with mostly American Twitter users. Its focus is on digital health and EHRs. The second largest in the lower left corner is mainly for Spanish tweets. The top right is a large network of mostly Dutch tweets. Those two clusters are well connected to the U.S. group but less so to each other. (Courtesy Marc Smith.)

health records. Visual temporal summaries of single-patient visual histories have been inspired by the early Lifelines prototype (Plaisant et al., 1998) (Figure 12.5), as are body maps showing the location of previous and current conditions, surgeries, or injuries, but no strategy has emerged to be widely accepted. While clinical trials remain the work horse of clinical research, there is now a shift toward the use of existing clinical data for discovery research, leading researchers to analyze large warehouses of patient histories (e.g., http://btris.nih.gov). Visualization can reveal data quality problems, which are common when reusing data created for other purposes. Temporal patterns are critical to this research, so novel visualizations now support powerful graphical temporal queries and summarization of clinically relevant temporal patterns hidden in the data (Monroe and del Olmo, 2013). Visualizations can also help

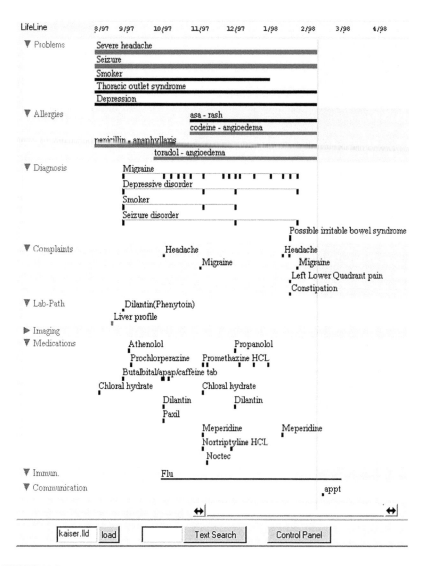

FIGURE 12.5

The Lifelines prototype shows a timeline summary of one patient. Users can zoom in and out or click on any graphic element to reveal more details. (Plaisant et al., 1998.)

clinicians identify cohorts of patients who match selection criteria for clinical trials (e.g., using http://i2b2.org).

After this quick review of the many opportunities for information visualization in health informatics we will focus on a detailed description of one example tool, EventFlow, and will then illustrate the use of EventFlow in the study of patterns of asthma drug prescriptions.

EVENTFLOW FOR TEMPORAL SEQUENCE ANALYSIS OF EHR DATA

EventFlow (http://www.cs.umd.edu/hcil/eventflow) builds on the past research by the Human Computer Interaction Laboratory (HCIL) on the visualization of temporal sequences of point events (i.e., events with a single time stamp), including LifeLines2 (Wang et al., 2009), and LifeFlow (Wongsuphasawat et al., 2011). With LifeLines2, researchers used event operators (align, rank, filter, and group by) to specify queries on point event data. This early effort focused on searches for patterns specified by users, for example, "Find all the patients who bounce back to the ICU within 24 hours of leaving the ICU," or "Find patients with high creatinine readings within 14 days of the administration of radiographic contrast materials" (in an effort to find patients who experienced reduced renal function after infusion of contrast materials). Our research showed that such temporal queries require users to refine their queries iteratively after seeing the results (e.g., by seeing the results they immediately realized that they needed to remove patients with too many creatinine highs before the contrast—as they probably had chronic renal failure—or that they needed to remove patients without normal readings before the contrast). See video demonstrations at http://www.cs.umd.edu/hcil/lifelines2.

The next step was to provide compact visual summaries of all sequences found in the data (Wongsuphasawat et al., 2011). This breakthrough technique allows users to explore questions such as, "What happens to patients after they leave the emergency room?" or, combined with the align operator, "What happens before and after patients are admitted to the ICU?"

While those tools have been successfully used by clinical researchers and quality assurance administrators to answer many questions, they operated only on point event data (e.g., diagnoses, orders, admission) and therefore had no notion of episodes, partial or complete overlaps, or gaps between events. EventFlow introduces the ability to interactively search and visualize interval data, which is an important step forward. Intervals, such as uninterrupted periods of medication use or episodes of disease, are a central aspect of the analysis of medication use.

In a broader context, temporal database storage, retrieval, interpretation, analysis, and visualization constitute a huge set of research topics. Still, the relational database model can be too limiting for many temporal queries. Extensions such as Temporal Structured Query Language (SQL/Temporal), and other temporal database query languages solve some problems, but the semantics of meaningful temporal queries is difficult or impossible to express in these temporal languages and logics, especially in the presence of interval events. Data-mining strategies that can extract common patterns in baskets of items have been cleverly extended to deal with categorical sequences. However, when events in a sequence have different amounts of time between them, data-mining approaches become difficult to apply, leading researchers to adopt more selective approaches that include interestingness measures that often puzzle end users.

EVENTFLOW INTERFACE

The interface of EventFlow consists of three main components: interactive including controls, legend, overview, and timeline (Figure 12.6).

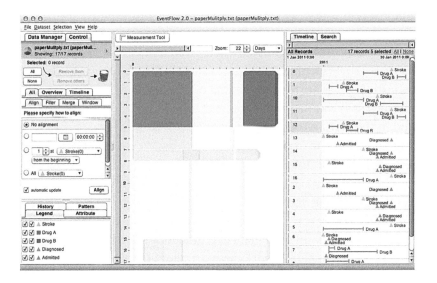

FIGURE 12.6
The EventFlow interactive analysis tool (http://www.cs.umd.edu/hcil/eventflow) with a small sample data set. On the left are found controls and legend, in the middle is the overview of all sequence patterns in the data set, and on the right is a scrollable timeline browser showing all the individual records. The top sequence in the overview is selected (drug A, followed by stroke, followed by drug B). The distance between event bars corresponds to the average time between events. The height of the bar corresponds to the proportion of records with that sequence. The records with the selected sequence are highlighted at the top in the timeline view.

Individual Records

On the right the timeline shows details of individual records; each patient is shown on a separate timeline. Triangle icons represent point events, whereas line segments represent intervals (and condense to a single rectangle when the interval duration is small). The legend shows all event categories, enabling users to change the color and order of the categories. Figure 12.6 shows only patients 0–16, forcing users to scroll to see all patients.

Overview of Sequences

In the center, the overview aggregates all records with the same sequence of events into a single bar. This method was first introduced in LifeFlow (Wongsuphasawat et al., 2011) and has now been extended to interval data in EventFlow. The height of a bar is determined by the number of records in the group, and the horizontal gap between events is proportional to the mean time between the two events among the records in the group. Users can select other metrics such as the median, and the distribution of values is overlaid on the display when the cursor hovers over a time gap element. Multiple interval events can occur concurrently, and EventFlow handles this occurrence by rendering overlapping intervals using the combined color of the two overlapping categories. Colors selected for interval categories default to primary colors, resulting in intuitive overlap colors. For example, when a red interval intersects a blue interval, the resulting overlap is purple. When two intervals of the same category intersect, the color saturation is increased. While this technique works best when limited to a small number of event categories (i.e., colors) our experience suggests that being able to see overlaps of just two or three event categories is already an important improvement over existing techniques for many users.

The two views (overview and timeline) are coupled so that when users select an event sequence (i.e., bar) all records with that sequence are selected on the timeline view (shown in light gray column to left of 2011 in Figure 12.6) and moved to the top of the timeline. Similarly, selecting a record on the right will highlight the corresponding event in the summary. The legend allows users to select or deselect which event categories they want to display on the overview or the timeline. After selecting records users can also remove either the selected or unselected records from the display. These two simple techniques allow users to easily narrow the focus of an analysis on records exhibiting particular event sequences of interest.

Search

EventFlow includes two separate search interfaces. The basic menu-based search interface gives users easy access to either before and after relationships (Subsequence module) or during relationships (Overlap module). The Advanced Search allows users to specify more complex temporal features such as absolute time constraints and absence of events scenarios (Monroe and del Olmo, 2013). The advanced search interface uses a visual query language to draw the desired sequence of event relationships. Matching records are selected in the timeline display and moved to the top, while those that do not match remain at the bottom. This allows users to quickly see not only the records that match their query but also records that did not match so they can check that the search behaved as expected (see Figure 12.8 in next section.).

A set of simplification operations allows users to focus on patterns of interest (Monroe, Lee et al., 2013), for example by selecting event categories or applying search-and-replace operations.

Finally, the control panel gives access to many more powerful operators to zoom and filter, rank and cluster the records, adjust parameters of the views, and manage data sets.

CASE STUDY: PATTERNS OF PRESCRIPTIONS OF ASTHMA MEDICATIONS

A case study was conducted with the U.S. Army, Office of the Surgeon General, Pharmacovigilance Center, where an epidemiologist worked with the EventFlow developers to understand the prescribing patterns of asthma medications. A particular question of interest was whether a type of asthma medication—long-acting beta-agonists (LABAs)—was being correctly prescribed according to guidelines. Visualizing the temporal patterns of asthma medication use surrounding a LABA prescription with EventFlow was a quick way to detect possible suboptimal use. The ultimate goal of the study was to understand LABA use to inform interventions to prevent morbidity and mortality from suboptimal use.

In layman's terms, the National Asthma Education and Prevention Program clinical guidelines for the diagnosis and management of asthma (NAEPP 2007) and safety alerts published by FDA (2010a, 2010b) recommend that LABAs should be prescribed only in combination with a particular other medication (a long-term asthma controller medication) and be used only after the use of other drugs have failed. Similarly, the guidelines recommend that LABA therapy should be deescalated once asthma has been adequately controlled. In other words, we were looking for the proportion of LABA used concomitantly with appropriate other therapies and escalation/deescalation patterns. For more information on the guidelines and overall study, please see Meyer et al. (2013).

The epidemiologist selected a sample of 100 asthma patients, extracted all of their asthma medication prescriptions for the 365 days surrounding a LABA prescription, and categorized the asthma medications into groups. The file included for each prescription a deidentified patient identifier, the type of asthma medication, the start date of the prescription, and the end date of the prescription derived from the start date plus days supply of the prescription. Figure 12.7 shows what it looked like when first

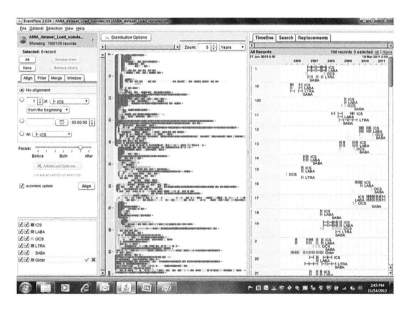

FIGURE 12.7
Initial EventFlow overview of 100 patients' prescription records. LABAs are shown in bright red, ICS is dark (and supposed to always overlap with LABA), while the other drugs that should be prescribed before and after the LABA therapies are shown in other colors (light blue, pink or yellow).

loaded in EventFlow. The color legend in the lower left corner indicates that LABAs appear as bright red intervals, inhaled corticosteroids (ICS; supposed to overlap with the LABA prescriptions) are blue, while the other drugs that should be prescribed before and after the LABA therapies are shown in other colors (i.e., light blue for oral corticosteroid bursts [OCS], pink for leukotriene receptor antagonists [LTRA], yellow for short-acting beta-agonists [SABA], and orange for other older drugs).

At first the display appeared very busy and did not reveal clear patterns, but we could immediately see that most of the patients had more than one LABA prescription. To compare with the guidelines, we needed to find the "new" LABA prescriptions, which are defined in simple terms as "new LABA prescriptions for patients who did not have a LABA in the previous 90 days." EventFlow graphical Search and Replace feature was found to be very helpful for that (see Figure 12.8). By using menu selections we placed the set of events and constraints on the search control panel to specify the search pattern (i.e., a red LABA interval, followed by no LABA for at least 90 days, then another red LABA interval.) and then specified that a new type of event be created ("Index LABA," colored black) and that this event be inserted at the time of the start of the second interval. After the insertion was completed we realized, by looking at the visualization, that we had forgotten the cases where patients had never

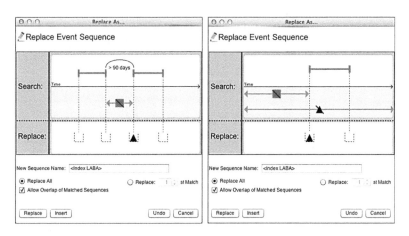

FIGURE 12.8

EventFlow advanced search interface. Using menus to select event type and control panels to set constraints users specify search patterns. For example, on the left the search pattern is to be a red LABA interval, followed by no LABA for at least 90 days, then another dark gray LABA interval. If needed users specify what the pattern should be replaced by, here a black "index LABA" event.

had a LABA before, so we repeated the search and replace with a second pattern (Figure 12.8, right side).

The search results separate the records that match the search pattern from those that do not match. Because we were able to quickly and visually inspect the nonmatches we could see that several patients had a LABA more than 90 days but less than a year before the index LABA, suggesting that using a longer "washout" period (i.e., period without LABA) may be useful in future analyses. Still, we decided to stick with the 90-day washout period because washing out for 365 days resulted in similar patients included.

Next, since we wanted to examine patterns surrounding the index LABA we used the powerful alignment tool in EventFlow to align all records by the time of the index LABA prescription (Figure 12.9).

We showed this display to specialists in asthma treatment, and they were immediately able to pick out troubling patterns of asthma treatment. For example, patients with a lot of yellow and light blue should most likely have been targeted for earlier step-up to a LABA. Patients with a lot of light blue or yellow after the LABA may need to be brought in for evaluation for continued LABA or other medications.

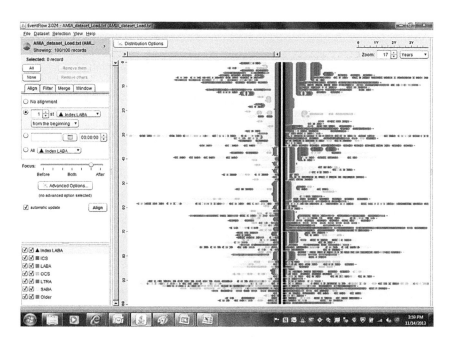

FIGURE 12.9
All records are now aligned by the black event "New LABA."

Next we wanted to check that the red LABAs were not prescribed without a blue ICS, so we started by searching for prescriptions of LABA that occurred at the same time as a prescription for an ICS. Then we decided to replace all the overlapping red and blue intervals with one brown LABA + ICS interval to more easily be able to find the remaining LABA prescriptions that did not fit the search criteria. This simplified the display so we could see that very few red LABAs were left. Looking at the detail timeline view of individual records we could review those exceptions. For example, one remaining red LABA was a patient with a LABA prescription that occurred during a longer ICS prescription, so that was still according to treatment guidelines.

Another way we could simplify the display and focus on the prescriptions immediately preceding and following the LABA was to set a time window of three months on either side of the alignment point (Figure 12.10). This really highlighted the LABAs that were prescribed without the appropriate step-up and step-down therapy. For example, we could see patients that were given only one LABA with no other asthma therapy before or after. A possible follow-up investigation would be to see if the LABAs were being prescribed for something other than asthma like an episode of bronchitis, flu, or cold.

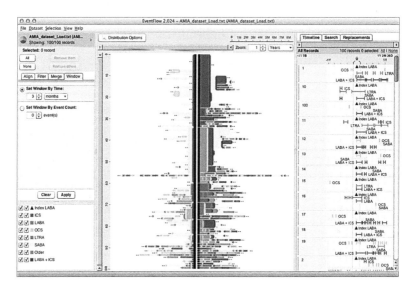

FIGURE 12.10

Setting a windowing limit of three months on each side of the Index LABA reduces the number of patterns and leads to a simplified display. On the right we can also see the detailed view, which allows users to review abnormal patterns.

We then used several search and replace steps to find patients that had appropriate step-up and step-down therapy. First, we looked for patients who had a blue ICS before and after their index LABA. That resulted in six selected patients. Then we found patients who were taking a pink LTRA before and after the LABA. The LABA could have been started during an existing pink LTRA event (Figure 12.11) or with prescriptions for LTRA before and after the index LABA. At the end we found the 27 of 100 patients that appear to have been treated according to treatment guidelines based on prescription patterns of step-up and step-down therapy.

We could remove those patients from the display and inspect the remaining 73 patients who may not have been treated according to treatment guidelines. We could see that this group still had some patterns that appear to be according to guidelines. The ones with multiple yellow SABA before the LABA or the light blue OCS before the LABA may indicate a severe asthma exacerbation that was appropriately treated with a LABA. There were also blue ICS before the LABA that switched to pink LTRA after the LABA. We were able to go back and add that pattern to our search

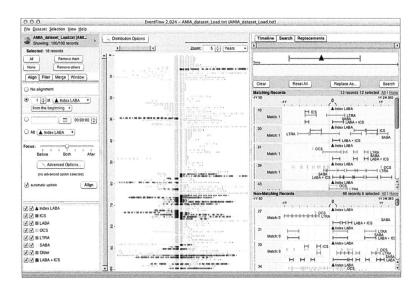

FIGURE 12.11

Find Patients with pink LTRA before and after Index LABA. On the right we see the search panel. On the top right is the pattern being searched, below it are the records that match the pattern (also highlighted on the overview in the center of the screen), and further below the records that do not match the pattern.

of appropriate treatment patterns. Of course other patients could also have been appropriately treated, but such analysis would require a full review of the clinical notes.

Because the exploration was done on a sample of 100 patients, to confirm these exploratory findings the entire patient population was evaluated using traditional SQL and SAS queries based on the queries that had been found useful during the rapid interactive exploration. These analyses supported the exploratory results. The epidemiologists and clinicians commented that the interface was much easier to learn and use than the command-based, statistical software that they normally employ. Furthermore, these command-based languages offered no way of reviewing the results in a meaningful way—while the visualization allowed rapid hypothesis generation, refinement of the queries, and review of the results.

CONCLUSIONS

While there are many opportunities, challenges for information visualization remain. Some are specific to health informatics such as characterizing and understanding similarity of patients or visualizing comparative effectiveness and cause-and-effect relationships. Others are general visualization problems such as scaling to larger data sets or maintaining of provenance (i.e., records of the source of the data and of the analysis process used). Additionally, traditional evaluation metrics for interactive systems—such as task time completion, number of errors, or recall and precision—are insufficient to quantify the utility of visual analytics tools that may be used for days or months, and new research is needed to improve our visual analytics evaluation methodology.

Still, the growing number of successful applications and case studies provides evidence that the use of electronic health records databases for research and quality assurance could be dramatically expanded when easy-to-use interfaces allow clinical researchers to specify queries, review results, and find patterns. We believe that the future of user interfaces is moving toward larger, information-abundant interactive visual displays similar to EventFlow, and this will help researchers compare populations, discover relationships, and spot anomalies that are medically actionable.

ACKNOWLEDGMENTS

We appreciate the partial support of the Oracle Corporation and the University of Maryland Center for Health-Related Informatics and Bioimaging (CHIB) for this research. Funds for the LABA study were received from FDA Safe Use Initiative. We wish to thank Drs. Cecilia Mikita and Maureen Petersen, clinicians with Walter Reed National Military Medical Center, Bethesda, Maryland, for their input into pattern recognition of suboptimal therapy, and we also thank Kris Wongsuphasawat and David Wang for their major contributions to our early work (as part of their PhD thesis work on LifeLines2 and Lifeflow).

REFERENCES

Afzal, S., R. Maciejewski, and D. Ebert. 2011. Visual Analytics Decision Support Environment for Epidemic Modeling and Response Evaluation. *IEEE Conference on Visual Analytics Science and Technology*, pp. 191–200.

Card, S., J. Mackinlay, and B. Shneiderman. 1999. *Readings in Information Visualization: Using Vision to Think*. San Francisco, CA: Morgan Kaufmann Publ.

Centers for Disease Control and Prevention (CDC). 2004. Framework for Evaluating Public Health Surveillance Systems for Early Detection of Outbreaks: Recommendations from the CDC Working Group. *MMWR* 53(RR-5). Available at http://www.cdc.gov/MMWR/preview/mmwrhtml/rr5305a1.htm

Christakis, N.A., and J.H. Fowler. 2011. *Connected: The Surprising Power of Our Social Networks and How They Shape Our Lives—How Your Friends' Friends' Friends Affect Everything You Feel, Think, and Do*. Boston, MA: Back Bay Books.

Faisal, S., A. Blandford, and H.W.W. Potts. 2013. Making Sense of Personal Health Information: Challenges for Information Visualization. *Health Informatics Journal* 19(3): 198–217.

Food and Drug Administration (FDA). 2010a. FDA Drug Safety Communication: New Safety Requirements for Long-Acting Inhaled Asthma Medications Called Long-Acting Beta-Agonists (LABAs). Available at http://www.fda.gov/Drugs/DrugSafety/PostmarketDrugSafetyInformationforPatientsandProviders/ucm200776.htm

Food and Drug Administration (FDA). 2010b. FDA Drug Safety Communication: Drug Labels Now Contain Updated Recommendation on the Appropriate Use of Long-Acting Inhaled Asthma Medications called Long-Acting Beta-Agonists (LABAs). Available at http://www.fda.gov/Drugs/DrugSafety/PostmarketDrugSafetyInformationforPatientsandProviders/ucm213836.htm

Hansen, M., B. Shneiderman, and M.A. Smith. 2011. *Analyzing Social Media Networks with NodeXL: Insights from a Connected World*. Boston, MA: Morgan Kaufmann Publishers.

Hesse, B.W., D. Hansen, T. Finholt, S. Munson, W. Kellogg, and J.C. Thomas. 2010. Social Participation in Health 2.0. *IEEE Computer* 43(11): 45–52.

Institute of Medicine (IOM). 2011. Committee on Patient Safety and Health Information. *Health IT and Patient Safety: Building Safer Systems for Better Care*. Washington, DC: National Academies Press. Available at http://www.nap.edu/catalog. php?record_id=13269

Kielman, J., and J. Thomas (Guest Eds.). 2009. Special Issue: Foundations and Frontiers of Visual Analytics. *Information Visualization* 8(4): 239–314.

Meyer, T., M. Monroe, C. Plaisant, R. Lan, K. Wongsuphasawat, T. Coster, S. Gold, J. Millstein, and B. Shneiderman. 2013. Visualizing Patterns of Drug Prescriptions with EventFlow: A Pilot Study of Asthma Medications in the Military Health System. *Proceedings the of Workshop on Visual Analytics in HealthCare* (VAHC2013), pp. 55–58.

Monroe, M., R. Lan, H. Lee, C. Plaisant, and B. Shneiderman. 2013. Temporal Event Sequence Simplification. *IEEE Trans. Visualization and Computer Graphics* 19(12): 2227–2236.

Monroe, M., R. Lan, J. Morales del Olmo, B. Shneiderman, C. Plaisant, and J. Millstein. 2013. The Challenges of Specifying Intervals and Absences in Temporal Queries: A Graphical Language Approach. *Proc. of ACM Conf. on Human-Computer Interaction*, pp. 2349–2358.

National Asthma Education and Prevention Program (NAEPP). 2007. Guidelines for the Diagnosis and Management of Asthma. Available at http://www.nhlbi.nih.gov/ guidelines/asthma

Plaisant, C., R. Mushlin, A. Snyder, J. Li, D. Heller, and B. Shneiderman. 1998. LifeLines: Using Visualization to Enhance Navigation and Analysis of Patient Records. *Proceedings of the American Medical Informatics Association Symposium*, pp. 76–80.

Rind, A., T. Wang, W. Aigner, S. Miksch, K. Wongsuphasawat, C. Plaisant, and B. Shneiderman. 2013. Interactive Information Visualization to Explore and Query Electronic Health Records. *Foundations and Trends in Human–Computer Interaction*. 5(3): 207–298.

Shneiderman, B., C. Plaisant, and B. Hesse. 2013. Improving health and healthcare with interactive visualization tools. *IEEE Computer*, May 2013, 46(5): 58–66.

Wang, T.W., C. Plaisant, B. Shneiderman, N. Spring, D. Roseman, G. Marchand, V. Mukherjee, and M. Smith. 2009. Temporal Summaries: Supporting Temporal Categorical Searching, Aggregation and Comparison. *IEEE Transactions on Visualization and Computer Graphics* 15(6): 1049–1056.

Ward, M.O., G. Grinstein, and D.A. Keim. 2010. *Interactive Data Visualization: Foundations, Techniques, and Application*. A.K. Peters, Ltd., Natick. MA.

Wongsuphasawat, K., J.A. Guerra Gómez, C. Plaisant, T.D. Wang, M. Taieb-Maimon, and B. Shneiderman. 2011. LifeFlow: Visualizing an Overview of Event Sequences. *Proceedings of the 2011 Annual Conference on Human Factors in Computing Systems*, pp. 1747–1756.

13

Driving Successful Population Health Management and Achieving Triple Aim with Clinical Analytics

Kim S. Jayhan

CONTENTS

OBJECTIVES

After reading this chapter, the reader shall be able to:

- Explain what the Triple Aim is
- Distinguish among utilization, comparative, and predictive analytics
- Apply analytics to patient care
- Understand the role of analytics in patient health management
- Describe the role of analytics in achieving greater return on investment

ABSTRACT

This chapter explores how clinical analytics impact care of patients, drive success in population health management and Triple Aim, and identify efficiencies of physicians with unbiased clinical analytics. Comparisons of traditional utilization-based analytics with predictive analytics demonstrate where enhanced value is, to enable more success in engaging patients and providers, and ultimately controlling costs while improving outcomes. We have come a long way while experimenting with different approaches and payments for care. The health care industry has had its biggest impact from the Patient Protection and Affordable Care Act of 2010. Those health care stakeholders using analytics will succeed with health reform initiatives and requirements.

INTRODUCTION

In a recent presentation at an American Health Insurance Plans (AHIP) conference, Peter Edelstein, who is chief medical officer (CMO) of Elsevier and leading author and renowned public speaker, drew analogies to the U.S. economics related to material expenses when compared with health care expenditures. "If you want a fancy car, you pay more. If you want a fancy gourmet meal, you pay more. If you want better health care, you pay less," he said. Then he paused, waiting for the reaction—the audience clearly nodding in agreement but amused at the same time.

Edelstein went on to share stories of his experiences in health care, performing surgery at a leading institution and being rewarded for more volume. He cited examples of the volume-based reimbursement across health care for many years and how it rewarded facilities for readmissions, surgeons for return surgeries, and primary physicians for sicker patients. He also related his experiences as a CMO and medical director at a large integrated delivery network (IDN), using clinical analytics for the first time—first learning to trust them and then gaining value from them.

Health care continues to evolve, risk continues to shift, and all stakeholders are learning ways to become more engaged and more focused on outcomes and results rather than simply cost. Health information is more readily available, and while walls have fallen to enable more sharing, there are needs beyond sharing of raw data to fully power a successful Triple Aim or population health management initiative. Technology exists today to drive powerful decisions in health care with informatics and analytics created from aggregated raw data. But it isn't only what you know; it's also how business intelligence or analytics are used to enhance every part of patient care that will set the path for success.

Achieving better care, improved outcomes, and increased patient satisfaction requires analytic data to incorporate enterprise level aggregated information to ensure the best insights. This chapter focuses on how enterprise health analytics are used to transform the care experience, inform the clinical care team on the not so obvious risks, and really zone in on what is driving patient risk.

As health care reform influences more decision-making, payers, providers, and policy analysts have turned their attention to the use of big data and analytics to drive better care and reduce costs. Much confusion abounds when it comes to big data and analytics: Are they the same? Can either (or both) really make a difference to patient care? Physicians and health care executives may challenge each other on the specifics of which information should be used to measure clinical effectiveness, outcomes, and reimbursements, but there is no longer any question that big data and analytics are here to stay.

Big data is defined in many ways. More than 12 years ago, Gartner first coined the term and defined it as "high-volume, high-velocity and high-variety information assets that demand cost-effective, innovative forms of information processing for enhanced insight and decision making" (2013). This is the definition (in its simplest form) that will be used in this chapter.

At its primary level, analytics are derived using big data. Derivation can come from a variety of statistical methods, but what will be focused on in this chapter is not the different methods to create the analytics but rather the variety of analytics available in health care and how they can be used to impact the patient's health and the related costs of care.

UTILIZATION VERSUS PREDICTIVE ANALYSIS

Health care analytics exist in two varieties: those created based on utilization data (retrospectively, looking backward) and those created based on statistical predictive models (prospectively, looking forward). Each has its own value, but as health care evolves it becomes increasingly important to use prospective predictive analytics to drive clinical decisions on patients.

Utilization analytics have long been used to find high-cost and high-utilization patients. Retrospective in nature, utilization analysis will often focus on those patients who cost the most money or used the most resources in the last x period (typically 6 or 12 months). Stratifying by cost and usage is typically tied to primary diagnosis or primary and secondary diagnoses—understood through claims data and allocating dollars spent by a diagnosis, or resources (e.g., pharmacy, lab services, radiology, therapeutic services, inpatient, surgical) used to maintain or heal the patient for these conditions.

Analytic models based on utilization are very strong at identifying the obvious prior risks. What cannot be identified by utilization analytics are the not-so-obvious risks—those things that may be causing the patients to become more ill and need very costly treatment, including emergency room (ER) visits and inpatient care. It is difficult with utilization analytics to identify what hasn't been done but could have been done—which impact the patient's health. Therefore, utilization analytics are valuable for the backward glance and knowledge of patient history of what services were provided for each condition, but not for less apparent or derivative informatics.

Predictive analytics begin with retrospective data but also include complex statistical modeling to identify the likelihood of future events. Predictive analytics also tend to rely less on a single primary diagnosis and more on episodes. Episodes are the aggregation of events over time, related to specific conditions, for the purpose of identifying a progression or larger sequence of services expended for a patient. Because episodes are the combination of services for the treatment and management of patients, the clinical units created are often used as a foundation for predictive analytics.

By creating clinical measures through episode analysis, different statistical methods (both linear and nonlinear) can analyze the relationships of episodes to each other, thus creating the ability to assess risk (rather than just cost predictions). When nonlinear methods are used for predictive modeling, patterns create the ability to translate possible risks into defined indices that can be used by providers and care managers to stratify patients by risk rather than, or in addition to, cost.

Predictive analytics may not always identify a correlation between high cost and high risk. While there is no argument that high-cost patients are riskiest, they are not always the most actionable. Their care has to be coordinated, monitored, and managed, but it is mostly to hold to a status quo rather than to reach any significant improvement. Other high-cost patients will get better through their treatments (e.g., trauma, acute events), and their major health issues will resolve through standard protocols of care. What then becomes the most curious and impactable of the high-risk patients are those whose costs may not have been significant in the last year but who are now predicted to be very risky, very costly in the following year. Therein lay the path to actionable patients—those patients for whom interventions, monitored care, programs targeted to their needs, and providers who understand their underlying risk can actually realize a significantly positive change in health and costs.

Analytic models based on predictions are very strong at identifying future risks of patients and populations. In contrast to utilization analytics, which don't address the not-so-obvious risks, predictive analytics provide insights beyond what can be gained through raw data utilization analysis. Predictions can identify risks of ER visits and inpatient stays as well as overall costly care. Comparisons used to analyze what should have occurred but hasn't yet occurred in treatment are also valuable to identify gaps in care that impact the patient's health.

The combination of predictive analytics with comparison analytics for evidenced-based medicine provides the strongest foundation for providers and clinicians who treat patients and participate in population health management programs. These analytics also help drive assessments on quality of care by those treating the patients. The ultimate goal is to find the most actionable patients and to enable the best care for the best cost. Actionable patients are the cornerstone of the population health management initiative and will be discussed as we explore how to apply analytics to individual patients as well as populations.

Key Thoughts

Combining predictive analytics with evaluation of evidence-based medicine protocols net the best actionable patients. Actionable patients are the cornerstone to the population health management initiative.

Utilization analytics

Retrospective, based on past events and driven by primary diagnosis for each individual.

Often cannot identify who is most actionable because it is driven by high costs and high utilization only.

Are unable to identify the not-so-obvious risks of patients.

Comparative analytics

Identification of noncompliance to evidenced-based medicine, these analytics identify where gaps in care exist. When those gaps are closed, it typically results in healthier patients, through early detection of deficiencies and opportunities for intervention.

Predictive analytics

Prospective, based on past events plus statistical modeling for likelihood of future events.

Identifies most actionable patients, since it is driven by risk in addition to cost and utilization.

Are able to identify the not-so-obvious risks of patients, including risks attributed to noncompliance and motivation.

APPLYING UTILIZATION AND PREDICTIVE ANALYTICS IN PATIENT CARE

First launched in 2007 by the Institute for Healthcare Improvement (IHI), the Triple Aim initiative soon became a beacon for many as solid goals in future health care delivery. Embraced by Centers for Medicare and Medicaid (CMS), as well as many payer and academic health care

FIGURE 13.1
The Triple Aim.

institutions, many initiatives have been created using the Triple Aim as its foundation.

Triple Aim (Figure 13.1) is centered on three key goals: improving health of populations, improving individual experience of care, and reducing per capita costs of care for populations. While seemingly simple in its concept, achieving these goals requires changes in culture and policy, collaboration among providers and payers, and creative approaches to engage patients deeper in their own health care.

Berwick, Nolan, and Whittington (2008) asserted that the goals of Triple Aim should not be viewed as independent but rather interdependent. Further discussions in the article deal with the acknowledgment that reaching these goals is no longer prevented by technology but rather policy issues and access to the medical information across settings. Since 2008, much has changed in the way of policy and culture. Providers are now expecting, rather than resisting, sharing of data and collaboration with other providers and clinicians. Technology helped advance the sharing of data. Analytics become a key part of the shared data, driving better care for reduced costs. Health reform through the Patient Protection and Affordable Care Act of 2010 (ACA) has driven more competition for the health care dollar as well as the recognition that Triple Aim initiatives are key to success under health reform.

To achieve success with Triple Aim, patient-centered medical homes (PCMH), and health reform, analytics are needed to assist in the navigation on where to spend time, focus for success, and impact patients.

Long-range plans and patient engagement depend on first understanding the provider's population and then, at the detail level, each patient and his or her risks and motivation. Preventing visits to the ER, inpatient admissions and readmissions are just a few of the goals common to each PCMH.

Primary care physicians (PCPs) are now taking a larger role as the coordinator of care across the health care enterprise. The evolution of the PCMH has meant a greater level of respect for the role of the integrator of care. Therefore, PCPs are at the center of many risk-sharing, cost-sharing, value-based payment models.

PCPs, often assisted with nursing staff, nurse practitioners, and case/care managers, can use analytic information to utilize patient risk to engage patients at various points of care. Specialists and hospitalists also benefit by using analytics at the point of care. The various touch points where there is value in using analytics include the following:

- During office visits for either preventive or acute care
- While performing deliberate outreach based on proactive risk assessment
- During ongoing case, disease, and care management programs
- At admission and for concurrent stay coordination
- During inpatient discharge planning and follow-up after inpatient stay

Office Visits for Preventive or Acute Care

Many health care organizations establish and update evidence-based medicine guidelines on an annual basis. Guidelines exist for both recommended preventative care as well as chronic condition care. Examples include the HEDIS Measures by National Committee for Quality Assurance (NCQA) for breast cancer screening, medication management for people with asthma, and controlling high blood pressure and guidelines from other commonly used organizations such as Physician Quality Reporting System (PQRS), American Diabetes Association Clinical Practice Guidelines, American Heart Association, and American Medical Association (AMA). These guidelines serve as practice protocols for good and optimal care. By advising patients which diagnostic and lab tests are needed for their conditions, which medications need to be taken and why, identifying medication adherence, and advising on consequences to noncompliance, the primary care physicians and associates in the PCMH become the leaders in engaging patient adherence to guidelines, thus improving health through compliance. During office visits, the analytic information can be used to initiate discussions with patients on their gaps in care—those gaps created by noncompliance with evidenced-based medicine.

Retrospective analyses on past services easily highlight areas for improvement. The guidelines are often available through analytic tools used at the point of care, enabling the clinician to create a list of noncompliance guidelines for each patient or the entire practice panel. Analytics tools used at the point of care are available to easily print lists of recommended care to close the noncompliance and can be given to the patient as a reminder of where they need to engage in their own care. Predictive analyses will further enhance the lists of noncompliance by providing insights on risks being driven by the patient's noncompliance. Combining the two analytics creates a stronger case for motivating the patient into compliance and improve their health. By engaging the patient to comply and improve their health, future costs related to degradation of health will be avoided. Subsequent follow-up office visits can be enhanced by continued review of guideline compliance and updated assessment of predictive risks.

Deliberate Outreach Based on Proactive Risk Assessment

PCMHs have the opportunity to use analytics to understand the risks across their population. While analytics enhance the office visits that are periodic, preventive, or acute in nature, many patients are trending toward high risk (or are already there) and are not seeking medical care or intervention. These patients are perhaps the most at risk, as they will continue to become sicker without intervention, resulting in health degradation, rising future costs, and complex polymorbid conditions.

Both comparative and predictive analytics are used to stratify patients across the provider's panel. Using analytics to find which patients are going to be high risk in the next 12 months, the clinicians can also determine what is driving their risk as well as where they are most vulnerable (e.g., inpatient admission risk, ER visit risk, worsening health due to noncompliance). Costs can also be used as stratification criteria, but this serves only to set tiers of patient groups and create action plans to deliberately reach out to these patients. Some might be more motivated than others—which will be apparent in the analytics. Those might just need a postcard or phone call to encourage them to make an appointment to be seen in the office. Others might need continuous reminders and outreach.

Analytics can also be used simply to identify preventive services that are missing for each patient. By using analytics with outreach programs, patients are more encouraged to be seen and screened for any possible emerging problems. By finding medical issues earlier, there is always more opportunity for improved health and reduced costs.

Since one of the tenets in Triple Aim is an improved patient experience, the proactive contact from the primary physician and staff will often result in a better perception of caring by the patient and of the PCMH achieving that goal. Making access and communication easier and more frequent, there are more chances that patient engagement will increase.

Managing Case and Disease/Care Management Programs

Case Management

Patients with extraordinary costs and a high degree of complications are often designated to case management programs, where costs are managed and brought in line using methods from alternate service providers to negotiation of high hospital bills. Often case management programs enable the medical management staff to offer a care plan to a patient (requiring a multidisciplinary team)—and in return for compliance to the plan a reduced amount of out of pocket costs for the patient.

These programs can be successful at controlling costs for catastrophic events such as posttrauma, malignancies, complex conditions, end stage renal disease (ESRD), and hospice. Case management programs often do not take into account future risk, except to cap costs as much as possible in the future. Future clinical risk and future cost estimates are typically not part of the analytics used in case management but can make differences to levels of care needed for patients.

Disease/Care Management

Programs addressing disease and chronic conditions are often referred to as disease management or care management. Care management can also encompass coaching and behavior modification programs for patients with certain risks that may lead to chronic conditions (e.g., tobacco use, obesity). Even wellness programs sometimes have an appointed care manager to mentor patients and maintain preventive, low-risk, overall good health. Disease/care management programs will often focus on the most common chronic conditions (i.e., asthma, diabetes, hypertension, chronic heart failure, chronic obstructive pulmonary disease, coronary artery disease, and depression).

High-cost and high-utilization retrospective analytics are also used to power disease management programs. With a view toward containing costs and controlling certain conditions, disease management programs have succeeded in demonstrating patient improvements in specific conditions and their related costs. Most analytics driving disease management decisions are specific to the relevant disease in the program; that is, for diabetes disease management programs, analytic data are usually the patient's utilization and costs related to diabetes as well as adherence to evidenced-based medical guidelines (e.g., HEDIS Comprehensive Diabetes Care guidelines published by NCQA). Traditionally using a microfocus on specific conditions, a plan is created to engage the patient to become more compliant and enable the payer/health plan to monitor costs more easily and eventually improve the health of the patient while controlling costs. These programs are designed with the goal of self-management in mind, encouraging greater health through compliance and engagement with care.

Analytics for disease and care management help identify patients with episodes related to chronic conditions or risks and then help rank the patients by their relative risk, including gaps in care and future risk of hospitalization and ER visits. While these programs in the past relied only on past history and utilization data, analytics now provide a more holistic view of the patient, which in turn results in more appropriate placement of programs and care givers. Patients who also have mental illness, comorbid with other chronic disease, are further stratified into programs encompassing involvement with mental health and social service professionals. Because of the holistic approach in disease and care management programs, enabled by advanced analytics, care planning no longer has to focus on just a specific condition but rather *all of the risks* that are preventing the patient from achieving optimal health.

Understanding underlying risks and also motivation of the patient further rounds out the ability to prescribe the best plan of action for improved outcomes. Not only used for stratification, analytics also help drive prioritization of care plans. Analytics can deliver a deep understanding of true risk drivers, which enable the clinical staff to prioritize the multitude of treatments that apply for each patient. For example, two patients can each be of the same approximate age, gender, and risks due to chronic conditions. They may each have similar projections of future cost

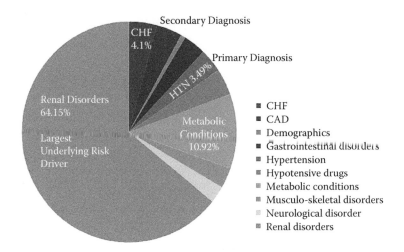

FIGURE 13.2
Risk drivers and contributions to risk.

and inpatient stays as well as ER visits. Even their medication projected costs and usage may be similar. But these two patients could have very different underlying risks. In Figure 13.2, note an example of one patient's risk drivers. This patient's primary diagnosis is hypertension. Hypertension contributes 3.49% to the patient's underlying risk. Chronic heart failure contributes a slightly higher portion of the risk. Metabolic conditions contribute even more at 10%. However, what is really driving the risk for this patient is the patient's renal issue (likely as a result of hypertension—but still demonstrates the biggest risk to this patient) at over 64%. This is a remarkable example of why using primary diagnosis and utilization as analytics are not as insightful as using predictive and advanced analytics, which uncover risk drivers. Using analytics to understand the true risk drivers will help the care management team and the PCMH prioritize the care related to renal disease to ensure that this patient does not get any sicker and hopefully will see an improvement in health.

Payers who employ disease and care management programs often report their adherence to industry standards through annual HEDIS reports to NCQA. Using analytics enhance the ability to have accurate reporting and enable the care and disease management staff to know which guidelines are critical to meet the annual certification needs.

Last, in the realm of disease and care management, analytics play a critical role in the ability to manage caseload and resources. Using analytics to tier patient risks, the care planners can easily distribute the appropriate number of patients for each disease or care manager. For those patients who are self-managing or progressing toward this goal, a care manager can take on a heavier load. Care teams that have more challenging, less motivated patients will need a lighter load to achieve the best success. Analytics can be used in the workload planning to assist in appropriate distribution.

Applying Analytics to Achieve Greater Return on Investment: Medicaid Patients

Challenges exist for providers caring for Medicaid patients, who tend to be a transient population, needing social services in addition to medical care to achieve optimal (or maintain) good health. Reimbursement follows CMS guidelines (2013). This population's analytics are critical— particularly those analytics that can provide insights on motivation of the patient to engage in their own care. Physicians and care managers often have a difficult time engaging Medicaid patients in self-management. Using analytics to understand the motivation level for self-management as well as future risks can accelerate the analysis needed to perform outreach or engage the beneficiaries while they are being seen in the office.

In one state Medicaid program, analytics were used to target three specific subpopulations: disabled adults with chronic conditions, asthmatics (both adult and children), and frequent ER users. By combining analytics with social services, primary care, outreach campaigns, and education, the state was able to save $569 million (Figure 13.3) over a four-year period. This program also helped the state Medicaid realize significant compliance improvements in beneficiary compliance with standards of care as well as a 33% reduction in inpatient stays for asthmatics. By steering the beneficiaries to primary care services, they reduced ER visits as well, which is always a challenge within the Medicaid population (Mitrakos, 2011).

During Admission and Concurrent Review Coordination

As data sharing and collaboration have become more common, payers and providers are using analytics to inform decisions at key critical times in patient care, specifically during inpatient admissions, readmissions, and the inpatient stay to enhance concurrent review coordination.

For those patients already in a program (case, disease, or care management), collaboration at admission is key to understand the progress of the patient with care plan goals, including significant events that

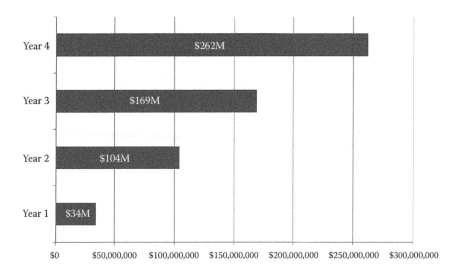

FIGURE 13.3

Savings realized in four years by state Medicaid plan using analytics for program stratification.

have occurred outside of the inpatient setting. Additionally, risks can be communicated so that the facility staff treating the patient can understand underlying risks. This patient-centered approach strengthens the ability for care across the continuum, including discharge planning and post-discharge care. Analytics can also be used to avoid unnecessary medical tests, thus also driving costs down for the inpatient stay.

Discharge Planning and Follow-Up Post-Inpatient Stay

The ACA added new parameters to the hospital readmissions reduction program, requiring CMS to reduce payments (beginning October 2012) to those hospitals with excessive readmissions that also participate in the inpatient prospective payment system. For three targeted conditions (acute myocardial infarction, heart failure, and pneumonia), a negative adjustment is made to the base DRG payment when a readmission is identified within 30 days of discharge from an acute care hospital.

Additionally, as payment models exit the fee-for-service reimbursements (where hospitals and physicians increase revenue with readmissions) in favor of value-based reimbursement (where hospitals and physicians are rewarded for lower costs and healthier patients and are often penalized for unnecessary readmissions), all providers of care are more motivated to avoid readmissions and, in fact, any admissions at all, unless absolutely necessary.

Many studies have shown positive outcomes when a patient is contacted within 7 days of hospital discharge and is seen within 14 days in a physician office postdischarge. Because health care models are evolving into continuum of care models, the positive outcomes can be proactively started at the time of discharge through the use of analytics in the collaborative model.

Using analytics to identify future risks of admission and ER visits as well as risks due to medication adherence and follow-up care, discharge planners can engage patients with actionable information to encourage their participation in following recommended postdischarge instructions. Sharing both the discharge instructions and the risk information with the PCMH strengthens the ability to succeed in follow-ups and preventions of further unnecessary admissions.

Once engaged in a follow-up visit, patients can be presented with future risk profiles to help them understand how best to engage in their own care, including what to avoid and why medication adherence is critical, and to encourage easy communication with the PCMH. This is especially true for the Medicare population, who tend not to communicate problems or questions until they are in a situation requiring acute or emergent care.

Key Thoughts

Significant savings as well as increased compliance and improved health have been demonstrated in programs using analytics for stratification and management of patients.

Analytics in primary care—office visits for preventive or acute care

Comparative analytics identifying gaps in care for evidence-based medicine are used during visits to educate patients on where they can improve their health through increased compliance.

Predictive analytics are used to assess the future risk of patients (e.g., inpatient stay, ER visit, increased costs) and the motivation of patients (ability to self-manage) and recommend plans of treatment based on future risks.

Analytics driving deliberate outreach

Both comparative and predictive analytics are used to stratify the provider's population for identification of patients who need to close gaps in care, who may be trending higher risk and need more monitoring, or even those who need to be put into care or disease management programs.

Analytics are also used to identify those patients who may need health coaching for behavior modification.

Analytics in case and care/disease management programs

Utilization, comparative, and predictive analytics are used to identify those patients who have had significant events and need immediate care coordination (case management).

Comparative and predictive analytics provide stratification of tiers of patients who need various levels of care. Stratification can also be done using the analytics to target for specific programs.

Predictive analytics also identify underlying risk drivers that are at the core of the patient's risk. This often may be different from the primary condition.

Predictive analytics are used to assist in workload assessments and distributions.

Analytics used at admission and during inpatient stay for concurrent coordination

Predictive analytics used at admission and during inpatient stays help inform the acute care staff of risks that may not be readily apparent from the intake. Using analytics throughout the inpatient stay enables a clean transition to discharge planning and postdischarge care.

Analytics used during discharge planning and follow-up postdischarge

Predictive analytics are used to inform the discharge plan as well as to communicate with the PCMH on the risks at the time of discharge. By using and sharing the risk analytics, enhanced coordination of care across the continuum leads to better care, improved outcomes, and lower costs.

PROVIDER PROFILING AND EVALUATION ANALYTICS

Much of the attention of analytics is currently focused on caring for the patient, with goals to improve outcomes and reduce overall costs. Triple Aim three tenets–combining improved outcomes and reduced costs with better patient experiences—are all treated equally and are inter-dependent. Complete population health management programs assess patient care in every way—care management and appropriate services for conditions, with fair and severity adjusted analytics related to measuring quality and efficiency of provider care. So we cannot just focus on caring for the patient, stratifying the patients into appropriate programs, and coordinating care. We must also evaluate the efficiency of the care provided to make improvements over time and also influence reimbursements as well as (for employers and payers) influence benefit design.

As health care moves away from volume-based (e.g., fee-for-service) reimbursement and toward value-based payments (e.g., incentive based, risk and cost sharing, bundled care), analytics take on a more important role in influencing where and how payments get distributed.

Under a volume-based model, it was important to verify only that a valid service was rendered and that the provider was in or out of network to navigate the reimbursement for the service. With a value-based model, new contracts identify specific targeted areas for key performance objectives. If those objectives are met, then the provider receives the maximum reimbursement, which may be a standard plus incentive or qualification for a bundled payment. Providers also can enter into contracts where risk is shared between the payer and provider (and consumer), and then metrics for the distribution of funds is articulated, typically based on outcomes and adherence to goals.

Analytics related to physician care first address attribution of patients. It is critical that accurate attribution occur, based on the physician's role of the patient care. Primary physicians and specialists are measured in different ways but do have one thing in common: measurements through episodes of care. Just as it is critical in stratifying patients, episodes play an equally important role in physician profiling.

Next, the evaluation of the illness burden of the population (i.e., how sick are the physicians' patients relative to industry norms and benchmarks) is analyzed. Then, for the level of sickness in the population, what is the case mix of the provider's population? That is, how many resources (e.g., tests, procedures, inpatient stays, surgery) would be the norm or expected for this illness burden?

Finally, the efficiency of the physician is determined by examining how many resources were expended for specific conditions in the population or at each patient level. Deviating from the norm requires further analysis to investigate whether low or high usage of resources was warranted.

There was a time where low resource usage was rewarded based on utilization only analytics. Early HMO models encouraged resources to be strictly monitored and often avoided. However, health care approaches have evolved to recognize not only that certain preventive and maintenance care is to be encouraged but also that some specialist care is sometimes required to maintain optimal health, or to identify problems sooner for earlier intervention. Advanced analytics identify where low resource usage may indicate much higher future risk of the physician's population. By not receiving the appropriate level of services, patients could indeed be trending sicker and leading to a complex set of conditions that will be hard to reverse.

Conversely, high resource usage is also subject to further analysis, since higher usage means higher costs. Achieving improved care while reducing costs means that the cost factor is still important. Analyzing resource categories (e.g., inpatient, ancillary, surgical, management, and pharmacy) often enables the insights to determine appropriateness of care as well as opportunities for savings or improvements. For instance, a provider's efficiency may be influenced by high pharmacy and ancillary costs but overall his patient population is not using excessive inpatient or surgical resources. In this instance, drilling down to the patient level in some areas will validate that the overall efficiency of the provider is good, with perhaps just a few areas to improve in the ancillary category. On the other hand, if the analysis shows high resource usage in most of the categories, this may be a physician or practice that needs mentoring or feedback to improve patient care. Efficiency metrics are not clearly identified yet in most provider contracts, but as the industry moves toward bundled payments and shared risk it will become critical that the providers understand how the metrics are derived and be able to monitor them through some kind of feedback loop—whether through provider reports, portals, or even the electronic medical records—with visual displays of performance assessments.

Provider efficiency metrics are not complete without including the ability to exclude clinical outliers—those patients who are anomalies, who have such complexities that no managed care approach is going to fully address costs of care. Therefore, most analytics provide the ability for the provider or the provider contracting/network staff to be able to exclude those outliers in calculating overall efficiency scores.

Physician analytics can be done at the individual or practice level and are typically done within the specialty (e.g., primary, orthopedic, cardiac, endocrine). Often benchmarks are used for comparison, and these include local, regional, within specific network, and also designated peer groups. Typically, value-based payment methodologies are using local, regional, or specific network benchmarks to ensure that regional differences don't skew the evaluation of the provider.

Last, to address the improvements of patient experience (Triple Aim), payers are often utilizing patient satisfaction surveys to assess the satisfaction of patients with their providers. These analytics are evolving and because of their subjective nature will continue to be refined until fair objectives can be measured and compared across providers.

Key Thoughts

Physician evaluation analytics are vital to value-based reimbursement programs as well as overall population health management initiatives.

Considerations in evaluation of physician performance

Illness burden of population: addresses "my patients are sicker" response from physicians.

Case mix: for the illness burden in the physician population, what is the resource usage expected to be (benchmarks)?

Efficiency: for the illness burden and case mix of the population, how many resources are being used when compared with norms in benchmarks?

Patient surveys are utilized to identify patient satisfaction. Feedback loops will drive better patient experiences. Surveys need to evolve to find fair measurements in patient satisfaction.

Comparison levels in physician analytics

Individual physician, practice, and peer groups evaluations.

Local, regional, national, and peer group benchmarks.

Typically comparisons are done within each specialty and not across specialties.

The ability to exclude outliers (patients who are considerably complex patients who are outside of the norms) is vital to fair efficiency analysis.

CONCLUSION

Population health management and Triple Aim are closely connected and have the same goals. Successful population health management includes both patient and provider analysis. Patient-centric analytics focus on stratification of risk to use programs, determining appropriate care, enhanced coordination across the care continuum, and reduction or avoidance of unnecessary costs.

While stratification has traditionally relied on retrospective utilization-based analytics for disease management, it is now possible to use every type of analytic to stratify patients for possible intervention through disease management and set tiers of care.

Care management has become a standard in value-based health care models. Analytics used in care management are often a hybrid of retrospective and predictive models. While it is critical to know past costs and utilization for a patient, it becomes ever more important to be able to judge future risk of the patient and, more important, what is actually driving the risk. Predictive analytics enable more accurate stratification of patients into care management programs, which allows additional value to the insights. When care is closely coordinated, there are improved outcomes and increased patient satisfaction.

Optimal care for patients also means being able to fairly assess the quality and efficiency of provider care. Physicians will respect analytics if they are fair and unbiased and will allow for exclusions of episodes or patients when judging the overall analysis. By excluding outliers, provider analytics are more balanced and more accepted, leading to deeper physician engagement.

Achieving the best outcomes requires analytics to address feedback to those responsible for medical and social care of the patients to promote provider and patient engagement.

As time goes on, other analytic assets will be combined with clinical analytics to achieve even more excellence in care. These analytics include identity verification and management, provider integrity and management, contact management, fraud, waste, and abuse analysis of both providers and members/beneficiaries.

Embracing analytics and the power they bring to health care is a large step forward in realizing genuine value-based care, superior outcomes—all for reasonable costs. Integration of multiple analytic assets with tools used by physicians, care managers, and clinicians in their workflow will be the next step of success. When physicians can ingest all of the clinical, administrative and analytic risk information for a patient in one place, one instance, there will be greater adoption of the use of analytics. Analytics are already being integrated into care management systems—with risk data elements as well as single sign-on, easing the access to analytics in the care management workflow.

Clinical analytics with clinical integration will equal successful Triple Aim accomplishments. It won't be a fancy car or a gourmet meal, but we will achieve better health care.

REFERENCES

Berwick, D.M., T.W. Nolan, and J. Whittington. 2008. The Triple Aim: Care, Health, and Cost. *Health Affairs* 27(3): 759–769.

Centers for Medicare and Medicaid (CMS). 2013. Acute Care Hospital Inpatient Prospective Payment System, April. Available at http://www.cms.gov/Outreach-and-Education/Medicare-Learning-Network-MLN/MLNProducts/downloads/AcutePaymtSysfctsht.pdf

Elliott, T. 2013. *7 Definitions of Big Data that You Should Know About*, July 5. Available at http://timoelliott.com/blog/2013/07/7-definitions-of-big-data-you-should-know-about.html

Gartner, Inc. 2013. *IT Glossary, Big Data*. Available at http://www.gartner.com/it-glossary/big-data/

Mitrakos A. 2011. State Shift in Patient-Care Programs Leaves Chicagoans without Coverage. *Chicago Health Care Dailey*, May 16. Available at http://www.chicagobusiness.com/article/20110516/NEWS03/110519915

14

Improving Decision-Making Using Health Data Analytics

Margrét V. Bjarnadóttir, Ritu Agarwal, Kenyon Crowley,
QianRan Jin, Sean Barnes, and Kislaya Prasad

CONTENTS

OBJECTIVES

After reading this chapter, the reader shall be able to:

- Assess opportunities to apply analytics for improved decision-making across multiple health care domains
- Explain how cost and quality data may be used to improve pricing transparency
- Illustrate how comprehensive survival prediction models can be used to support critical treatment decisions

285

- Describe how prediction models, and cost and benefit characteristics of different intervention programs, can be combined to optimize decisions about program design and patient enrollment
- Demonstrate opportunities to use predictive analytics to improve the detection of fraud, waste, and abuse in health care billing claims

ABSTRACT

The increasing availability of data in the health care industry is creating striking opportunities to apply sophisticated analytical techniques to address persistent problems in health care related to cost, quality, and patient safety. Data from across the health care sector, including from clinical systems, administrative records, and open government initiatives, are being used to support decision-making by a wide range of stakeholders. This chapter provides illustrations of four opportunities to support better decision-making, including evaluating health care cost, making informed treatment decisions, improving the design and selection of intervention programs, and combatting fraud, waste, and abuse in health care billing practices.

INTRODUCTION

The availability of data in the health care industry is rapidly expanding, driven by the increased use of information technology such as electronic health records, support from federal policy initiatives such as the open data movement, and efforts to standardize data and technical requirements. Promising opportunities abound to improve decision-making by health care providers, payers, consumers, researchers, population health administrators, entrepreneurial innovators, and governmental organizations.

The market has taken notice. The global health care analytics market is forecast to grow at a compound annual growth rate (CAGR) of 25.2% from 2013 to 2020. In 2013, this market was valued at an estimated $4.4 billion, and by 2020, is expected to total over $21 billion (Markets and Markets, 2013). Driving this growth is the demand for predictive and prescriptive analytics, which decision-makers require to take evidence-based actions and navigate a changing reimbursement environment. However, market growth may be constrained by lingering challenges such as the high costs of information technology implementation and maintenance, interoperability issues, shortages of health data professionals, and a complex regulatory environment stemming from poorly understood protocols such as the Health Insurance Portability and Accountability Act (HIPAA) and new regulations under the Patient Protection and Affordable Care Act (ACA).

The field of health data analytics is poised at an important tipping point of sharp growth enabled by the increase in data availability in health care. The opportunities created for improving decision-making are promising. In this chapter, we provide four illustrations of the use of health care data across a spectrum of health care decisions:

- Evaluating health care cost and quality
- Making informed treatment decisions
- Improving the design and selection of intervention programs
- Combatting fraud, waste, and abuse in health care billing practices

We conclude by identifying potential risks inherent in applying advanced analytics to health care data and areas where future research is needed.

COST AND QUALITY TRANSPARENCY THROUGH PUBLICLY AVAILABLE DATA

Aggregated health care data can help build a picture of the overall functioning of the health care system and has the potential to support health care decisions for a wide range of stakeholders. For example, a patient choosing where to have an operation could benefit from information about quality, patient satisfaction, and prices of different treatment options. A primary care provider would benefit from the same information when suggesting a specialist to his/her clients. For the policy maker, a detailed understanding of costs and benefits drivers in the system can help advance the right policies such as when determining reimbursement rates or selecting which public programs to incentivize.

In recent years there has been a concerted movement to make the health care system more transparent, in large part, through the liberation of data. As a result, greater amounts and variety of data are being made available to anyone wishing to analyze it (*Economist,* 2014). In the United States, the website http://healthindicators.gov, the health data flagship of the open government effort by the Barack Obama administration, exemplifies and is leading the data liberation movement. Managed by the U.S. Department of Health & Human Services, the goal of the website is to highlight valuable health care data and make it available to researchers, entrepreneurs, and other parties who may benefit from it. In January 2014, the website had close to 1,300 data sets, of which over 500 originate from the Medicare and Medicaid systems. Other useful federal health data resources being made publicly available include the Health Indicators Warehouse (HHS, 2014), Data.gov, and the Centers for Medicare and Medicaid (CMS) Data Navigator (http://dnav.cms.gov/). Data resources at the state and local levels include the New York Open Data Portal (https://data/ny.gov/) and the City of Chicago Data Portal (https://data.cityofchicago.org/) and public–private initiatives such as the Health Data Consortium (HDS, 2014b) and the Robert Wood Johnson Foundation (RWJF, 2014b) are also providing robust new data resources. These include the Health Data All-Stars (HDS, 2014a) and state and local level county health rankings and roadmaps (RWJF, 2014a), respectively.

Unsurprisingly, the release of previously proprietary data that results in transparency and visibility of actions has created controversy. An example of public data that has stirred considerable debate is the payment data release by CMS. On May 9, 2013, CMS made public data containing information on average provider charges and average payments (i.e., the amount that providers get reimbursed) for the 100 most common inpatient services for the fiscal year 2011 (FY 11) (CMS, 2013). The goal of the release, fueled in part by negative coverage of the opacity of rising health care costs in popular media such as *Time* magazine's special report on health care pricing practices (Brill, 2013), was to promote transparency and accountability. The press release highlighted the large variation in charges by providers by geographical location. Figure 14.1, published as a part of the press release, vividly illustrates the geographical variation for one of the inpatient services. However, it was not simply the variation across the United States that made headlines, but rather variation between providers only miles apart (Tribble, 2013) and the large gap between charges to the CMS on one hand and the payments made by CMS on the other, especially in light of the fact that the payments

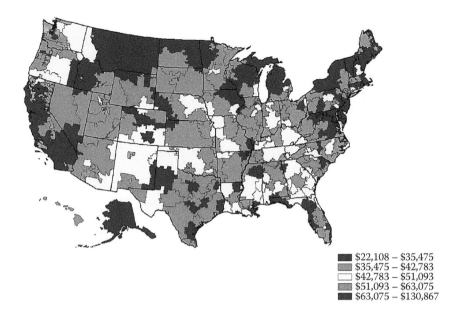

$22,108 – $35,475
$35,475 – $42,783
$42,783 – $51,093
$51,093 – $63,075
$63,075 – $130,867

FIGURE 14.1

The average hospital inpatient charges for major joint replacement or reattachment of lower extremity without major complications or comorbidities. The data is presented by hospital referral region, and providers with fewer than 10 discharges in the FY 11 are excluded from the calculations. (Source: CMS, 2013.)

from CMS are "intended to cover the costs that reasonably efficient providers would incur in furnishing high quality care" (Medicare Payment Advisory Commision, 2011).

Researchers have begun to perform analyses on these data to gain further insight into the nature and distribution of costs and charges (Barnes and Bjarnadóttir, 2013). In a study on the composition of sticker prices (i.e., the charges to the CMS), it has been estimated, everything else held constant, that hospitals operating under special circumstances (e.g., rural and sole community hospitals) receive higher CMS payments on average (which is a result of extra subsidy payments to those providers in CMS's payment system). At the same time, the researchers estimated that these same providers' sticker prices are lower on average than other providers, again everything else held constant. In a follow-up paper (Barnes and Bjarnadóttir, 2014), the researchers show that, even after accounting for different levels of quality, patient satisfaction, and outcomes, in addition to provider and procedure specific variables, over 25% of the variation in sticker prices remains unexplained. As a result, one can conclude that there is no clear uniform way providers set their sticker prices; rather, there is a large part that cannot be explained using a uniform model. As the researchers demonstrated, using models specially built for certain types of providers does not clarify these differences.

The CMS payment data release was important from many perspectives. It improved transparency of hospital charges, which is especially critical for those who are uninsured or underinsured (and the unfortunate international tourist and may end up paying the actual charges). It also demonstrates the large gap between charges and payments, which can only improve the negotiating position of those paying sticker prices, especially given the small fraction of the sticker prices the CMS actually reimburses. The large, unexplained variation in sticker prices, coupled with the public outcry and information availability, has the potential to lead to a more rational price setting in the health care system. But an interesting question remains unanswered: Will the information release affect the providers' charging strategies?

The example of the CMS payment data is just one of the many instances of how publicly available data can help guide decisions, in this case by the individual consumer, and how it has the potential to affect the behavior of health care providers. The movement toward transparency is focusing on health care quality as well. Data resources such as http://hospitalcompare. gov and the physician quality reporting websites under development by CMS and assessments by private organizations (e.g., HealthGrades and Castlight Health) are also likely to have a significant influence on consumer decisions in the future and will enable more informed cost–quality trade-offs. And, the burgeoning use of social media by patients reflected in the striking increase of online reviews of physicians may further illuminate the quality of health care services as experienced by individual patients (Gao et al., 2012).

MAKING INFORMED DECISIONS USING INDIVIDUAL-LEVEL CLINICAL DATA

In the past decades, decision-making in the context of health care has become increasingly complex. Multiple factors contribute to this increased complexity, among them changes in the payer systems and policies and the staggering increase in treatment options driven by advances in clinical and pharmaceutical research. Each of these has exacerbated the complexity of well-informed health care decisions. In addition, there are multiple stakeholders, including health care delivery organizations, providers, payers, and patients, whose incentives are not fully aligned and whose needs and decision support differs.

Decision models constructed from individuals' data have the potential to alleviate the challenge of better decision-making. Every day, providers and payers collect more and more individual-level health care data, including clinical information (e.g., diagnoses, medical history, and treatments) in electronic health records and mobile health applications; medication regimens and adverse events in medication management systems or modules; lab values in laboratory information systems; hospital admission, discharge, and transfer (ADT) events in health information exchanges; administrative payment information in claims databases; and most recently, health insurance enrollment information in health insurance exchanges. This increased data availability coupled with increasing computing power has resulted in an avalanche of research focusing on deriving insight and building prediction models from individual-level health data. At the same time, researchers and practitioners alike are using increasingly sophisticated models; in a field once dominated by linear and logistic regression and perhaps an occasional classification tree, now sophisticated machine learning methods are being utilized to create knowledge and predict risk. However, it is important to point out that deriving new knowledge or accurately predicting risk does not automatically lead to better decisions; rather, the new models need to be translated into actionable information.

We discuss two cases that illustrate the use of individual-level data to support decision-making. First, we present the use of advanced analytics for constructing comprehensive survival prediction models that can contribute to better decisions by patients, providers, and policy makers. Second, we discuss an approach to take advantage of prediction models to decide the appropriate scale of intervention and prevention program in the health care system, that is, which patients to enroll based on their individual characteristics. These two cases reflect recent developments and issues currently being addressed by researchers.

Supporting Treatment Decisions in Cancer Care

One of the first questions a newly diagnosed cancer patient asks herself is: What is my prognosis under the different treatment options? And what is important for short- and long-term survival? These are key questions for the patient and her provider, and clear answers to those questions can help guide treatment decisions. A natural start for answering these questions would be to search the literature; however, that search may leave the knowledge seeker confused as conflicting and often equivocal findings are brought to the surface. As an example, when searching the literature on colorectal cancer, one study finds that age is a significant predictor of mortality (Fiscella et al., 1976), while another found no difference between survival between young and old patients (O'Connell et al., 2004). While one study finds that those who are married have higher survival rates (Goodwin et al., 1987), it is reported as not significant in another (Greenberg et al., 1987). Multiple additional examples of inconsistent findings exist (Zia, 2013). These inconsistencies are rooted in differences in independent variables included from one study to the next, differences in survival horizons considered, and differences in a study's starting and end points.

A research team at Stanford University and University of Maryland has, over the past few years, used modern data-mining models and detailed patient data to build comprehensive models of colorectal cancer survival, with the goal of providing patients and providers with insights and knowledge to support treatment decisions (Bjarnadóttir, Rhoads, and Zia, 2012). Crucial modeling decisions to be made during such analysis include deciding what variables to include in the model and what the specific analytical form of the model will be. In their study the researchers use data on over 100,000 patients and independent variables that span patients' diagnosis, demographics and socioeconomic status, information on their hospital stays, their treatments (the characteristics of the hospital that provided the first line of care which in the case of colorectal cancer is often surgery), and tumor characteristics. The researchers used classification trees, multiple adaptive regression trees, and regularized logistic regression to predict survival over multiple horizons ranging from 30 days to 5 years. Using regularized logistic regression the researchers report an area under the receiver operating characteristic (ROC)* curve (AUC) of above .9 for all time horizons and AUC of .88 and above for classification trees. However, accurate prediction models are not enough, the models

---

* An ROC curve is a plot of the true positive rate against the false positive rate that highlights the trade-off between the achievable sensitivity and specificity of a classifier. As the sensitivity increases (we move away from the lower left corner of the curve), the specificity decreases, reaching zero when the sensitivity is 1 (the upper right-hand corner of the curve).

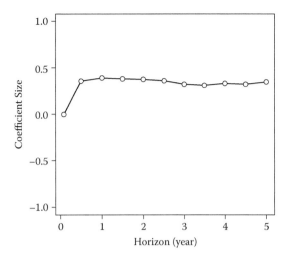

FIGURE 14.2

The importance of age as estimated by the coefficient size in regularized logistic regression models for each survival horizon. (Source: Zia, 2013.)

need to be translated into actionable information, such as a picture of survival probabilities, and information about factors that influence both short- and long-term survival.

Figures 14.2 and 14.3 illustrate how results of prediction models are being translated into information that can help drive treatment choices. Figure 14.2 depicts the importance of age as represented by the size of coefficients in a regularized logistic regression model on normalized data. What is noteworthy is that for 30-day survival age does not play a role, but for survival horizons six months or longer age plays a constant and significant role in the prediction.

Figure 14.3 shows a different approach to measuring variable importance. Rather than deriving importance from coefficient size, the figure depicts the classification improvement a variable makes when it is added into a model. An important modeling decision when measuring the variable importance using this approach is: To which model is the variable added? Figure 14.3 shows the two extreme answers to that question. The solid line represents the improvement in reclassification when the variable is added to a baseline model that predicts the average for all members. The dashed line represents the classification improvement when the variable is added to a model containing all other variables. The first approach represents the predictive strength of a variable ignoring all other information,

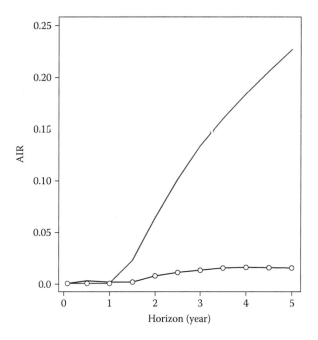

FIGURE 14.3

The importance of stage of the tumor at the time of diagnosis, as estimated by the Additional Improvement in Reclassification (AIR). The solid line corresponds to the increase in AIR when stage is added to the baseline model and the dashed line represents the improvement when stage is added to the full model. The x-axis is the survival horizon. (Source: Zia, 2013.)

while the second approach represents the additional value of the variable after accounting for all other independent variables. Figure 14.3 contrasts these two approaches for a variable indicating the stage of the tumor. As the figure shows, there is a stark difference in the measured importance by these two approaches. The figure also highlights that the stage of the disease is not a strong predictor of short-term survival, but increasingly so for longer-term survival.

The previous discussion highlights the complexities involved with interpreting variable importance in a health care setting. Due to the increasing number of variables available for today's prediction models, determining what is the "right" definition of variable importance is an open question, and like many questions in data analytics the answer may be both application and data dependent.

Finally, as an example of how the output of prediction models can be used as a policy tool or by a health care organization, consider the case of chemotherapy in the last 30 days of life, which has been a topic of debate due to the toxicity of the treatment and patients' reduced quality of life, with very limited to no curative benefit (Harrington and Smith, 2008; Magarotto et al., 2011). In addition to the often very limited (if any) benefits for these late-in-life treatments, oncologists tend to be overly optimistic about their patients' survival (Glare et al., 2003) and avoid discussions about end-of-life decisions (Wright et al., 2008). As a result, patients often receive aggressive treatment close to their death. For example, it is reported that more than 20% of patients on Medicare who had metastatic cancer started a new chemotherapy treatment regimen within two weeks of death (Harrington and Smith, 2008). It is clear that in this difficult decision scenario accurate prediction models are needed to reduce the variability in survival predictions and are key for reducing bias in conversations about treatment and end-of-life choices.

At an organizational level, the prediction models can also help decision-makers. There is anecdotal evidence that policies that limit or eliminate therapy toward end of life often face resistance as these therapies are very profitable. Therefore, if the use of prediction models enables researchers to identify a group a people that will almost surely die within 30 days with a high level of accuracy, that may be a chance to change the conversation and recommend more appropriate treatment regimens for individuals in this group.

Figure 14.4 depicts the ROC curve for 30-day survival for colorectal cancer patients. Traditionally the focus is on the upper right corner of the curve, as often those points represent the maximum accuracy; however, if the issue at hand is identifying patients for whom treatment is not appropriate, the trade-off between false positives and false negatives is very skewed. In particular, it may not be desirable to refuse treatment to someone who may benefit. Referring back to Figure 14.4, focusing on the lower left part of the ROC curve, these points corresponds to a group of identified members with very low false positive rates (inaccurately identifying a patient as dying when she is not). At the same time, the points capture more than 20% of the population who will not survive beyond 30 days, with a false positive rate of almost zero. These are the population that may be offered alternatives to treatment.

In summary, in the absence of accessible information for patients and providers, honest conversations about treatment options and survival cannot take place between the provider and her patient, and the trade-off between aggressive treatments with perhaps limited benefit and palliative

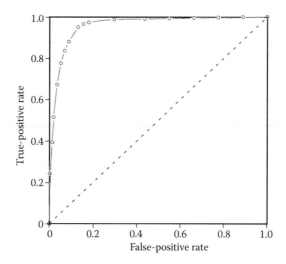

FIGURE 14.4

The ROC curve for 30-day mortality from the time of hospital discharge for colorectal cancer patients. (Source: Adapted from Zia, 2013.)

care are difficult to discuss. Comprehensive prediction models have the potential to provide information for these difficult decisions as well as guide general treatment options.

Supporting the Selection of Intervention Programs with Risk Prediction Models

In recent policy discourse, in part a result of reimbursement changes, there is a strong focus on reducing preventable readmissions to hospitals, often modeled as readmissions within 30 days. Multiple studies have analyzed the efficacy of different preventive care models and programs to avoid preventable readmissions (Pal, Babbott, and Wilkinson, 2013; Spruce and Sanford, 2012; Walsh and McPhee, 1992). Hospitals report using quality monitoring, medication management programs, and discharge and follow-up processes (Bradley et al., 2012) as strategies to reduce readmission. Risk prediction models, which estimate individuals' risk of readmission, have been built using large administrative databases and, with greater success, with data available from the electronic health care records or other internal provider data (Englander et al., 2011). However, what most of these studies do not provide is a cost–benefit estimation of running the prevention programs, and none consider the fact that the cost effectiveness of an intervention or prevention program is a function of the population enrolled in it. This is important as enrolling all patients into a prevention program may not be an economical use of resources, whereas offering enrollment to a high-risk population may lead to better outcomes and at the same time improve the bottom line.

A recent study (Bjarnadóttir and Zia, 2014) addresses how prediction models and cost and benefit characteristics of different intervention programs can be combined to optimize decisions about which programs to run and which patients to enroll. By formulating the problem as an optimization problem the proposed methodology balances operational aspects of the programs such as start-up costs and variable costs, the economics of running programs such as economies of scale, and the risk characteristics of the population selected based on a risk prediction model. To maximize the benefit from the program, the riskiest patients are enrolled first, and as the program expands patients of increasing lower risk are added. As a result there may be competing objectives, decreasing the cost per person enrolled as a program is expanded and, at the same time, decreasing the risk of adverse events as the risk threshold for being included in the program goes down.

The hospital manager or the health care provider not only has to decide on the right scale of the program but may also have to choose which programs to run. In general, intervention programs are never 100% effective. In other words, even if all members are enrolled in a prevention program, 30-day readmissions will not be completely eliminated. Multiple programs are available; some cost more than others, and in most cases the more expensive programs have higher efficacy (otherwise they would be dominated by cheaper programs and not used). Using the optimization methodology presented in Bjarnadóttir and Zia (2014), the manager is able to select the menu of programs that she should run. In particular, assume there is a high-cost, high-efficacy program that has nurses calling recently discharged patients to follow up on their medications, adherence, and their general health state and a low-cost, lower-efficacy program that sends recently discharged patients automated reminders to contact the hospital in case the member's health condition is not progressing in the right direction. What the hospital manager may discover is that from an economic standpoint the best decision may be to enroll high-risk patients in the high-cost program, medium-risk patients in the lower-cost program, and not to enroll the lowest risk patients in any program. This is shown schematically in Figure 14.5.

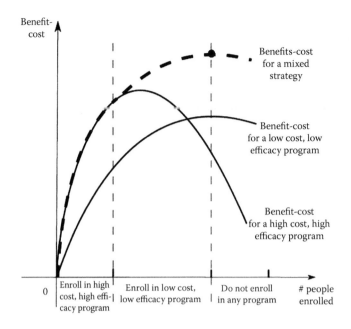

FIGURE 14.5
Benefits minus costs for three prevention strategies. On the x-axis is the fraction of the population included in a program. On the y-axis is the overall benefit-costs. The dashed vertical lines note the switch in the mixed strategy.

To maximize the value of prediction models for the decision-maker, tools such as optimization need to be used to apply the risk predictions in an operational setting.

PREDICTIVE ANALYTICS FOR DETECTION OF FRAUD, WASTE, AND ABUSE USING CLAIMS DATA

Fraud, waste, and abuse (FWA) in health care billing is a major problem that has been implicated as a significant contributor to the excessive costs in the U.S. health care system. The Institute of Medicine estimates the U.S. health care system squanders approximately $750 billion a year—roughly 30 cents of every medical dollar—through unneeded care, byzantine paperwork, fraud, and other waste (Kaiser Health News, 2012). The Federal Bureau of Investigation (FBI) estimates that fraudulent billings to public and private health care programs in fiscal 2009 equal approximately

3-10% of total health spending, or $75–$250 billion (Parente et al., 2012). FWA not, only affects health system financial sustainability but also can negatively impact patient care and safety, such as when patients cannot get the care they need because fraudulent charges have exhausted their benefits or when unnecessary medical interventions put patients at risk. Policy and technical efforts are being undertaken to combat this serious problem.

The ACA has put in the hands of fraud fighters tools that include new rules and sentencing guidelines, new technologies, and resources for fighting fraud. Legislation enacted in the 2010 Small Business Act (H.R. 5297) compels Medicare to apply predictive analytics to prevent improper payments (Parente et al., 2012). Resources for fighting fraud are not insignificant; in the 2012 fiscal year, the Department of Health & Human Services, Office of Inspector General, and Department of Justice directed $583.6 million toward the Health Care Fraud and Abuse Control programs including the development and use of new technologies that use predictive analytics (Government Accountability Office, 2013).

The use of predictive analytics to detect fraud is not new; the credit card industry pioneered fraud classification techniques over 20 years ago (Ghosh and Reilly, 1994; Leonard, 1993). In health care, the application of predictive analytics to FWA detection is a relatively nascent phenomenon, enabled by the complementarities arising from the availability of health care data and sophisticated computing resources. A key advantage of powerful computing infrastructures is that fraud detection can occur at speeds that make it possible to analyze vast volumes of claims in real time, enabling the identification of a fraudulent claim before it is paid. In the traditional pay-and-chase method of fighting FWA, a potential fraud is identified after the claim has been settled and the payer then has to recoup the loss from the payee.

As has been documented in prior studies, FWA can occur in a variety of ways. It may be committed by a health care provider, by an insurance subscriber, or in more rare cases by an insurance company. FWA by health care providers typically involves billing for services either not rendered or incorrectly billing for services. When the fraud is not initiated by providers, it is usually committed by the insurance subscriber or on his or her behalf. Insurance carrier FWA is the least widely observed among the three parties involved. A summary of the type of fraud classified by the perpetrator is provided in Table 14.1.

TABLE 14.1

Types of FWA Classified by Perpetrator Class

FWA Scenario	Description
Types of Fraud Committed by Providers	
Phantom billing	The practice of billing for services not provided (Coalition Against Insurance Fraud 2013b, Travaille et al. 2011a, Arash Rashidian 2012)
Unbundling	The practice of submitting several claims for various services that should have only been billed as one master claim including ancillary services (Barrett 2004, Kemp 2010, Travaille et al. 2011b, Verisk_Health 2012)
Upcoding	To the practice of billing for a service with a higher reimbursement rate than the service rendered (Travaille et al. 2011a, Bolton and Hand 2002, Li et al. 2008, False Claims Act Resource Center 2013, Barrett 2004, Kemp 2010)
Double billing	The practice of submitting similar claims more than once (Coalition Against Insurance Fraud 2013b, Barrett 2004, Kemp 2010, Travaille et al. 2011a)
Overutilization	Provides unnecessary services or ordering unnecessary tests (AllMed 2013, Thorpe et al. 2012, E. Emanuel 2008)
Ghost patient	Cases when a claim is submitted on behalf of a patient that doesn't exist or never received the services (False Claims Act Resource Center 2013, Bolton and Hand 2002)
Kickbacks	Improper payments to reward a referral or health care services. For example, an independent hospital is involved where physicians have an ownership interest in the practice (Barrett 2004, Kemp 2010, Arash Rashidian 2012, False Claims Act Resource Center 2013, Bolton and Hand 2002)
Types of Fraud Committed by Insurance Subscribers	
Identity theft	A third party stealing the identification information from providers or beneficiaries and using the information to submit fraudulent bills to health care providers (Coalition Against Insurance Fraud 2013b, Arash Rashidian 2012, Travaille et al. 2011a, Coalition Against Insurance Fraud 2013a)
Doctor shopping	A patient bouncing from one doctor to another simultaneously to obtain multiple prescriptions without making effort to coordinate care or informing the physicians of the multiple caregivers (Aral et al. 2012)
Misuse of an insurance card	The act of allowing unauthorized person to use the subscriber's medical insurance card and ID to obtain medical services or drugs (Aral et al. 2012)
Falsifying records of employment or eligibility	Enables the subscriber to obtain a lower premium rate (Li et al. 2008)
Types of Fraud Committed by Insurance Subscribers	
Falsification	Falsifying reimbursement and benefit/service statements (Li et al. 2008)

The problem of FWA in health care settings is complex and multi-faceted. To the degree that FWA can take on many forms, it is highly unlikely that there exists one universal detection algorithm. Rather, specialized algorithms need to be built to detect each scenario—and other abnormal behavior that may indicate anomalous claims and perhaps new types of fraud. There are several additional challenges in creating detection algorithms to identify FWA in health care settings. First, the underlying fraction of FWA claims (i.e., those that are "anomalous") is usually low so one is looking for rare events, which makes the classification of FWA claims more challenging. A second challenge relates to the availability of appropriate data—while claims data are widely available, labeled data sets that are a critical prerequisite for the application of supervised data-mining methods to train the models are rare. These labeled data sets are extremely difficult to find and expensive to create. Exacerbating this challenge is the essential information asymmetry in health care settings. In contrast to financial transactions where customers can usually spot an invalid charge (Zimmerman, 2013), the typical patient does not usually have enough knowledge to determine whether the procedure is necessary or not, thus making it hard to label data.

Third, there are also manpower constraints to support the review and adjudication of claims by human experts. It is difficult for human experts to identify all of the fraudulent claims because various styles of fraud can co-occur (Phua et al., 2010), and the fraud characteristics change as fraudsters develop new methods once experts learn how to spot existing methods. Yet, despite these challenges, tools are entering the market and are expected to increase in use and efficacy over time.

Researchers have tackled the challenge of health care fraud detection using a mix of supervised and unsupervised techniques. The key difference between the two is that while the former uses labeled data that classify cases as good or bad to learn about the structure of the data, the latter apply algorithms without the availability of labeled data, for example to detect outliers (Dougherty, Kohavi, and Sahami, 1995). In addition, published studies differ in the level of detection, while some focus on identifying fraudulent providers based on their overall claims patterns, others isolate fraud at the claims level.

Liou, Tang, and Chen (2008) apply popular data-mining algorithms to detect providers of diabetic patients whose contracts were terminated due to severe fraud, using a data set provided by Taiwan's Bureau of

National Health Insurance (BHNI). Based on a limited data set of three fraudulent providers, and using providers' summary statistics, they show that classification trees have the fewest false positives followed by neural networks and then logistic regression trees.

Shin et al. (2012) built a detection system that processes large amounts of data to detect patterns of abusive behavior of outpatient providers (clinics), as a first step toward initiating further investigation into the flagged providers. Their model is based on a weighted composite score of the abnormality of 38 care indicators such as the costliness of service as well as the rates of utilization, selected based on their individual association with fraudulent behavior (as observed during a training period). The authors then propose a segmentation using classification trees to communicate the score and the reasons for the flagged providers to the investigators. The researchers validated their finding in an out-of-sample experiment, where labeling was based on the action of official oversight authority in the testing period, which investigated close to 11% of the clinics. The model achieves a lift of close to two, that is, when selecting the top 10% highest scoring clinics, the true positive rate is about 19%, and over 80% of the fraudulent clinics go undetected. The method may be appropriate to help prioritize the efforts of the human investigators but at the same time highlights the challenges of the fraud detection problem.

Aral et al. (2012) used an unsupervised approach on an unlabeled data set to identify risky claims based on a ranking empirically derived from the distribution of claims. The researchers validated their analysis by having a medical expert label a random sample of 249 claims from a cardiac surgery database, therefore overcoming the challenge of unlabeled data. The underlying fraud percentage in their test sample was 36%, and true positive rate of 77.4% and a false positive rate of 6% with an AUC of 85.7%. Other researchers have explored combinations of multiple algorithms and approaches to improve classification performance, including the mixing of unsupervised and supervised learning methods. For example, Chan and Lan (2001) used fuzzy sets theory and Bayesian classifier to detect fraudulent claims in Taiwan's BHNI.

The potential payoff from being able to accurately detect even a small proportion of fraudulent claims is significant, and researchers continue to seek better techniques and methods for predictive analytics in this domain.

CONCLUSION

In this chapter we underscored the pace at which big data is being generated in the domain of health and medicine from a staggering variety of sources. The digital transformation of health care currently under way is capturing extensive health data and history in electronic medical records that are now becoming available for analysis. Patients routinely exchange information about disease conditions, treatment experiences, and the effectiveness of medications in online health communities and provide feedback on interactions with clinicians through social media and online reviews. The quantified self movement is accelerating the tracking and capture of granular activities of daily living such as exercise and nutrition, all of which have the potential to provide unique insight into relationships between health, wellness, and lifestyle. The human genome project and the rapidly falling cost of genomic testing are enabling the linking of individual genes to the prediction of disease risk. We presented four domains in health care where data availability and analytical modeling can create value: in enabling cost and quality transparency, assisting patients and providers to make more informed treatment decisions, helping administrators evaluate the cost-effectiveness of different intervention programs, and detecting fraud, waste, and abuse in health care claims. Each of these domains represents a robust opportunity for improving the overall performance of the health care system.

We conclude by noting that while the benefits of such big data in health are incontrovertible, risks exist and many questions remain unanswered. Significant future work is needed in the following areas:

1. What is the relationship between big data analytics and the traditional mode of clinical research? To what extent is one superior to the other, and what are the conditions that determine how and when each is appropriate? What are the complementarities between the two models of science?
2. What adverse consequences do big data analytics pose for individuals? For example, health information privacy violations can result in employment discrimination, the denial of health insurance, and the potential for social stigma. Are individuals aware of these consequences, and do they take adequate protection against such risks? How are privacy attitudes evolving in the health context?

3. If patterns discovered in big data are used as the basis for the diagnosis and treatment of health conditions, what are the safety and assurance mechanisms for certifying the veracity of conclusions? How will causality be established?
4. What is the role of trust in the context of health information privacy? How does/will the security infrastructure across various health care transactions support the protection of health information privacy?
5. What is the willingness and cognitive capacity of individuals to learn about their health through discoveries enabled by big data? Does such knowledge trigger fear, anxiety, and other negative emotions, or does it spur greater engagement with health and wellness?
6. What is the willingness of individuals to disclose personal health information for the purposes of scientific discovery? Is there variation in this willingness based on demographic, socioeconomic, and disease conditions? What challenges does this raise for the generalizability of findings and the potential for statistical bias in the data collections used for research (Anderson and Agarwal, 2011)?
7. To what extent are clinicians willing to believe findings from big data compared with the traditional model of learning from randomized control trials? How will this affect their diagnosis and treatment decisions?

We hope the academic and policy communities are vigilant to these questions and risks in future work on big data in health care contexts.

REFERENCES

AllMed. 2013. Overutilization, Abuse and Fraud within Cardiac Departments. Available at http://allmedmd.com//landing-pages/hpr-landing-pages/AuditsinCardioDeptWP.pdf
Anderson, Catherine L., and Ritu Agarwal. 2011. The Digitization of Healthcare: Boundary Risks, Emotion, and Consumer Willingness to Disclose Personal Health Information. *Information Systems Research* 22(3): 469–490.
Aral, Karca Duru, Halil Altay Güvenir, İhsan Sabuncuoğlu, and Ahmet Ruchan Akar. 2012. A Prescription Fraud Detection Model. *Computer Methods and Programs in Biomedicine* 106(1): 37–46.
Arash Rashidian, Hossein Joudaki, and Taryn Vian. 2012. No Evidence of the Effect of the Interventions to Combat Health Care Fraud and Abuse: A Systematic Review of Literature. *Plos One* 7(8).
Barnes, Sean, and Margrét V. Bjarnadóttir. 2013. The Composition of Sticker Prices: An Analysis of CMS Provider Charge Data. In *Proceedings of the 8th INFORMS Workshop on Data Mining and Health Informatics,* Minneapolis.

Barnes, Sean, and Margrét V. Bjarnadóttir. 2014. Unexplained Variation in Sticker Prices: An Analysis of CMS Provider Charge Data. Working Paper.

Barrett, Stephen. 2004. Insurance Fraud and Abuse: A Very Serious Problem. www.quackwatch.com/02ConsumerProtection/insfraud.html

Bjarnadóttir, M.V., K. Rhoads, and L. Zia. 2012. A Comprehensive Study of Prediction Models for Colorectal Cancer. In *Proceedings to the 7th Informs Workshop on Data Mining and Health Informatics,* Phoenix.

Bjarnadóttir, M.V,. and L. Zia. 2014. Optimizing Intervention Program in Healthcare. Working Paper.

Bolton, Richard J., and David J. Hand. 2002. Statistical Fraud Detection: A Review. *Statistical Science* XX: 235–249.

Bradley, Elizabeth H., Leslie Curry, Leora I. Horwitz, Heather Sipsma, Jennifer W. Thompson, MaryAnne Elma, Mary Norine Walsh, and Harlan M. Krumholz. 2012. Contemporary Evidence about Hospital Strategies for Reducing 30-Day Readmissions: A National Study. *Journal of the American College of Cardiology* 60(7): 607–614.

Brill, Steven. 2013. Bitter Pill: Why Medical Bills Are Killing Us. *Time Magazine,* March 4.

Centers for Medicare and Medicaid Services (CMS). 2013a. HHS Releases Hospital Data on Charge Variation to Promote Transparency. Available at http://www.cms.gov/apps/media/press/factsheet.asp?Counter=4597

Centers for Medicare and Medicaid Services (CMS). 2013b. Medicare Provider Charge Data. Available at http://www.cms.gov/Research-Statistics-Data-and-Systems/Statistics-Trends-and-Reports/Medicare-Provider-Charge-Data/

Chan, C.L., and C.H. Lan. 2001. A Data Mining Technique Combining Fuzzy Sets Theory and Bayesian Classifier—An Application of Auditing the Health Insurance Fee. In *Proceedings of the International Conference on Artificial Intelligence.*

Coalition Against Insurance Fraud. 2013a. Emerging Issues. Available at http://www.insurancefraud.org/white-paper-emerging.htm-.Ulf46Rb3BvY

Coalition Against Insurance Fraud. 2013b. False Medical Claims. Available at http://www.insurancefraud.org/scam-alerts-false-medical-claims.htm-.Ulal7xb3BvY

Dougherty, James, Ron Kohavi, and Mehran Sahami. 1995. Supervised and Unsupervised Discretization of Continuous Features. ICML.

Economist. 2014. Measuring Health Care: Need to Know, February 1. Available at http://www.economist.com/news/international/21595474-improve-health-care-governments-need-use-right-data-need-know

Englander, Honora, Amanda Salanitro, David Kagen, Cecelia Theobald, Sunil Kripalani, Michele Freeman, O.R. Portland, and Devan Kansagara. 2011. Risk Prediction Models for Hospital Readmission: A Systematic Review. *Journal of the American Medical Association* 306(15): 1688–1698.

Ezekiel, J. Emanuel, and Victor R. Fuchs. 2008. The Perfect Storm of Overutilization. *Journal of the American Medical Association* 299(23).

False Claims Act Resource Center. 2013. Health Care Fraud and False Claims. Available at http://www.falseclaimsact.com/common-types-of-fraud/health-care-fraud

Fiscella, Kevin, Paul Winters, Daniel Tancredi, Samantha Hendren, and Peter Franks. 1976. Racial Disparity in Death from Colorectal Cancer: Does Vitamin D Deficiency Contribute? *Medical Laboratory Sciences* 33(1): 13.

Gao, Guodong Gordon, Jeffrey S. McCullough, Ritu Agarwal, and Ashish K. Jha. 2012. A Changing Landscape of Physician Quality Reporting: Analysis of Patients' Online Ratings of Their Physicians over a 5-Year Period. *Journal of Medical Internet Research* 14(1).

Ghosh, Sushmito, and Douglas L. Reilly. 1994. Credit Card Fraud Detection with a Neural-Network. In *Proceedings of the Twenty-Seventh Hawaii International Conference on System Sciences.*

Glare, Paul, Kiran Virik, Mark Jones, Malcolm Hudson, Steffen Eychmuller, John Simes, and Nicholas Christakis. 2003. A Systematic Review of Physicians' Survival Predictions in Terminally Ill Cancer Patients. *British Medical Journal* 327(7408): 195.

Goodwin, James S., William C. Hunt, Charles R. Key, and Jonathan M. Samet. 1987. The Effect of Marital Status on Stage, Treatment, and Survival of Cancer Patients. *Journal of the American Medical Association* 258(21): 3125–3130.

Government Accountability Office (GAO). 2013. http://www.gao.gov/assets/660/658334.pdf

Greenberg, Raymond S., Deborah A. Baumgarten, W. Scott Clark, Peter Isacson, and Kathleen McKeen. 1987. Prognostic Factors for Gastrointestinal and Bronchopulmonary Carcinoid Tumors. *Cancer* 60(10): 2476–2483.

Harrington, Sarah Elizabeth, and Thomas J. Smith. 2008. The Role of Chemotherapy at the End of Life. *Journal of the American Medical Association* 299(22): 2667–2678.

Health Data Consortium (HDS). 2014a. Health Data Allstars. Available at http://www.healthindicators.gov

Health Data Consortium (HDS). 2014b. Health Data Consortium. Available at http://www.healthdataconsortium.org/

Kaiser Health News. 2012. IOM Report: Estimated $750B Wasted Annually in Health Care System. Available at http://www.kaiserhealthnews.org/Daily-Reports/2012/September/07/iom-report.aspx

Kemp, Hannon. 2010. Combating Medicaid Fraud in New York State. Available at http://www.nysenate.gov/files/pdfs/Combating_Medicaid_Fraud_in_NYS.pdf

Leonard, Kevin J. 1993. Detecting Credit Card Fraud Using Expert Systems. *Computers & Industrial Engineering* 25(1): 103–106.

Li, Jing, Kuei-Ying Huang, Jionghua Jin, and Jianjun Shi. 2008. A Survey on Statistical Methods for Health Care Fraud Detection. *Health Care Management Science* 11(3): 275–287.

Liou, Fen-May, Ying-Chan Tang, and Jean-Yi Chen. 2008. "Detecting Hospital Fraud and Claim Abuse through Diabetic Outpatient Services." *Health Care Management Science* 11(4): 353–358.

Magarotto, Roberto, Gianluigi Lunardi, Francesca Coati, Paola Cassandrini, Vincenzo Picece, Silvia Ferrighi, Luciana Oliosi, and Marco Venturini. 2011. Reduced Use of Chemotherapy at the End of Life in an Integrated-Care Model of Oncology and Palliative Care. *Tumori* 97(5): 573–577.

Markets and Markets. 2013. Healthcare Analytics/Medical Analytics Market by Application, December. Available at http://www.marketsandmarkets.com/Market-Reports/healthcare- data-analytics-market-905.html

Medicare Payment Advisory Commision. 2011. Hospital Acute Inpatient Services Payment System. Available at http://www.medpac.gov/documents/MedPAC_Payment_Basics_11_hospital.pdf

O'Connell, Jessica B., Melinda A. Maggard, Jerome H. Liu, David A. Etzioni, and Clifford Y. Ko. 2004. Are Survival Rates Different for Young and Older Patients with Rectal Cancer? *Diseases of the Colon & Rectum* 47(12): 2064–2069.

Pal, Aroop, Stewart Babbott, and Samaneh Tavalali Wilkinson. 2013. Can the Targeted Use of a Discharge Pharmacist Significantly Decrease 30-Day Readmissions? *Hospital Pharmacy* 48(5): 380–388.

Parente, Stephen T., Brian Schulte, Allen Jost, Thomas Sullivan, and Allan Klindworth. 2012. Assessment of Predictive Modeling for Identifying Fraud within the Medicare Program. *A Klindworth.*

Phua, Clifton, Vincent Lee, Kate Smith, and Ross Gayler. 2010. A Comprehensive Survey of Data Mining-Based Fraud Detection Research. *arXiv preprint arXiv:1009.6119.*

Robert Wood Johnson Foundation (RWJF). 2014a. County Health Rankings and Roadmaps. Available at http://www.countyhealthrankings.org/

Robert Wood Johnson Foundation (RWJF). 2014b. Robert Wood Johnson Foundation. Available at http://www.rwjf.org/

Shin, Hyunjung, Hayoung Park, Junwoo Lee, and Won Chul Jhee. 2012. A Scoring Model to Detect Abusive Billing Patterns in Health Insurance Claims. *Expert Systems with Applications* 39(8): 7441–7450.

Spruce, Lisa R., and Julie Tanner Sanford. 2012. An Intervention to Change the Approach to Colorectal Cancer Screening in Primary Care. *Journal of the American Academy of Nurse Practitioners* 24(4): 167–174.

Thorpe, Natalie, Stacie Deslich, Andrew Sikula Sr., and Alberto Coustasse. 2012. Combating Medicare Fraud: A Struggling Work in Progress. Marshall University Management Faculty Research.

Travaille, Peter, Roland M. Müller, Dallas Thornton, and Jos Hillegersberg. 2011a. Electronic Fraud Detection in the US Medicaid Healthcare Program: Lessons Learned from Other Industries. *Proceedings of the Seventeenth Americas Conference on Information Systems.*

Travaille, Peter, Roland M. Müller, Dallas Thornton, and Jos Hillegersberg. 2011b. Electronic Fraud Detection in the US Medicaid Healthcare Program: Lessons Learned from Other Industries.

Tribble, S.J. 2013. Cleveland Clinic May Charge $22,000 for Chest Pain, but Parma is $10,000. *Cleveland.com,* May 8. Available at http://www.cleveland.com/healthfit/index.ssf/2013/05/cleveland_clinic_may_charge_22.html

U.S. Department of Health and Human Services. 2014. Health Indicators Warehouse (HIW). Available at http://healthindicators.gov/

Verisk Health. 2012. Solving $400 Billion Problem of Fraud in Medicare & Medicaid. Available at http://www.veriskhealth.com/whitepaper-and-research/solving-400-billion-problem-fraud-medicare-medicaid

Walsh, Judith M.E., and Stephen J. McPhee. 1992. A Systems Model of Clinical Preventive Care: An Analysis of Factors Influencing Patient and Physician. *Health Education & Behavior* 19(2): 157–175.

Wright, Alexi A., Baohui Zhang, Alaka Ray, Jennifer W. Mack, Elizabeth Trice, Tracy Balboni, Susan L. Mitchell, Vicki A. Jackson, Susan D. Block, and Paul K. Maciejewski. 2008. Associations between End-of-Life Discussions, Patient Mental Health, Medical Care Near Death, and Caregiver Bereavement Adjustment. *Journal of the American Medical Association* 300(14): 1665–1673.

Zia, L. 2013. Prediction Models in Health Care Systems: Applications and Insights. PhD dissertation, Stanford University.

Zimmerman, Noah. 2013. Data Science Labs: Predictive Modeling to Detect Healthcare Fraud, Waste, and Abuse. Available at http://blog.gopivotal.com/case-studies-2/data-science-labs-predictive-modeling-to-detect-healthcare-fraud-waste-and-abuse

15

Measuring e-Health Impact: An e-Health Evaluation Framework that Leverages Process Control Theory and Big Data Analytics*

Derek Ritz

CONTENTS

---

* This work heavily leverages elements of the author's graduate thesis ("HALE and Healthy," University of Edinburgh, 2012), presentations made at the 2013 Canadian National e-Health Conference (Ottawa, June 2013) and the Asia e-health Information Network (AeHIN) general meeting (Manila, October 2013), and content developed in support of his advisory services on national e-health infrastructure projects in Canada, southern Africa and in southeast Asia.

OBJECTIVES

After reading this chapter, the reader shall be able to:

- Understand the complexity of health systems
- Explain frameworks for measuring health systems
- Describe measures of health systems
- Understand the role of e-health in evaluating health systems

ABSTRACT

There is, at present, a genuine challenge in answering the direct question: What is the health impact of implementing e-health? This is a problem— and a significant one. For any minister of health, regional administrator, or hospital chief executive officer (CEO) to invest in e-health, it should be clear that the expenditure of funds on information and communication technology (ICT) will yield a demonstrable health benefit for the population of interest. Today, however, this is not at all clear, and there is a dearth of evidence that such benefits are to be realized. We know that part of the art of problem solving is to frame a problem in such a way that it lends itself to being solved. This chapter describes a way to frame the *e-health impact* problem. It describes an evaluation framework that may be employed to explicitly measure the population health impact of e-health implemented at scale.

INTRODUCTION

Why Is e-Health a Challenging Problem?

The evaluation of e-health's impact on health is confounded by three core issues:

1. Health systems are complicated—or complex—or both.
2. It is difficult to measure *health*.
3. The workings of the health production function are not well understood.

What Do We Mean by the Term *Health System?*

Defining the term *health system* is, as it turns out, nontrivial. Many sources, especially in North America, use health system as a synonym for the medical care delivery network composed of primary, tertiary, acute, and long-term care and the financial models that may be employed to fund these (Hsiao, 2003). The World Health Organization (WHO), as one would expect (see Figure 15.1), posits a broader definition:

> A health system consists of all organizations, people and actions whose primary intent is to promote, restore or maintain health. This includes efforts to influence determinants of health as well as more direct health-improving activities. A health system is therefore more than the pyramid of publicly owned facilities that deliver personal health services. It includes, for example, a mother caring for a sick child at home; private providers; behaviour change programmes; vector-control campaigns; health insurance organizations; occupational health and safety legislation. It includes inter-sectoral action by health staff, for example, encouraging the ministry of education to promote female education, a well known determinant of better health. (WHO, 2007, p. 2).

In its widely cited 2007 framework document, WHO defines six interrelated building blocks of a well-functioning health system:

> *Good health services* are those that deliver effective, safe, quality personal and nonpersonal health interventions to those that need them, when and where needed, with minimum waste of resources.

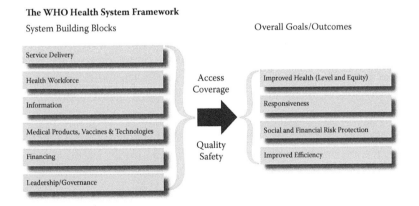

The WHO Health System Framework

FIGURE 15.1

The World Health Organization System Framework. (2007. Everybody's Business: Strengthening Health Systems to Improve Health Outcomes: WHO's Framework for Action. Production. Geneva, Switzerland: WHO.)

A *well-performing health workforce* is one that works in ways that are responsive, fair, and efficient to achieve the best health outcomes possible, given available resources and circumstances (i.e., there are sufficient staff, fairly distributed; they are competent, responsive, and productive).

A *well-functioning health information system* is one that ensures the production, analysis, dissemination and use of reliable and timely information on health determinants, health system performance, and health status.

A *well-functioning health system* ensures equitable access to essential medical products, vaccines, and technologies of assured quality, safety, efficacy, and cost-effectiveness and their scientifically sound and cost-effective use.

A *good health financing system* raises adequate funds for health in ways that ensure people can use needed services and are protected from financial catastrophe or impoverishment associated with having to pay for them. It provides incentives for providers and users to be efficient.

Leadership and governance involve ensuring strategic policy frameworks exist and are combined with effective oversight, coalition building, regulation, attention to system design, and accountability.

The WHO building blocks model implies a cogs-in-a-machine view of health systems. In contrast, the World Bank, in its definition of a health system, explores the nature of health systems as complex adaptive systems. Unlike a mechanical system, whose response to stimuli can be predicted, "adaptive systems… have the freedom to respond to different stimuli in different and unpredictable ways and are interconnected with the actions of other parts of a system" (World Bank, 2007). The World Bank report (2007) suggests complex adaptive systems have key characteristics:

Adaptable elements. They can learn and change themselves. In mechanical systems, change is imposed, whereas under adaptive systems they can happen from within.

Context. Systems exist within systems, and this context matters because one part of a system affects another. In health systems, changing the financing system may change availability and performance of health workforce, the use of other inputs, and the relationship with patients. In adaptive systems, optimizing one part of the system may lead to poor overall system performance. In a hospital, for example, reducing the length of stay of patients in one ward may lead to queuing and readmission in other parts of the hospital, compromising overall quality or cost.

Inherent order. Systems can be orderly even if there is no central control, often because they self-organize. Health systems are self-organizing; different types of provider organizations, associations, and behaviors emerge continually, either formally or informally.

Not predictable in detail. Changes are not linear or easily predictable. For example, a large health program may have little impact, but a rumor may spark a strike or a riot at a clinic. Forecasting and modeling in health systems can be done to predict effects on health and poverty, but they are not predictable in detail because the elements and relationships are changeable and nonlinear, often in creative ways. The only way to know what complex adaptive systems will do is to observe them (World Bank, 2007, pp. 27–28).

Nobel laureate H. A. Simon advocated for a nested hierarchies approach to describing and dealing with complex adaptive systems. Less than five years after confirmation of the DNA theory of replication, Simon (1962) asserted that "correlation between state description and process description is basic to the functioning of any adaptive organism" with the generalizability of such thinking illustrated by an example based on the highly mechanical process of watch-making. Simon was truly visionary. Decades ahead of the development of genetic algorithms and pattern matching software, Simon postulated that in "their dynamics, hierarchies have a property, near-decomposability, that greatly simplifies their behaviour."

Clearly, health systems are interesting creatures. Taken as a whole, health system models could be compared to the wave and particle theories of light. These systems can be seen to exhibit complex adaptive properties yet are often amenable to classic process control in ways that seem to indicate the workings of underlying mechanistic models.

WHAT IS HEALTH AND HOW CAN WE QUANTIFY IT?

There is a business axiom, which is sometimes attributed to W. Edwards Deming and sometimes to Peter Drucker: You can't manage what you don't measure. It is generally accepted that a universal measure of health is long life. Indeed, life expectancy at birth is a very common measure of population health. However, when informing the management of a health system, length of life alone is too crude a metric; one must also account for the quality of that life and the morbidities that may diminish that quality.

Fryback (2010) lays out a useful landscape for quantifying health: "Health may be measured at the population level, or for a group of individuals, or at the level of the individual person. These measures are not mutually exclusive, as most individual measures can be aggregated in some fashion to represent a group or population. Health measures may be roughly classified as indicators, disease-specific measures, generic health profiles, and summary health-related quality of life index" (p. 3). Fryback references a hierarchy of health measures (after Wolfson). This hierarchy is illustrated in Figure 15.2, which shows that health-related quality of life (HRQoL) indicators are the most aggregated measures of population health. It is important to note, however, that most population measured may be expressed as aggregations of individual measures.

There is significant scholarly literature on the calculation of HRQoL indices (Arnesen, 2004; Arrow et al., 2012; Billingham, Abrams, and Jones, 1999; Brouwer et al., 2005; Davidson, 2009; Dobrev et al., 2008; IOM, 2011; Peters et al., 2009; Robberstad, 2005; Robine et al., 2000; Sorenson, Drummond, and Kanavos, 2008; WHO, 2003a, 2003b, 2011; Williams and Bryan, 2007; World Bank, 2006). Generally, there is consensus that the two main types of HRQoL metrics are (1) quality-adjusted life-years

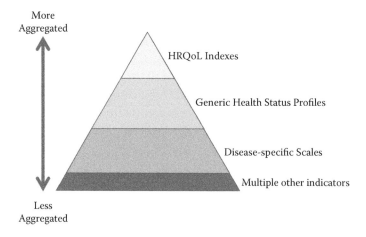

FIGURE 15.2
Data Pyramid for population health. (Fryback, Dennis G. 2010. *Measuring Health-Related Quality of Life*. Washington, DC: The National Academies.)

(QALYs) and (2) disability-adjusted life-years (DALYs). Both metrics are measures of time that are adjusted based on a simple premise: health may be considered on a scale from 0–1, where 0 indicates death, and 1 indicates full health. Therefore, a life-year at full health equals a full year. A life-year at 75% of full health (0.75) would equal a health-adjusted life-year valued at 9 months. A sum of QALYs, therefore, is a measure of lifespan that has been adjusted to reflect diminished health or hastened death due to adverse health impacts. A population-averaged sum of the expected QALYs at birth yields a health-adjusted life expectancy (HALE) for the population of interest.

As a complementary metric, one can also determine what should have been a person's life expectancy, at full health, had they not suffered the adverse health impacts. Graphically, one can think of this as the gap between the quality-adjusted life years and the theoretical life years at full health. This gap represents the DALYs that have been lost due to the adverse health impact or impacts. An example from Robberstad (2005) is shown in Figure 15.3.

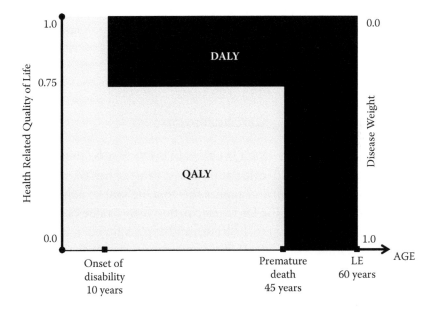

FIGURE 15.3
Illustrating QALYs and DALYs. (From Robberstad, Bjarne. 2005. QALYs vs DALYs vs LYs gained: What are the differences, and what difference do they make for health care priority setting? *Norsk Epidemiologi* 15(2): 183–191. http://www.ntnu.no/ojs/index.php/norepid/article/view/217e)

Figure 15.3 graphically illustrates the life-years of a person who suffers the onset of some disability at the age of 10, lives with the condition for 35 years, and suffers premature death at the age of 45. If the statistical life expectancy (LE) for a member of this population is 60 years and the health-related quality of life weight associated with the condition is 0.75, the lifetime QALYs for the person may be calculated as the gray area shown in the figure:

$$(10 \text{ years} * 1.0 \text{ health/year}) + (35 \text{ years} * 0.75 \text{ health/year})$$
$$= 36.25 \text{ health-years}$$

Conversely, the gap (DALYs) is illustrated by the black area on the graphic:

$$60 \text{ years} * 1.0 \text{ health/year} - 36.25 \text{ health-years} = 23.75 \text{ health-years}$$

The DALYs may also be calculated as the years of life lost due to premature death (YLL) plus the years of diminished health due to living with disability (YLD):

$$DALY = YLL + YLD$$
$$= (60 - 45) + (35 * (1.00 - 0.75))$$
$$= 15 + (35 * 0.25)$$
$$= 15 + 8.75$$
$$= 23.75 \text{ health-years}$$

As illustrated by Figure 15.3, QALYs and DALYs may be thought of as complementary. The QALY calculation uses a value of health, rated from 0 (death) to 1 (full health), and applies this to a life year to adjust for the quality of the lived year. The DALY calculation uses a value of disability, rated from 0 (no disability) to 1 (death), and applies this to a life year to determine the impact of the disability on what would have otherwise been full health.

The development of a "health scale" bears scrutiny. The process used by WHO, for instance, is described in detail in its cost-effectiveness handbook (WHO, 2003a, p. 51):

> While death is not difficult to define, non-fatal health states are. Nonfatal outcomes of disease differ in their impact on the individual, and the

impact on the individual is mediated by contextual factors including personal characteristics and the physical and social environment. Nonfatal outcomes involve multiple domains such as mobility, anxiety and pain: health state valuations provide the means to weight and then aggregate individual functioning on these domains of health.

To develop health state values, WHO recommends use of a short and simple visual analog scale (VAS) questionnaire to capture ordinal ranking of multiple health states from the general population. A smaller sample of the population (with high levels of educational attainment) would answer a more detailed, multistate, multimethod survey. The purpose of the second survey is to provide the precisely articulated intervals that may then be combined with the results of the first study to model the appropriate measures of health state values for the population of interest. Fryback (2010) and Kopec (2003) have advocated the use of common, standardized health status survey that may be employed to automatically generate the preference weights (the 0–1 health scale). Although there are differences between the tools, they may be accounted for using transform functions (Fryback, 2010).

Another approach to employing health state values is to develop HALE metrics based on a population's statistical expectation of years lived without disability. The Centers for Disease Control and Prevention (CDC) develop such a HALE using their Healthy Days (CDC, 2000) surveys. The European Health Expectancy Unit's calculation (Robine et al., 2007) of disability-free life expectancy (DFLE) is similar and may also be employed to develop a rudimentary HALE based on the premise that a healthy year is fully weighted (worth 1.0 health-year) and each unhealthy year is worth zero.

Many scholars address the important concept of discounting in the calculation of adjusted life-years (Arnesen, 2004; Billingham et al., 1999; Brouwer et al., 2005; Davidson, 2009; Gold, Stevenson, and Fryback, 2002). Similar to the application of future value discounting in economics, it is common to discount the future value of life-years gained (through a health intervention, for instance). Discounting can have a significant impact on the relative perceived cost-effectiveness of candidate health interventions—especially for public health or preventive measures which may not yield health benefits until later in a person's life.

Unlike QALYs, DALYs are also sometimes age weighted. Age weighting is used to mathematically reduce the value of lost life-years in the very young and the very old. Although such weighting is generally reflective of societal beliefs, it has drawn criticism on ethical grounds (Gold et al., 2002). Many organizations (e.g., WHO, World Bank) now report calculated DALYs with and without age weighting to address the ethical controversy that may surround such weighting.

In its 2000 HALE report (Mathers et al., 2000, p. 310), WHO outlined the minimum set of desirable properties for HRQoL metrics:

1. If age-specific mortality decreases in any age group, everything else being the same, then a summary measure should improve (i.e., a health gap should decrease and a health expectancy should increase).
2. If age-specific prevalence of some health state worse than ideal health increases, everything else being the same, a summary measure should get worse.
3. If age-specific incidence of some health state worse than ideal health increases, everything else being the same, a summary measure should get worse.
4. If age-specific remission for some health state worse than ideal health increases, everything else being the same, a summary measure should improve.
5. If the severity of a given health state worsens, everything else being the same, then a summary measure should get worse.

To these, two other overarching attributes were added (Mathers et al., 2000):

1. Summary measures should be comprehensible and feasible to calculate for many populations. Comprehensibility and complexity are different. Life expectancy at birth is a complex abstract measure but is easy to understand. Health expectancies are popular because they are also easily understood.
2. Summary measures should be linear aggregates of the summary measures calculated for any arbitrary partitioning of subgroups. Many decision-makers, and very often the public, desire information that is characterized by this type of additive decomposition. In other words, they would like to be able to answer what fraction of the summary measure is related to health events in the poor, in the uninsured, in the elderly, in children, and so on. Additive decomposition is also often appealing for cause attribution.

HOW DOES THE HEALTH PRODUCTION FUNCTION WORK?

The concept of a *health production function* was first postulated by the American economist Michael Grossman over 40 years ago. Put simply, Grossman (1972) described health as a "durable capital stock that produces an output of healthy time" (p. 223). According to Grossman's model, health stock and its production are described as a function of genetic endowment and resource expenditure at the individual level.

On a macrolevel, Grossman's theoretical model may be leveraged to describe population health in terms of per capita variables expressing economic, social, and environmental factors (Fayissa and Gutema, 2005). The literature regarding the concept of a health production function usefully embraces the notion that a health production *system* incorporates much more than what is normally considered part of a care delivery network (a *health care system*), including things like population-level behaviors (healthy eating habits, exercise), education, and wealth (Fayissa and Gutema, 2005; Lessard and Birch, 2009; Mwabu, 2007; Ogunleye, 2012; WHO, 2009).

How might we depict the workings of a health production system? WHO's (2010) monitoring and evaluation (M&E) framework is, not surprisingly, aligned with their health system model. This framework is shown in Figure 15.4. From the figure we may note that the WHO framework is based on the classic M&E pipeline model of inputs, outputs, outcomes, and impact.

The World Bank Health System Analysis (HSA) model (Berman and Bitran, 2011) is shown in Figure 15.5. This framework, sometimes referred to as the control knobs model, importantly illustrates the idea that some manner of process control may be exerted upon a health system. As indicated in the figure, this control is exerted through system-level control knobs including health system financing, payments schemes, and regulation.

The underlying concepts and theories of process control are not always well understood by those outside of the engineering disciplines. To give a brief illustration of these concepts, a graphical depiction of process control techniques is shown in Figure 15.6. From Figure 15.6a we see that a generic system may be thought of in terms of inputs and outputs across an arbitrary system boundary. Some system inputs are measured, some are controlled; others are unmeasured or uncontrolled (shown as dashed-line arrows). Likewise, some outputs are measured and some are not.

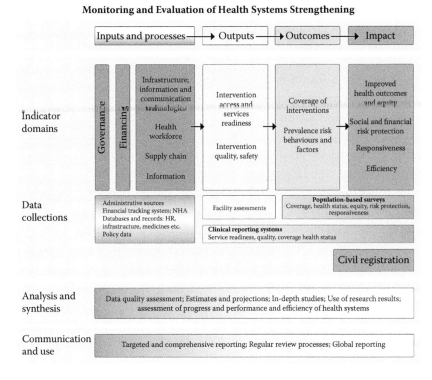

FIGURE 15.4
WHO monitoring and evaluation framework. (From Who, 2010. Monitoring the Building Blocks of Health Systems: A Handbook of Indicators and Their Measurement Strategies. Geneva, Switzerland: WHO, p. vii.)

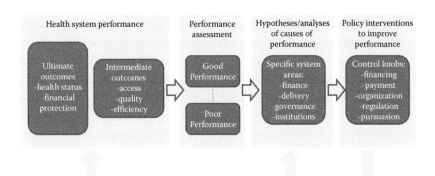

FIGURE 15.5
World Bank health system performance model. (From Berman, Peter, and Ricardo Bitran. 2011. *Health Systems Analysis for Better Health System Strengthening*. Washington, DC: The World Bank, p. 7.)

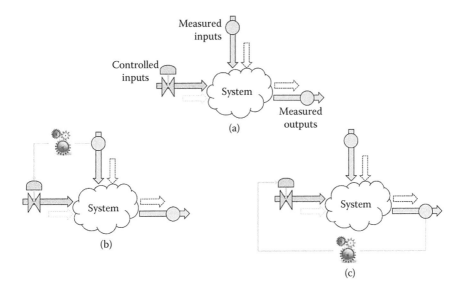

FIGURE 15.6
Generic representation of system process control.

Figure 15.6b illustrates *feedforward process control*. In feedforward control, a measured input drives a control logic (indicated by the gear train), which in turn provides a control signal to a controlled input. If the measured input is being used to infer the value of an unmeasured input, it is called *inferential feedforward process control*. Figure 15.6c illustrates *feedback process control*. In feedback control, a measured output drives a control logic (indicated by the gear train), which provides the control signal to a controlled input. As before, in a configuration where a measured output is being used to infer the value of an unmeasured output, it is called *inferential feedback process control*. The World Bank control knobs model is an example of feedback control.

When thinking of process control, it is useful to use the analogy of filling the bathtub (Figure 15.7). The system is the bathtub. To get just the right temperature, if you put your hand in the tub of water and adjust the faucets accordingly—that is feedback control. If you put your hand in the input stream and adjust the faucets, that is feedforward control. If you watch the steam rise from the tub (feedback) or from the stream (feedforward) and adjust accordingly, that is inferential process control.

In closing this section, we return to the idea of health production. For our purposes, it will be accepted that systemic health production is impacted by the care delivery network (primary, community, and tertiary/acute care),

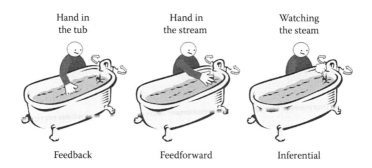

FIGURE 15.7
The "Bathtub Analogy" for process control theory.

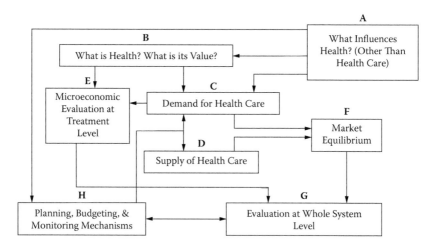

FIGURE 15.8
Williams' health production "plumbing" diagram. (From Williams, Alan. 1987. Health economics: The cheerful face of a dismal science. In *Health and Economics,* edited by Alan Williams. London: Macmillan.)

by public health interventions (e.g., immunizations, nutritional education, tobacco taxation), and by process control mechanisms at the micro/individual and the macro/system levels. Conceptually, this idea is illustrated by Alan Williams' (1987) plumbing diagram (Figure 15.8).

In the following section, a framework is described that relates investments in pervasive, standards-based e-health infrastructure and how these impact upon population health. This framework embraces and operationalizes concepts of health process control and population-level health metrics and importantly leverages recent advances in big data analytics to drive the crucial process control logic.

WHAT IS THE NEW APPROACH, AND HOW IS IT DIFFERENT?

The previous section outlined key issues that impede efforts to discern the health impact of e-health:

1. It is difficult to define and describe what a health system is, let alone what role e-health plays within that system.
2. There are genuine challenges in describing what health is and in measuring it at an individual or population level.
3. There are a lot of moving pieces in a health system, and it is hard to understand how they operate to execute the health production function.

Using Patton's (2011) ontology, as illustrated by Figure 15.9, some aspects of a health system may be considered to lie within the zone of complexity. Indeed, such is the case for almost any sociotechnical system. It is noteworthy that various elements of a health system will fall into the simple area, the complicated areas, and the zone of complexity. The management

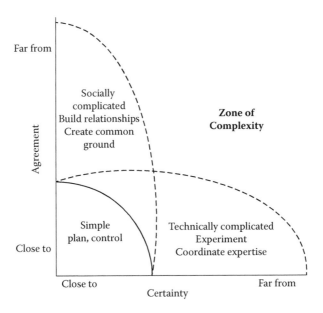

FIGURE 15.9
Illustration of the zone of complexity.

of complex systems will favor *sense and adapt* over *plan and control.* Simon's (1962) concept of characterizing complex systems as nested hierarchies can usefully inform such an approach.

Based on the preceding, a new evaluation framework is proposed for describing the role of e-health within a health production system. It is reflective of the dual nature of health systems as both complex adaptive yet exhibiting near-decomposability amenable to process control. It leverages big data analytic techniques to develop a HALE metric from person-centric e-health transactions. On a hierarchical, recursive basis, both feedforward and feedback process control is employed to operationalize a virtuous cycle of continuous quality improvement. This framework is illustrated in Figure 15.10. It depicts how national-scale, standards-based e-health infrastructure impacts upon population health. Tracing the paths of the arrows, the system behaviors may be described as follows:

1. Health interventions yield population health. It is the role of public health and curative care interventions (health interventions) to positively impact upon the health of the nation's citizens

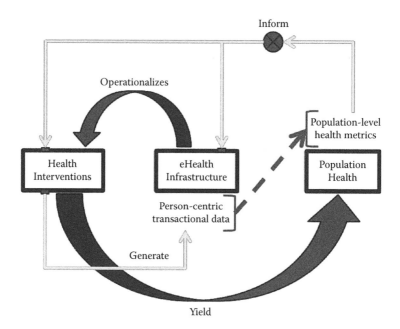

FIGURE 15.10
An evaluative model for describing the health impact of eHealth.

(population health). Insecticide treated bed nets reduce the spread of malaria; antiretroviral medications are used to manage individual patients' HIV; immunizations help reduce childhood morbidity and mortality. Such interventions, especially clinical interventions, are typically supported by strong evidence such as randomized controlled trials (RCT).

2. e-health infrastructure operationalizes health interventions. The e-health infrastructure is an industrial engineering intervention; its job is to improve the efficiency and effectiveness of the health interventions. Systematic SMS reminders reduce loss to follow-up; coded health observations raise alerts if readings are outside of antenatal care guidelines; longitudinal, person-centric information supports evidence-based chronic disease management.

3. Health interventions generate person-centric transactional data. e-health applications meter the system. The use of standards-based ICTs to support care delivery workflows lays down transactional data that are in a computable format.

4. Person-centric transactional data may be aggregated to generate population-level health metrics. Standards-based data may be employed to calculate statistics and support analyses across subpopulations or on a national basis. Information aggregated at an individual level is, by definition, a longitudinal electronic health record (EHR) for that citizen. Aggregated information at a care provider level may be employed for human resource management and to support payment initiatives such as performance-based financing (PBF). District or regional-level data can support health system management and, at a national level, population health indicators can be developed and reported.

5. Population-level health metrics inform both e-health infrastructure and health interventions. We can use the aggregated indicators to create feedback loops. This enables us to exert process control upon the system to continuously improve both our e-health applications and the health interventions they support. Such feedback, over time, creates what is referred to by the U.S. National Institutes of Health as a learning health system (Grossman, Powers, and Mcginnis, 2011).

It is useful to specifically explore the pivotal role played by the e-health infrastructure. Through a pervasive, standards-based e-health infrastructure, we both meter the health production system and afford ourselves a mechanism to exert process control upon it. A caricature of a health system is depicted in Figure 15.11 to illustrate this important point.

WHY IS THIS IMPORTANT?

Recall the axiom: You can't manage what you don't measure. Couched inside this common sense imperative are crucial insights into the value of e-health and the crucial role it can play in impacting health.

Measure Health

Big data analytics affords us a mechanism to measure health. We can leverage statistical techniques to develop a population-level HRQoL from person-centric e-health transactions (Helfand et al., 2012). This opportunity presents itself, however, only when e-health infrastructure is pervasive

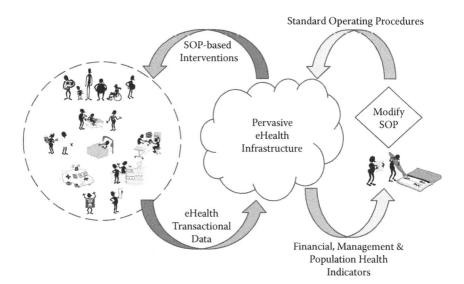

FIGURE 15.11

An eHealth-supported health production system. This figure may be read in a counterclockwise fashion starting from the top right of the diagram. Following are comments pertaining to such a reading. *(Continued)*

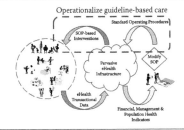

Based on public health and care delivery priorities (the system health "vision"), standard operating procedures (SOPs) are developed and operationalized within the eHealth infrastructure. Such SOPs could include guideline-based chronic disease management or maternal care, for example. Operationally, the eHealth infrastructure exerts feedforward process control regarding these SOPs.

Individual health outcomes are significantly positively impacted by continuity of care, over time and across different care sites. Shared health record infrastructure, such as a Health Information Exchange (HIE), supports such continuity of care and the health impacts that arise from it.

eHealth transactions record the activities of health system actors (both subjects of care and care providers). Comparisons between SOPs and actual actions provide management metrics at the individual level (e.g. medications adherence), provider level (e.g. guideline adherence), facility level, district level, etc. Management actions based on such comparisons exert feedback process control on the health production system.

Standards-based eHealth transactions are computable and may be employed to develop population-level metrics from the person-centric transaction logs. In the face of pervasive eHealth infrastructure, big data analytic techniques may be leveraged to express HRQoL indicators.

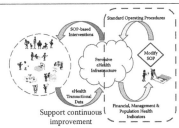

For the health production system as a whole, an appropriate HRQoL metric may be employed as a feedback process control signal. In this way, SOPs may be evolved to operationalize health production activities sympathetic to improved population health and to disincentivize those that are antithetical to improved health.

FIGURE 15.11 (Continued)

An eHealth-supported health production system. This figure may be read in a counter-clockwise fashion starting from the top right of the diagram. Following are comments pertaining to such a reading.

and when the person-centric transactions are in a computable (standards-based) form. The U.S. Health Information Technology for Economic and Clinical Health (HITECH) Act (formally part of the American Recovery and Reinvestment Act of 2009) is an example of how public policy and health system financing may be used as control knobs in incenting such pervasive infrastructure and reflects the important notion that *scale is the innovation.*

Manage for Health

Although it may be true that you can't manage what don't measure, that doesn't necessarily mean you *can* manage what you *do* measure. Especially in a complex adaptive system, command and control measures are often difficult to introduce and can have unintended consequences (Ash et al., 2007; Coiera, 2007; Hsiao and Siadat, 2009). At the individual, patient level, it has been shown that guideline-based care will yield the best health outcomes (Freedman et al., 2005; Kupersmith et al., 2007; Mechael and Sloninsky, 2008). Leveraging Simon's decomposability simplification, e-health may be employed to increase adherence to guideline-based interventions at the point of care. At the health production system level, iterative, sense and adapt techniques need to leverage provider compensation, drug formulary, public health education, school fitness, and other interventions are largely operationalized by public policy and health system financing. The key is for the HRQoL control signal to guide the evolution of interventions expressed in the standard operating procedures (SOPs). Techniques relying on the natural variability within a large population open up important opportunities to leverage the big data analytics to discern interventions that are having the greatest health impact (Grossman et al., 2011).

Optimize Health

When optimizing any system, one must answer the fundamental question: optimal with respect to what? From a public policy standpoint, a health production system is optimal if it generates the maximum quantity of health that may be produced based on the resource constraints within which it operates. Such an obvious statement masks the quite controversial assertion that health systems, when characterized as very large commercial markets, will naturally evolve toward optimization of financial return.

This underlines the crucial importance of being able to support measuring and managing for health.

FUTURE DIRECTIONS

At present (2014), only a few countries have implemented e-health infrastructure at national scale; almost all of these are deployed in developed countries. Many of these bellwether implementations have experienced issues regarding broad uptake by providers and adoption of e-health standards. As issues are sorted out, national governments are launching initiatives specifically tasked with leveraging benefits from their infrastructure investments. Organizations such as the UK's National Institute for Health and Care Excellence (NICE), the U.S. Patient Centered Outcomes Research Institute (PCORI), Canada Health Infoway, and others are actively engaged in programs around benefits realization.

In the coming years, national-scale e-health infrastructure projects in lower- and middle-income countries will begin to come on stream. Projects in Rwanda, South Africa, the Philippines, Brazil, and India are under way, and many others are in the project planning stages. Many of these new projects are aligned with national aspirations regarding universal health coverage (UHC), and the infrastructure investments will be leveraged to support health insurance schemes as an integral part of the health production system. Many of these infrastructures will also, out of necessity, leverage technology platforms based on mobile phones and their associated mobile networks. In these settings we have already seen the significant benefits from health production systems that leverage mobile technologies to more closely engage with individual patients (Lester et al., 2010; Mapham, 2008).

The present model represents a rethinking of e-health and its role in a complex health production system. Reframing the approach helps us address the important question: What is the health impact of e-health? Standards-based e-health infrastructure, at scale, provides us with a mechanism to meter our health production system and, at the same time, a way to exert process control upon it. By leveraging big data analytical techniques, we can use population health as a system-level control signal, and in this way we can optimize for it. By embracing the complex nature of our health systems, we can recursively evolve and improve them and operationalize the concept of a learning health system.

REFERENCES

Arnesen, T.M. 2004. Counting Health? A Critical Analysis of Cost Utility Analysis as a Tool for Setting Priorities in Health. *Health Services Research*. PhD thesis. Available at http://scholar.google.com/scholar?hl = en&btnG = Search&q = intitle:COUNTIN G+HEALTH?+A+critical+analysis+of+Cost+Utility+Analysis+as+a+tool+for+setti ng+priorities+in+health#0

Arrow, K., K. Bilir, S. Brownlee, and R. Califf. 2012. *Valuing Health Care: Improving Productivity and Quality*. Kansas City, MO.

Ash, Joan S., Dean F. Sittig, Richard H. Dykstra, Kenneth Guappone, James D. Carpenter, and Veena Seshadri. 2007. Categorizing the Unintended Sociotechnical Consequences of Computerized Provider Order Entry. *International Journal of Medical Informatics* 76(Suppl 1): S21–7. Available at http://www.ncbi.nlm.nih.gov/pubmed/16793330

Berman, Peter, and Ricardo Bitran. 2011. *Health Systems Analysis for Better Health System Strengthening*. Washington, DC: World Bank.

Billingham, L.J., K.R. Abrams, and D.R. Jones. 1999. Methods for the Analysis of Quality-of-Life and Survival Data in Health Technology Assessment. *Health Technology Assessment* 3(10): 1–157.

Brouwer, W.B.F., L.W. Niessen, M.J. Postma, and F.F.H. Rutten. 2005. Need for Differential Discounting of Costs and Health Effects in Cost Effectiveness Analyses. *BMJ* 331(7514): 446–448. Available at http://www.bmj.com/content/331/7514/446.extract

Centers for Disease Control and Prevention (CDC). 2000. Measuring Healthy Days. Atlanta, GA: Centers for Disease Control and Prevention.

Coiera, Enrico. 2007. Putting the Technical Back into Socio-Technical Systems Research. *International Journal of Medical Informatics* 76(Suppl 1): S98–103. Available at http://www.ncbi.nlm.nih.gov/pubmed/16807084

Davidson, Thomas. 2009. How to Include Relatives and Productivity Loss in a Cost-Effectiveness Analysis. *Linköping University Medical Dissertations* (1101). Available at http://hj.diva-portal.org/smash/get/diva2:200966/FULLTEXT01

Dobrev, Alexander, Tom Jones, Anne Kersting, Jorg Artmann, Karl Streotmann, and Veli Stroetmann. 2008. Report on Methodology for Evaluating the Socio-Economic Impact of Interoperable EHR and ePrescribing Systems. Bonn.

Fayissa, Bichaka, and Paulos Gutema. 2005. Estimating a Health Production Function for Sub-Saharan Africa (SSA). *Applied Economics* 37(2): 155–164. Available at http://www.tandfonline.com/doi/abs/10.1080/00036840412331313521

Freedman, Lynn, Ronald Waldman, Helen de Pinho, Meg Wirth, Mushtaque Chowdhury, and Allan Rosenfield. 2005. *Who's Got the Power? Transforming Health Systems for Women and Children*. Summary Version of the Task Force on Child Health and Maternal Health. New York.

Fryback, Dennis G. 2010. *Measuring Health-Related Quality of Life*. Washington, DC: National Academies.

Gold, Marthe R., David Stevenson, and Dennis G. Fryback. 2002. HALYS and QALYS and DALYS, Oh My: Similarities and Differences in Summary Measures of Population Health. *Annual Review of Public Health* 23: 115–134. Available at http://www.ncbi.nlm.nih.gov/pubmed/11910057

Grossman, Claudia, Brian Powers, and J. Michael Mcginnis (Eds.). 2011. *Digital Infrastructure for the Learning Health System: The Foundation for Continuous Improvement in Health and Health Care*. Washington, DC: Institute of Medicine.

Grossman, Michael. 1972. On the Concept of Health Capital and the Demand for Health. *Journal of Political Economy* 80(2): 223–255. Available at http://www.jstor.org/stable/10.2307/1830580

Helfand, Mark, Alfred Berg, David Flum, Sherine Gabriel, and Sharon-Lise Normand. 2012. Draft Methodology Report: "Our Questions, Our Decisions: Standards for Patient-Centered Outcomes Research." Washington, DC. Available at http://preview.acr.org/~/media/ACR/Documents/PDF/Advocacy/Fed Relations/pcori_draftmethodologyreportforcomment_72012.pdf

Hsiao, W.C. 2003. What Is a Health System? Why Should We Care? Working Paper, Harvard School of Public Health, Boston, MA. Available at http://lingli.ccer.edu.cn/ahe2011/papers/5/Hsiao(2003).pdf

Hsiao, William C., and Banafsheh Siadat. 2009. In Search of a Common Conceptual Framework for Health Systems Strengthening. Washington, DC: World Bank. Available at http://siteresources.worldbank.org/INTHSD/Resources/376278-1114111154043/1011834-1246449110524/HsiaoSiadatInSearchOfaCommonConceptualFrameworkForHSSDraft62309.pdf

IOM. 2011. *For the Public's Health: The Role of Measurement in Action and Accountability. Measurement.* Washington, DC: National Academies Press.

Kopec, J. 2003. A Comparative Review of Four Preference-Weighted Measures of Health-Related Quality of Life. *Journal of Clinical Epidemiology* 56(4): 317–325. Available at http://linkinghub.elsevier.com/retrieve/pii/S0895435602006091

Kupersmith, Joel, Joseph Francis, Eve Kerr, Sarah Krein, Leonard Pogach, Robert M. Kolodner, and Jonathan B. Perlin. 2007. Advancing Evidence-Based Care for Diabetes: Lessons from the Veterans Health Administration. *Health Affairs (Project Hope)* 26(2): w156–68. Available at http://www.ncbi.nlm.nih.gov/pubmed/17259199

Lessard, Chantale, and Stephen Birch. 2009. *Complex Problems or Simple Solutions? Enhancing Evidence-Based Economics to Reflect Reality.* Hamilton, Ontario.

Lester, Richard T., Paul Ritvo, Edward J. Mills, Antony Kariri, Sarah Karanja, Michael H. Chung, William Jack, et al. 2010. Effects of a Mobile Phone Short Message Service on Antiretroviral Treatment Adherence in Kenya (WelTel Kenya1): a Randomised Trial. *Lancet* 376(9755): 1838–1845. Available at http://www.ncbi.nlm.nih.gov/pubmed/21071074

Mapham, William. 2008. Mobile Phones: Changing Health Care One SMS at a Time. *South African Journal of HIV Medicine* (Spring): 11–16.

Mathers, Colin D., Ritu Sadana, Joshua A. Salomon, Christopher J.L. Murray, and Alan D. Lopez. 2000. *Estimates of DALE for 191 Countries: Methods and Results.* Geneva, Switzerland.

Mechael, Patricia, and Daniela Sloninsky. 2008. *Towards the Development of an mHealth Strategy.* Geneva, Switzerland: WHO.

Mwabu, Germano. 2007. Health Economics for Low-Income Countries. *Handbook of Development Economics* 4. Available at http://www.sciencedirect.com/science/article/pii/S1573447107040533

Ogunleye, Eric Kehinde. 2011. *Health and Economic Growth in Sub-Saharan African Countries: A Production function Approach.*

Patton, Michael Quinn. 2011. *Developmental Evaluation.* New York: Guilford Press.

Peters, David H., Sameh El-saharty, Banafsheh Siadat, Katja Janovsky, and Marko Vujicic (Eds.). 2009. *Improving Health Service Delivery in Developing Countries.* Washington, DC: World Bank Publications. Available at http://www.worldbank.icebox.ingenta.com/content/wb/bk17888

Robberstad, Bjarne. 2005. QALYs Vs DALYs Vs LYs Gained: What Are the Differences, and What Difference Do They Make for Health Care Priority Setting? *Norsk Epidemiologi* 15(2): 183–191. Available at http://www.ntnu.no/ojs/index.php/norepid/article/view/217

Robine, Edited J.-m., C. Jagger, and V. Egidi. 2000. Selection of a Coherent Set of Health Indicators: A First Step Towards A User's Guide to Health Expectancies for the European Union. *Europe*, June.

Robine, Jean-Marie, Carol Jagger, Herman Von Oyen, Bianca Cox, Emmanuelle Cambois, Isabelle Romieu, Aurore Clavel, and Sophie Le Roy. 2007. *Health Expectancy Calculation by the Sullivan Method: A Practical Guide,* 3rd ed. Montpellier, France.

Simon, H.A. 1962. The Architecture of Complexity. *Proceedings of the American Philosophical Society* 106(6): 467–482. Available at http://www.jstor.org/stable/10.2307/985254

Sorenson, Corinna, Michael Drummond, and Panos Kanavos. 2008. *Ensuring Value for Money in Health Care: The Role of Health Technology Assessment in the European Union.* Geneva, Switzerland: European Observatory on Health Systems and Policies.

WHO. 2003a. *WHO Guide to Cost-Effectiveness Analysis.* Edited by T. Tan-Torres Edejer, R. Baltussen, T. Adam, R. Hutubessy, A. Acharya, D.B. Evans, and C.J.L. Murrary. Geneva, Switzerland: WHO.

WHO. 2003b. *Systems Performance Assessment Debates, Methods and Empriricism.* Edited by Christopher J.L. Murray and David B. Evans. Geneva, Switzerland: WHO.

WHO. 2007. *Everybody's Business: Strengthening Health Systems to Improve Health Outcomes: WHO's Framework for Action. Production.* Geneva, Switzerland: WHO.

WHO. 2009. *WHO Guide to Identifying the Economic Consequences of Disease and Injury. World Health.* Geneva, Switzerland: WHO.

WHO. 2010. *Monitoring the Building Blocks of Health Systems: A Handbook of Indicators and Their Measurement Strategies.* Geneva, Switzerland: WHO.

WHO. 2011. World Health Statistics 2011 Indicator Compendium. *World Health.* Geneva, Switzerland.

Williams, Alan. 1987. Health Economics: The Cheerful Face of a Dismal Science. In *Health and Economics*, edited by Alan Williams. London: Macmillan.

Williams, Iestyn, and Stirling Bryan. 2007. Understanding the Limited Impact of Economic Evaluation in Health Care Resource Allocation: A Conceptual Framework. *Health Policy (Amsterdam, Netherlands)* 80(1): 135–143. Available at http://www.ncbi.nlm.nih.gov/pubmed/16621124

World Bank. 2006. *Global Burden of Disease and Risk Factors.* Edited by Alan D. Lopez, Colin D. Mathers, Majid Ezzati, Dean T. Mamison, and Christopher J.L. Murray. Washington, DC: World Bank.

World Bank. 2007. Healthy Development: The World Bank Strategy for Health, Nutrition, & Population Results. Washington, DC: World Bank.

Author Biographies

Ritu Agarwal is professor and the Robert H. Smith Dean Chair of Information Systems at the Robert H. Smith School of Business, University of Maryland, College Park. She is also founder and director of the Center for Health Information and Decision Systems at the Smith School, the first research center within a business school to study the use and application of information technology in health care. Agarwal's current research is focused on understanding how information technology can be used to alleviate cost and quality challenges in health care and with identifying mechanisms through which information technology can be successfully incorporated into health care routines. She has worked extensively with Fortune 500 companies on a variety of research and consulting engagements, and her research has been sponsored by the Agency for Healthcare Research and Quality, the U.S. Food and Drug Administration (FDA), CMS, Society for Information Management, U.S. Department of Labor, National Science Foundation (NSF), Defense Advanced Research Projects Agency (DARPA), and the Robert Wood Johnson Foundation.

Margrét V. Bjarnadóttir is assistant professor of management science and statistics at the Robert H. Smith School of Business, University of Maryland, College Park. His research focuses on data analytics and surveillance system design with applications in health care and finance. He holds a BSc in mechanical and industrial engineering from the University of Iceland and a PhD in operations research from the Massachusetts Institute of Technology.

Christopher Broyles is a senior at Methodist University, where he studies financial economics, political science, and international business. He is inspired by his parents, Steven Broyles and Susan Sherman-Broyles. Broyles looks forward to entering a career in public policy.

Lanette Burrows is a PMP credentialed project director with over 14 years of experience, including approximately 3 years of overseas country experience. Burrows provides leadership in program development and management, information, communication and technology, public health, and organizational support of international and domestic projects. She provides technical leadership in monitoring and evaluation and health management information systems to ensure that strategic information is used for improving clinical and program management. She has led the development of electronic medical records and other e-health systems based on field requirements. Under Burrows' management, the team applies software best practices throughout development. Similarly, she has been integral in designing assessment tools and training curriculum to strengthen capacity of her team, partners, and clients. Burrows received her MPH in international health from Johns Hopkins and has worked in Burkina Faso, Guyana, Haiti, Kenya, India, Nigeria, Rwanda, South Africa, Swaziland, Tanzania, Uganda, and Zambia.

Dilhari R. DeAlmeida, PhD. Dr. DeAlmeida is an assistant professor with the Department of Health Information Management in the School of Health and Rehabilitation Sciences at the University of Pittsburgh. She received her BS degree in cell and molecular biology in Toronto, Canada. Over the past 12 years, Dr. Dilhari has worked in government, academic and the private sector in the field of Molecular Biology. She received her MS (HIS/RHIA option) and doctorate degrees (HIM) from the University of Pittsburgh. Her dissertation research highlighted evaluating the ICD-10-CM coding system for documentation specificity and reimbursement. During her doctoral research, she was the recipient of the Research and Development Award in 2011 and the Pennsylvania Health Information Management Association Student Scholarship in 2010. Her current research focuses on Research Use Case Development and Data Analytics in Healthcare which is conducted in collaboration with the Center for Assistance in Research using eRecords at UPMC.

Linda Dimitropoulos, PhD, is the director for the Center for the Advancement of Health IT at RTI International–Greater Chicago Area. She is a social psychologist and an expert in the use of health information and technology to improve care delivery. Key areas of interest include patient and provider engagement, wellness, and self-generated health information. Dr. Dimitropoulos leads the Center for the Advancement of Health IT, which includes a team of policy analysts, clinicians, informaticians, and health services researchers working to transform health care delivery to improve individual, population, and public health. The Center focuses on solving challenges to using interoperable health information to improve health and health care. She has more than 20 years of experience in qualitative research methods, survey research design, and evaluation and program planning. She specializes in large, complex project design and management. Recent work has focused primarily on interoperability, health information privacy, data governance, barriers to meaningful use, and the use of health IT and health information exchange to improve Medicaid programs.

Matthew Dobra holds a PhD and MA in economics from George Mason University, a graduate certificate in higher education from Monash University, and a BA in history from Loyola University, New Orleans. He is currently associate professor of economics in the Reeves School of Business at Methodist University in Fayetteville, North Carolina. His primary research interests lie in the field of public economics and political economy, with current research projects focused on the funding of higher education, natural resource economics, and health economics.

Donald A. Donahue, Jr. is president and CEO of Diogenec Group, a Washington, D.C., health care professional services firm. He previously served as director of Health Policy & Preparedness Programs at the Potomac Institute for Policy Studies, vice president with Jefferson Consulting Group, deputy surgeon for Plans and Fiscal Administration for the Army Reserve, senior marketing manager for Merit Behavioral Care, and emergency department administrator and consultant for New York City Health and Hospitals Corporation. Donahue is a fellow of the American College of Healthcare Executives and the University of Pittsburgh Center for National Preparedness. An adjunct assistant professor with University of Maryland University College and the University of Maryland Baltimore County, he holds a BS in sociology and political science, an MBA, and a PhD in health education. Other activities include board membership in the American Academy of Disaster Medicine/American Board of Disaster medicine, work as a peer reviewer for the Health Resources and Services Administration (HRSA), medical response director for Firestorm Solutions, a technical advisor for Quantum Leap Innovations, and immediate past chair of the board of directors for Melwood, an AbilityOne services agency.

Martine Etienne-Mesubi is director of health programs at the Institute of Human Virology, University of Maryland School of Medicine/PEPFAR program. She is a trained public health epidemiologist with special focus on health systems strengthening through the development and evaluation of global HIV programs for the last 10 years. Etienne-Mesubi has worked in more than 10 countries in sub-Saharan Africa implementing and managing HIV/AIDS community health programs. She has directed a comprehensive clinical and public health team in the development and implementation of medical records systems, including patient medical forms and database systems in support of international health agendas. She has been successful in leading international training and mentoring workshops with an emphasis on mother-to-child transmission, HIV/AIDS community care, treatment and prevention, and epidemiological research agendas. Using the data collected by the program implementers she supported the development of recommendations for policy changes and approaches to supporting HIV-related programs nationally and internationally, using evidence-based outcomes. She has published an adherence curriculum titled "A Guide to Providing Highly Supportive Antiretroviral Treatment and Maximizing Adherence in Resource-Limited Settings," which is currently being used as a resource in many HIV programs. She has also conducted focus group discussions to help target some of the factors associated with adherence of patients on antiretroviral treatment as well as identify specific social determinants of community health. Through this process, she designed and piloted the Patient Adherence Survey, which was used as an integral part of the evaluation of patient adherence in the UMSOM/IHV PEPFAR program and currently in programs that have transitioned to local country partners. Etienne-Mesubi has also published literature on the factors affecting successful patient outcomes.

Roland Grad is a practicing family doctor and associate professor of family medicine at McGill University. In his research, he studies how doctors, nurses, and pharmacists use clinical information to improve health care and the health of their patients. To improve the performance of health professionals, we need better ways to help health professionals learn, retain, and apply clinical information. Since 2001, Grad has worked to develop, validate, and implement the Information Assessment Method (IAM) for the continuing education of health professionals. The IAM was designed for this purpose and is used in the context of practice-based learning and for understanding how health professionals apply research-based clinical information to improve their practice.

Lynda R. Hardy is adjunct professor in the heath care administration master's program at the University of Maryland University College. She has an avid interest in health informatics working with several committees on data sharing and biomedical informatics training. She is also a senior health science administrator at the National Institutes of Health.

Kim S. Jayhan is a senior health care executive who believes that humor and common sense can be combined with technology to find remarkable solutions to today's health care challenges. With more than 32 years in health care information technology and nearly 10 years in analytics, Jayhan has worked with every aspect of the health care sector, including health care businesses (provider and payer), vendors and her own consulting practice for 10 years. Now the leader of LexisNexis Risk Solutions' Transformation Advisory Consulting group, Jayhan leads initiatives to assist clients in using health care analytics to transform their businesses and to realize ongoing value from their analytics investments. She and her team help clients react to and prepare for the impacts from health reform. Through her insights and leadership, companies have been able to turn reform challenges into additional revenue opportunities as well as transform their business as they might never have imagined. A strong advocate for combining analytics, technology, and process, Jayhan focuses on uncovering insights not available in raw data. Leveraging analytics into care management processes, provider network analysis, and new payment methodologies are common topics for her clients. She is a noted speaker at conferences and webinars and has authored white papers, e-books, and case studies. She is a passionate supporter of collaboration across health care to transform care.

Bruce Johnson is an information technology (IT) entrepreneur and architect who has spent most of his career focused on data architecture, analytics, and business intelligence. He is a frequent teacher and speaker at health care and analytics conferences. Having worked in a variety of industries, Johnson spent the last 11 years focused solely on helping health care leverage the tools and frameworks that highly effective businesses in other industries use for business optimization and growth. Johnson led the IT planning and design of the Enterprise Data Trust at the Mayo Clinic and was a cofounder of Recombinant Data Corp. He was an active member of HDWA for 10 years and served on the board as the education chair for 4 years.

David T. Marc is assistant professor and program director for the graduate program in health informatics at the College of St. Scholastica in the Department of Health Informatics and Information Management. Previously, Marc was an adjunct faculty at St. Scholastica where he taught courses on databases in health care, data analytics, and research design. Marc has a master's in biological sciences and has extensive experience working with large health care data sets. Prior to working for St. Scholastica, Marc was employed at a biotech company where he applied myriad analytic approaches to investigate the predictive value of potential biomarkers for psychiatric diseases. Currently, he is pursuing a PhD in health informatics at the University of Minnesota.

Peter Memiah is director of outcomes and evaluation at the Institute of Human Virology. His expertise spans from evaluation research to community outreach and support. For more than seven years, he has worked across several countries in Africa and the Caribbean implementing quality improvement programs and supporting governments, health facilities, and health professionals alike in using data to impact outcomes. This has allowed for comprehensive development and implementation of work plans used to support successful patient scale up. Memiah is a public health epidemiologist, and his fieldwork has been effective in combining clinical data with community strategies. These methods have allowed him to support health facilities in collecting and analyzing site-specific data and in providing support of the complete use of data through inclusive facility feedback and facility-specific interventions. He has also developed a broad spectrum of job aids and material for complete assessment, treatment, and continuity of care for the lifelong treatment of HIV. These materials are currently being used by local health care providers all over Africa and the Caribbean. His commitment to education and teaching is evident through the support he provides his staff in the field. Memiah has also published several manuscripts on quality improvement processes.

Tamra Meyer is epidemiologist at the Pharmacovigilance Center of the U.S. Army in Falls Church, Virginia, where she uses administrative claims data from the Military Health System to conduct drug safety studies.

Megan Monroe is a senior PhD student and graduate research assistant in the computer science department of the University of Maryland. As part of her PhD thesis research she is the main developer of Eventflow.

David E. Parkhill is vice president of consulting services with the Hitachi Consulting Corporation. He is a seasoned technology executive specializing in the creation and application of service solutions for the telecom industry. Mr. Parkhill was a founder of Network Effects, LLC and has previously held positions as CIO and CTO of Virgin Mobile USA; director of BT's Service Assembly Project; national director at Andersen Business Consulting; and principal with IBM Global Services. By combining his passion for leading edge software technology with delighting customers through innovative products and services, he has delivered products and systems projects that customers and clients have used to grow revenue, acquire new customers, and reduce costs.

Catherine Plaisant received the doctorat d'Ingénieur in France in 1982. She is a senior research scientist at the Human-Computer Interaction Laboratory of the University of Maryland Institute for Advanced Computer Studies. She enjoys working most with multidisciplinary teams on designing and evaluating new interface technologies that are useable and useful. She has written more than 100 refereed technical publications on the subjects of information visualization, evaluation methods, electronic health record interfaces, digital libraries, and online help. She coauthored with Ben Shneiderman the fifth edition of *Designing the User Interface.*

Derek Ritz is the principal consultant at ecGroup Inc. He is an advisor to international public and private sector clients regarding e-health strategy, enterprise architecture, informatics standards, and national-scale implementations of e-health infrastructure.

Ryan H. Sandefer is assistant professor and chair at the College of St. Scholastica in the Department of Health Informatics and Information Management. Previously, he was research coordinator for the Center for Healthcare Innovation at the College of St. Scholastica. Sandefer has a master's in political science and is completing a PhD in health informatics with a focus on consumer engagement in the use of health information technology. He is on the editorial advisory board and review panel for Perspectives in Health Information Management with the American Health Information Management Association (AHIMA). He is an elected board member and the chair-elect of the AHIMA Council for Excellence in Education and is chair of its research and periodicals workgroup.

Sandefer teaches research methods and health care data analytics and participates in the Minnesota e-health advisory workgroups.

Ben Shneiderman is distinguished university professor in the Department of Computer Science and was the founding director (1983–2000) of the Human-Computer Interaction Laboratory at the University of Maryland. He is a fellow of the ACM, AAAS, and IEEE and member of the National Academy of Engineering. He received the ACM SIGCHI Lifetime Achievement Award in 2001. His research interests are human–computer interaction, information visualization, and user interface.

Gregory D. Stevens is associate professor of family medicine and preventive medicine at the Keck School of Medicine, University of Southern California. He has been working to improve health care systems by enhancing the quality of primary care practice and integrating the fields of primary care and public health. He earned his doctorate and MHS from the Bloomberg School of Public Health at Johns Hopkins University.

Dorothy Weinstein has a long tenure working in Washington, D.C., on national, state, and local health policy. She has been employed at Georgetown University Institute of Health Policy Analysis, Association of American Medical Colleges, American Diabetes Association, Endocrine Society, American College of Cardiology, and National Health Council. Her various positions include research and writing, crafting legislation, and directing government relations departments at leading major nonprofit health organizations. Her most recent activities concentrated on designing and now implementing health care reform legislation. The focus of her efforts is on patient engagement in the health care delivery process. She also teaches health policy at the University of Phoenix. Weinstein also works in health care volunteer and philanthropic work at Children's National Medical Center (CNMC) and at the Prevention of Blindness Society in Washington, D.C. Dorothy has a BA in philosophy from the University of Maryland and a MA from Duke University's Sanford School of Public Policy. She is a member of Phi Beta Kappa and is a published author in areas including fetal tissue/stem cell research, environmental policy on noise abatement, de minimus standards in risk assessment, and personalized/genomic medicine and patient engagement.

Index